# *Smart Cooking*
## THE COSTCO WAY™

Grilled Sea Scallops with Arugula, Watermelon and Feta Salad can be found on page 138.

# *Smart Cooking*
# THE COSTCO WAY™

## *Delicious recipes using Costco products*

Tim Talevich
*Editorial Director*

*With a foreword by*
Tim Rose

Issaquah, Washington

# To Our Valued Members

We are delighted to offer this gift in time for the holidays—our ninth annual cookbook in our series of *Costco Way* cookbooks—to thank you for your business and loyal membership. This book has been made possible through the support of Costco's many food suppliers.

As in past years, we've asked our suppliers to develop recipes that showcase their products that we sell at Costco. We have also included recipes from many of our favorite celebrity chefs such as Mario Batali, Steven Raichlen and Anne Byrn in the "Chef's Choice" section in the center of the book. These top chefs have worked their magic to develop recipes using their favorite ingredients from Costco. Most of the recipes throughout the book have a short list of affordable, readily available ingredients and are quick and easy to prepare.

This year, you'll find a variety of helpful tips at the beginning of the chapters in the book. We have asked leading experts, such as Sandra Lee, Christopher Kimball and the crew at America's Test Kitchen, and David Murdock of the Dole Corporation, to share ideas on what foods to eat, how to best prepare them and how to safely store them.

Above everything else, the secret to all the great dishes featured in this book is top-quality ingredients. When you purchase your ingredients from Costco, you know that you are getting the best—and at a great price.

And about the title of this year's book: "Smart Cooking" pretty much sums up what we try to achieve with the food we sell at Costco. Our buyers work hard to find the best food products from around the country and the world. They place a lot of emphasis on convenience for you, and they do this all while keeping an eye on prices. I think that's a pretty smart approach to preparing meals for your family.

We hope you enjoy *Smart Cooking The Costco Way* and try out our recipes with your family and friends. You can also find our past years' cookbooks online at Costco.com. Just type "Costco Cookbooks" in the search window on our home page.

Bon appétit from all of us at Costco!

Ginnie Roeglin,
Senior Vice President,
E-commerce and Publishing

# Foreword

When Costco opened its doors with a single warehouse in Seattle back in 1983, one area that was very small was the food department. In support of our business members who ran restaurants and other businesses, we offered some large cuts of beef, packages of sliced deli meats and a few other products. But there was no produce or other fresh foods. In fact, in those early years we didn't think that food would be a big part of our business. I'm happy to report that we were wrong.

Today, food is at the top of the shopping list for many members, ranging from staples such as sugar, flour and canned goods to fresh fruit and vegetables; from fresh meats, seafood and poultry to muffins, pies and cakes that you can smell baking throughout the day. To see how big food has become in the warehouses, just look for the crowds around the sample tables. Many of our food products have become famous, such as our marvelous pumpkin pies. We sell more than 4 million of them during the holidays.

We've built our food program around the Costco philosophy of the best products for the lowest possible prices. We don't carry the thousands of food items you'll see in a typical grocery store. Instead, we focus on the everyday essentials, complemented by a variety of special products that come in at different times during the year, such as fine vanilla beans, unique olive oils and select wines. The emphasis is always on quality, whether the product comes from a leading manufacturer or carries our own label, Kirkland Signature.

This cookbook shows just how robust and exciting our food program at Costco has become. Thanks to the efforts of our buyers and the quality products from our suppliers, you can find everything you need to make great meals at Costco. A perfect place to start is with some of the 280 recipes featured here. We hope you enjoy them, and we appreciate the opportunity to serve you.

Tim Rose

Tim Rose,
Senior Vice President,
Foods and Sundries

# About This Book

This is the ninth year we have created a cookbook designed to showcase the exciting array of foods sold at Costco. As with the last six books, *Smart Cooking The Costco Way* will be handed out to members on a first-come, first-served basis the weekend after Thanksgiving as a token of our appreciation for their membership.

And as with Costco itself, the format of the book remains simple and direct. The book is arranged with sections for breakfasts, appetizers and beverages, salads and soups, side dishes, entrées and desserts.

The index at the back of the book contains listings by recipe and food item. We also have included a "Supplier Listing" section with contact information for all of the participating food suppliers.

Every recipe has been identified with the supplier's name and logo. We want to thank each of these suppliers for their support of this book. (Please note that some branded products may not be sold in your part of the country. In such cases, you should substitute a similar product.)

Again this year, some of the recipes have nutritional information listed with them. This is helpful for anybody watching calories and following a controlled, healthful diet.

Our popular "Chef's Choice" chapter offers nearly 30 pages of recipes developed by some of the country's most accomplished chefs. All of these chefs have achieved national or international renown with cookbooks of their own, television shows and/or exceptional restaurants. Thanks to all of them for helping to make this another exciting addition to *The Costco Way* cookbook series.

An innovation you will see this year is a "Quick & Easy" logo. It appears next to recipes that are particularly easy to prepare when your time is limited. I think you'll find these recipes handy for those busy days that we all have.

I hope you will enjoy this offering of culinary delights and that armed with these recipes, you will be able to demonstrate that you do indeed know something about smart cooking.

David W. Fuller,
Publisher

Note on brands

# *Smart Cooking*
## THE COSTCO WAY™

# Recipe for longevity

**David H. Murdock**
David H. Murdock is Chairman of the Dole Food Company. He recently published *The Dole Nutrition Handbook: What to Eat and How to Live for a Longer, Healthier Life*. It has been condensed into pocket-size booklets that can be ordered online at *www.dole.com/costco*.

**By David H. Murdock**

WHERE DO YOU find everything you need to live a long and healthy life? Not at the doctor's office, but at Costco.

Even as Chairman of the Dole Food Company, I shop every weekend at Costco—filling up my cart with large quantities of fruit and vegetables. Oprah Winfrey and I did a Costco run when she visited me as part of a show she devoted to longevity. My secret, at age 87, is plenty of fruit and vegetables, plus 50 or 60 minutes of exercise five days a week. It all starts with a good breakfast, and continues with a smart eating plan throughout the day.

I personally like to juice up several different kinds of fruit and vegetables—bananas, red bell peppers, apples, carrots, celery, broccoli, spinach, parsley, tomatoes and cucumbers. I include the rinds and even some banana peel because that's where most of the nutrition is.

For my daily diet, I stay with lean protein with every meal (fish, egg whites, beans and nuts), plus a half plate of fruit and vegetables.

Basically I recommend eating a substantial breakfast each day, one that includes a whole grain (such as oatmeal), plenty of fruit—berries, banana, pineapple—and topped with nuts (almonds, walnuts, pecans, all kinds of nuts). Sometimes I have an egg-white vegetable omelet, which Oprah joked is "mostly vegetables."

For lunch and dinner I like to have a fish rich in omega-3s, such as salmon, black cod or sardines. That is accompanied by either a salad or soup—and often both.

I eat a lot, but my weight rarely fluctuates more than one or two pounds. When you eat a diet that is primarily fruit and vegetables, the high water and fiber content really fills you up. Plus, by eating good quantities of fruit and vegetables every day, you're essentially getting all your nutrient needs met, and that helps you feel satisfied.

I recommend that you subscribe to Dole's *Nutrition News*, a free electronic monthly newsletter, for more food tips and information. Subscribe at *www.dole.com*.

## A day in the diet of Mr. Murdock

### Breakfast

- Steel-cut oatmeal with pineapple, bananas, raspberries, black raspberries, blueberries and sliced almonds
- Egg-white omelet with tomatoes, broccoli, red bell peppers, spinach, mushrooms and onions
- Pineapple juice

### Lunch

- Baby spinach salad with sliced apple and pecans
- Grilled salmon with mango salsa

### Dinner

- Broccoli soup
- Grilled halibut
- Roasted tomatoes with olives and capers
- Barley risotto
- Roasted pear halves in port

## Turkey 'n' Stuffing Strata

### Moark LLC/Hillandale Farms/ Hickman's Family Farms/Cal-Maine Foods/Oakdell Egg Farms/Wilcox Farms/NuCal Foods

- **Cooking spray**
- **4 cups (about 7-8 ounces) herb-seasoned stuffing cubes, divided**
- **1 10-ounce package frozen chopped broccoli, thawed and drained**
- **1 cup (about 5 ounces) diced cooked turkey**
- **1/2 cup (2 ounces) shredded Cheddar cheese**
- **3 tablespoons thinly sliced green onions with tops**
- **6 eggs**
- **1 1/2 cups skim or low-fat milk**
- **2 tablespoons sliced almonds**

Evenly coat an 8-inch square baking pan with cooking spray.

Sprinkle 2 cups of stuffing cubes in the pan. Layer broccoli, turkey, cheese and onions over the cubes. Top with the remaining 2 cups of cubes.

In a large bowl, beat together eggs and milk until well blended. Pour evenly over the stuffing mixture. Cover and refrigerate for several hours or overnight.

Preheat oven to 350°F.

Sprinkle the stuffing mixture with almonds. Bake, uncovered, until golden brown and a knife inserted near the center comes out clean, about 50-60 minutes. Makes 6 servings.

## Three-Cheese Egg Bake in Ham Cups

### Kirkland Signature/Michael Foods

- **12 slices (1/8 inch thick) Black Forest or Virginia ham (see note)**
- **3/4 cup whipped cream cheese**
- **2 cups (16 ounces) Kirkland Signature Real Egg Product**
- **1/3 cup milk**
- **1/4 teaspoon salt**
- **1 tablespoon finely chopped fresh basil**
- **1/2 cup chopped grape tomatoes**
- **1/2 cup shredded mozzarella cheese**
- **1/4 cup shredded Parmesan cheese**

Preheat oven to 400°F. Grease a 12-cup nonstick regular muffin pan.

Carefully place a ham slice inside each muffin cup; the ham will come up over the edges. Spoon 1 tablespoon cream cheese into the bottom of each cup.

Whisk together Real Egg Product, milk, salt and basil. Pour the mixture equally into the ham cups. Top with chopped tomatoes and shredded cheeses.

Bake for 14-16 minutes, or until a toothpick inserted in the center comes out clean. Let cool for 5 minutes before removing from the pan. Serve immediately. Makes 6 servings.

**Note:** Ham slices should be without holes.

## Breakfast Crepes
### Nutella

**3/4 cup whole wheat flour (or all-purpose flour)**
**3 tablespoons sugar**
**Pinch of salt**
**3/4 cup skim milk**
**2 large eggs, beaten**
**2 tablespoons butter, plus more for frying**
**Nutella* hazelnut spread**
**Fresh fruit, for serving**
**Confectioners' sugar, for serving**
**Whipped cream (optional)**

In a mixing bowl, blend flour, sugar and salt. Gradually whisk in milk. Add beaten eggs and continue mixing until the batter is smooth and creamy, with no lumps. Cover the bowl with plastic wrap and refrigerate for 2 hours (or overnight).

When ready to make the crepes, melt 2 tablespoons butter, add to the batter and mix thoroughly.

Heat a small pan over medium heat. Brush the pan lightly with butter or oil (repeat for each new crepe). Pour 2 tablespoons of batter into the pan and tilt to spread evenly. Cook until golden brown, flip over and cook until the other side is browned.

Let the crepes cool. Spread Nutella on each crepe and roll or fold. Serve with your choice of garnish, such as fresh fruit, confectioners' sugar and a dollop of whipped cream. Makes 10-12 crepes.

** Brands may vary by region; substitute a similar product.*

## Blueberry Oat Pancakes with Fruit Topping
### Nature's Partner

**3/4 cup low-fat milk**
**3/4 cup plain low-fat Greek yogurt**
**3/4 cup rolled oats**
**1/2 cup oat bran**
**3/4 cup flour**
**1 tablespoon baking powder**
**1 teaspoon salt**
**2 large eggs, beaten**
**1/4 cup honey**
**1/4 cup butter, melted**
**1 cup Nature's Partner* VitalBerry blueberries, washed**
**Chopped almonds or pecans, for garnish (optional)**

***FRUIT TOPPING***

**1 cup plain low-fat Greek yogurt**
**Honey to taste**
**2 Nature's Partner* kiwifruit, peeled and diced**
**2 Nature's Partner* peaches, washed and diced**
**1 cup Nature's Partner* green or red seedless grapes, washed and halved**

In a large bowl, mix together milk, yogurt, oats and oat bran. Let stand for 5 minutes.

Sift together flour, baking powder and salt.

Gently stir eggs into oat mixture. Stir in dry sifted ingredients, honey and butter. Set batter aside.

To prepare the fruit topping, mix yogurt with honey to taste in a bowl. Add kiwifruit, peaches and grapes, stirring to coat.

Drop batter by 1/3 cupfuls onto a greased or nonstick griddle or frying pan heated to medium-high. Dot the tops of the pancakes with blueberries. Cook until tops are bubbly and edges appear cooked. Flip over and cook the other side.

Top the pancakes with fruit mixture. Garnish with chopped nuts. Makes 8-10 pancakes.

** Brands may vary by region; substitute a similar product.*

NATURE'S PARTNER

## Black Velvet Apricot French Toast
### Kingsburg Orchards

- 4 ounces cream cheese, softened
- 3 tablespoons butter, softened
- 1 cup confectioners' sugar, plus more for serving
- 1/4 teaspoon vanilla
- 8 slices slightly stale bread
- 4-6 Kingsburg Orchards* Black Velvet apricots, pitted and sliced
- 3 large or extra large eggs
- 1 cup milk
- 1 teaspoon ground cinnamon

Heat a greased griddle to 300°F.

In a bowl, mix together cream cheese, butter, 1 cup sugar and vanilla. Spread a thin layer of this mixture on each slice of bread, then add a layer of sliced apricots on 4 of the slices. Top with the other 4 bread slices.

In a separate bowl, whisk together eggs, milk and cinnamon. Dip the stuffed French toast into the egg mixture.

Grill on the griddle until both sides are a crisp golden-brown—the cream cheese should be melted and the apricots warm.

Dust with confectioners' sugar and serve warm. Makes 4 servings.

** Brands may vary by region; substitute a similar product.*

# Cranberry Orange Scones

## Pure Via

- 2 cups all-purpose flour
- 12 packets Pure Via* All Natural Zero Calorie Sweetener
- 1 tablespoon grated orange peel
- 1 1/2 teaspoons baking powder
- 1/2 teaspoon baking soda
- 1/4 teaspoon salt
- 1/2 cup (1 stick) butter, cut into 8 pieces
- 1 cup buttermilk
- 1/2 cup sweetened dried cranberries
- 1 beaten egg (optional)

Preheat oven to 425°F.

In a medium bowl, mix flour, sweetener, grated orange peel, baking powder, baking soda and salt. Cut in butter with a pastry blender, until the mixture looks like fine crumbs.

Stir in buttermilk until the dough pulls away from the sides of the bowl. Stir in cranberries.

Drop dough by 1/3 cupfuls onto an ungreased cookie sheet. Brush with egg.

Bake for 12-15 minutes, or until light brown. Immediately remove scones from the cookie sheet.

Serve warm. Makes 10 scones.

**Nutritional information:** Each serving has 200 calories, 3 g protein, 27 g carbohydrates, 9 g fat, 25 mg cholesterol, 290 mg sodium, 7 g sugar.

** Brands may vary by region; substitute a similar product.*

# Double Orange-Walnut Muffins

## Quaker

- 1 1/2 cups all-purpose flour
- 1 cup Quaker Oats (quick or old fashioned, uncooked)
- 2/3 cup plus 1 tablespoon sugar, divided
- 2 teaspoons baking powder
- 1/2 teaspoon baking soda
- 1/4 teaspoon salt
- 3/4 cup coarsely chopped toasted walnuts, divided
- 2/3 cup plus 1/4 cup Tropicana Pure Premium orange juice or Naked 100% orange juice, divided
- 1/2 cup 1% or skim milk
- 1 large egg
- 1/4 cup butter or trans-fat-free vegetable shortening, melted and cooled

Preheat oven to 400°F. Spray bottoms only of 12 medium muffin pan cups with cooking spray or line with paper baking cups.

In a large bowl, stir together flour, oats, 2/3 cup sugar, baking powder, baking soda and salt. Add 1/2 cup walnuts; mix well.

In a medium bowl, beat 2/3 cup juice, milk, egg and melted butter until well blended. Add all at once to the dry ingredients; stir just until evenly moistened. Pour into muffin pan cups. Sprinkle with 1/4 cup walnuts.

Bake for 15-18 minutes, or until a wooden pick inserted in the center comes out clean.

Remove from the oven and immediately spoon 1/4 cup juice over the muffins. Let stand for 5 minutes. Sprinkle with 1 tablespoon sugar. Serve warm. Makes 12 muffins.

# Good Morning Apple Cake
## Borton & Sons

- 1 18.25-ounce package yellow cake mix
- 3 large eggs
- 1 1/3 cups milk
- 1/2 teaspoon ground cinnamon
- 2 medium-sized Borton* apples, the variety of your choice

*STREUSEL TOPPING*

- 3/4 cup old-fashioned oats
- 3/4 cup chopped pecans or walnuts
- 1/2 cup packed dark brown sugar
- 1/2 teaspoon ground cinnamon
- 1/2 cup melted butter

Preheat oven to 350°F. Grease and flour a 13-by-9-inch baking pan.

To prepare the streusel topping, combine all ingredients in a medium bowl and mix well. Set aside.

Beat cake mix, eggs, milk and cinnamon in a large mixer bowl until just moistened. Beat for 2 minutes at medium speed.

Core and slice apples; fold into the batter. Pour half of the batter into the prepared pan. Sprinkle with half of the streusel topping. Top with the remaining batter. Sprinkle with the remaining topping.

Bake for 40-45 minutes, or until a toothpick inserted in the center comes out clean. Makes 8-10 servings.

** Brands may vary by region; substitute a similar product.*

# Apple Pear Strudel
## Kingsburg Orchards

**2 sheets puff pastry (1 package)**
**2 tablespoons butter**
**4-5 Kingsburg Orchards* apple pears, peeled, cored and thinly sliced**
**1/2 cup firmly packed light brown sugar**
**Grated peel of 1 orange**
**1/4 cup chopped walnuts**

***GLAZE***
**3/4 cup confectioners' sugar**
**1 tablespoon milk**
**1/4 teaspoon vanilla extract**

Preheat oven to 350°F.

Remove puff pastry from the package to thaw.

Melt butter over medium heat in a large sauté pan. Add apple pears and cook until tender. When they are almost done, add sugar, grated orange peel and walnuts. Stir gently until the sugar has melted and the apple pears are glazed.

Place a sheet of puff pastry on a greased cookie sheet. Along each long side of the pastry, make angled slits 1 inch apart from the edge to within about 1/2-3/4 inch of the fold mark. Spread half of the apple pear mixture down the center. Fold the cut sides over the top in a crisscross pattern. Pinch the ends closed. Repeat for the second strudel.

Bake for 20-30 minutes, or until golden brown.

To prepare the glaze, combine all ingredients in a small bowl and whisk to blend. For a thinner consistency, add 1/2 teaspoon more milk. Drizzle over the warm strudel. Makes 8 servings.

** Brands may vary by region; substitute a similar product.*

# Blueberry Danish Delight
## Meduri Farms

4 ounces cream cheese (refrigerate until ready to use)
2 tablespoons sugar (or 1/4 cup Splenda)
1 egg
1/2 teaspoon grated lemon peel
1 teaspoon lemon juice
1/2 teaspoon vanilla extract
1/2 cup Kirkland Signature dried blueberries
1 Pillsbury Crescent refrigerated seamless dough sheet (1 package)
1 teaspoon honey
1/2 teaspoon water
Confectioners' sugar (optional)

Preheat oven to 375°F.

In a mixer, beat cream cheese and sugar until smooth. Add egg, grated lemon peel, lemon juice and vanilla; beat until well blended. Fold dried blueberries into the mixture.

Cover a cookie sheet with parchment paper. Roll out dough onto the cookie sheet.

Cut the dough into 8 squares.

Spread 1-2 tablespoons of the blueberry cream cheese mixture diagonally across each square.

Using your fingers, pick up the 2 opposite corners of the square and overlap to form each Danish.

In a small bowl, mix honey and water. Brush over the top of each pastry.

Bake on the cookie sheet for 13-15 minutes, or until golden brown. Remove from the oven and place on a cooling rack for about 15 minutes.

Sift confectioners' sugar over the top of each Danish and serve. Makes 4-8 servings.

**Tip:** These pastries are also good for dessert.

## Savory Pancake Bowls
### Continental Mills/Peterson Cheese

**1 cup Krusteaz Buttermilk Pancake Mix**
**1 1/4 cups water**
**1 tablespoon butter**
**3/4 cup 2-inch asparagus tips**
**1/2 cup chopped onion**
**1 cup fresh spinach, packed**
**6 eggs**
**2 egg yolks**
**1/4 cup milk or cream**
**Salt and pepper**
**1 cup shaved or grated EntreMont Comté Cheese**

Preheat a lightly greased griddle to 375°F (medium heat). Preheat oven to 350°F. Lightly grease a 12-cup muffin pan.

Stir together pancake mix and water (batter will be thin). Let stand for 2-3 minutes. Pour 1/4 cup batter per pancake onto the griddle. Cook for 1-1 1/4 minutes per side.

Place warm pancakes in muffin cups, pushing gently to form bowls. Bake for 4-5 minutes, or until lightly crispy around the edges. Set aside.

Melt butter in a skillet over medium heat. Add asparagus and onion; sauté for 3-4 minutes. Add spinach; cook for 3 minutes. Remove and drain well.

Whisk together eggs, yolks, milk, and salt and pepper to taste. Scramble in a lightly greased skillet over medium heat until eggs are set. Remove from the heat and fold in sautéed vegetables.

Fill pancake bowls with egg mixture. Top with cheese. Bake for 7-10 minutes, or until cheese has melted. Serve immediately. Makes 12 servings.

## Breakfast Wraps
### Del Monte Foods

**1 egg**
**2 egg whites**
**Nonstick cooking spray**
**1 15 1/4-ounce can S&W or Del Monte* whole kernel corn, drained**
**1 14 1/2-ounce can S&W or Del Monte* diced tomatoes, well drained, squeezing out excess liquid**
**1 cup diced zucchini**
**1/4 cup sliced green onions**
**3 ounces low-fat, low-sodium shredded jack cheese**
**8 warm corn tortillas**
**Toothpicks**

Beat together egg and egg whites. Spray a skillet with cooking spray and heat over medium heat. Add eggs and scramble, breaking up into small pieces.

Stir in corn, tomatoes, zucchini, onions and cheese.

Spoon the egg mixture down the center of each tortilla; roll up and secure with a toothpick.

Heat in the microwave for 30 seconds on high, or until warm and the cheese has melted. Makes 4 servings.

** Brands may vary by region; substitute a similar product.*

## Southwestern Sausage Pie
### Jimmy Dean

**1 refrigerated crust for a 9-inch pie**
**12 links Jimmy Dean Fully Cooked Turkey Sausage**
**1/2 cup chopped onion**
**2 jalapeños, seeded and chopped**
**1 cup Kirkland Signature Real Egg Product**
**1 cup milk**
**1 teaspoon ground cumin**
**1/4 teaspoon salt**
**1/8 teaspoon ground black pepper**
**1 cup (4 ounces) Kirkland Signature shredded Mexican cheese blend**

Preheat oven to 375°F.

Place crust in an ungreased 9-inch glass pie plate as directed on the package for a 1-crust filled pie.

Coarsely chop sausage. Cook and stir sausage, onion and jalapeños in a large skillet over medium-high heat until the vegetables are tender. Remove from the heat.

In a large bowl, beat egg product, milk, cumin, salt and pepper until blended. Stir in the sausage mixture and cheese. Pour into the piecrust.

Bake for 45-50 minutes, or until the eggs are set. Makes 8 servings.

**Variations**

**Cheddar:** Substitute 1/2 cup chopped red bell pepper for the jalapeños. Omit the cumin. Substitute shredded Cheddar for the Mexican cheese blend.

**Mediterranean:** Substitute 1 cup chopped mushrooms for the jalapeños. Omit the cumin. Add 1/2 cup chopped roasted red peppers or sun-dried tomatoes and 1 teaspoon dried basil. Substitute shredded Italian cheese blend for the Mexican cheese blend.

## Cowboy Breakfast
### Hormel Foods

**2 15-ounce cans Hormel* chili with beans**
**14 strips fully cooked bacon, chopped**
**4 eggs**
**4 green onions, chopped**

In a large skillet, heat chili over medium heat.

Place bacon on a paper towel; microwave for 30 seconds, or until crisp. Fold bacon into the chili.

Flatten the chili mixture with the back of a spoon. Make 4 indentations in the chili. Break 1 egg into each indentation.

Cover the skillet and cook for 12 minutes, or until the eggs are cooked to taste.

With a large spoon, scoop up 1 egg with a portion of chili and bacon for each serving. Sprinkle with green onions. Makes 4 servings.

** Brands may vary by region; substitute a similar product.*

# Appetizers and beverages

## The art of the appetizer ...

**The Purcell sisters**
The Purcell sisters, Lauren and Anne, offer timely entertaining advice and tips in their book, *Cocktail Parties, Straight Up!*, and on their website, *www.purcellsisters.com*.

**By Lauren Purcell and Anne Purcell Grissinger**

TWO THINGS are commonly said about first impressions: They're very important, and you don't get a second chance to make one. So as you can see, those delightful tidbits we call appetizers—the first culinary impression at a party—must come off perfectly.

We promise that your appetizers will be an outstanding opener for any party if you follow some simple, time-tested steps. Making as many preparations as you can in advance will help you relax when the actual party starts.

**1. Follow the foolproof Rule of Five, which calls for a menu of five types of appetizers:**

- One heavy (so that guests who skip dinner will feel satisfied)
- One heavy or medium (choose a heavy one if you expect your party to go long)
- One medium (typically a vegetarian dish or a dip)
- One lighter choice (such as crudités for nibbling)
- One bowl item (such as nuts or olives)

**2. For an accurate head count** to help you plan properly, provide an e-mail address with your invitation, along with your phone number. You can nudge the shirkers with a gentle e-mail reminder as the date draws near without being ill-mannered yourself ("We're just finalizing the guest list and are soooo hoping that you'll be there").

**To determine how much to prepare, follow this guide:**

- Heavy appetizers—4-5 pieces per guest
- Heavy/medium—4-5 pieces per guest
- Medium—4-5 pieces
- Light—5-6 pieces
- Bowl foods—place 1 bowl for every 7-8 guests and keep them filled

**3. For a sense of elegance in your rooms,** take a look at your lights. Keeping the lighting at a twilight level encourages easy mingling and conversation. Consider exchanging 100-watt bulbs with 40-watt bulbs, and add candles throughout (though avoid scented ones because they can interfere with the fragrance and flavor of the food).

**4. A smart way to chill Champagne** or wine, if you don't have enough room in your fridge, is to use the multi-ice-bucket method. Place a bottle in each bucket and add as many ice cubes as will fit. Place the buckets on counters and they'll be ready to go when guests arrive.

**5. Run out of food?** It's a compliment to your cooking! All you need is a backup dessert item, such as bunches of grapes, chocolates or after-dinner mints. Remove all serving trays as if to signal the end of the hors d'oeuvres portion of the evening, then put out the dessert platter. The trick is to act as though this is all part of your master plan.

# Grilled Vegetable and Hummus Pita Pizzas

Sabra

- **1 1/2 cups yellow and/ or green summer squash (about 2 medium sized) cut in 1/4-inch rounds**
- **4 tablespoons olive oil, divided**
- **Salt and freshly ground black pepper**
- **1 red onion**
- **2 vine-ripe tomatoes**
- **3 6-inch pitas**
- **1 cup Sabra* hummus**

Preheat the grill or a grill pan over medium heat.

Place squash in a bowl and add 2 tablespoons olive oil, 1/4 teaspoon salt and pepper to taste; stir to coat.

Peel and cut onion in half. Slice with the grain into 1/3-inch wedges. Place in a bowl with 1 tablespoon olive oil, 1/4 teaspoon salt and pepper to taste; stir to coat.

Cut tomatoes in half and slice each half into 4-6 half-moon wedges. Place in a bowl with 1 tablespoon olive oil, 1/4 teaspoon salt and pepper to taste; stir to coat.

Grill the squash for about 8 minutes, rotating once. Grill the onions for about 5 minutes, rotating once. Grill the tomatoes for about 5 minutes, rotating once.

Warm pitas on the grill for about 3 minutes on each side. Remove from the heat and slather each pita with 1/3 cup hummus. Top with summer squash, tomatoes and onions. Cut each pita into 8 pieces. Makes 6-8 servings.

**Tip:** The best pita for this is the flat variety. You can also use lavash.

*Recipe developed by Colombe Jacobsen.*

** Brands may vary by region; substitute a similar product.*

# Fresh Buffalo Mozzarella Caprese

Mucci Farms

- **8 Sapori tomatoes**
- **1 8-ounce ball of fresh buffalo mozzarella**
- **8 large basil leaves**
- **Extra-virgin olive oil**
- **Balsamic vinegar**
- **Sea salt**
- **Freshly cracked black peppercorns**

Wash tomatoes and cut into quarters. Tear mozzarella into rustic-style pieces. Hand-tear basil leaves.

In a bowl, combine tomatoes, mozzarella and basil. Toss with oil, a touch of balsamic vinegar, and salt and pepper to taste. Makes 4 servings.

**Tip:** Serve with toasted bread or crackers.

## Double-Tomato Healthy Bruschetta

Village Farms

- 8 Village Farms* Sinfully Sweet Campari tomatoes, diced
- 1/2 cup sun-dried tomatoes in oil, chopped
- 4 garlic cloves, chopped
- 1/4 cup chopped fresh basil
- 1/2 cup chopped red onion
- 1/2 cup extra-virgin olive oil, divided
- 3 tablespoons balsamic vinegar
- 1/2 teaspoon sea salt
- 1/2 teaspoon fresh ground black pepper
- 1 whole wheat baguette
- 1 cup grated Asiago cheese
- 1 cup grated Parmesan cheese

In a large bowl, combine tomatoes, garlic, basil and onion. Add 1/4 cup oil, vinegar, salt and pepper; mix well. Cover the bowl with plastic wrap and refrigerate for at least 2 hours and up to 24 hours to let the flavors develop.

Place the top oven rack 5 inches from the broiler element. Preheat the broiler to high.

Cut baguette into 1/2-inch-thick slices. Brush with the remaining oil and place on a cookie sheet. Set under the broiler and cook until golden brown, watching carefully to avoid burning. Remove from the oven, leaving the broiler on.

Spread a 3/4-inch-thick layer of the tomato mixture on each baguette slice.

Sprinkle with grated cheese.

Place under the broiler once again until the cheese melts and begins to bubble.

Remove from the oven, let cool and serve. Makes 6 servings.

** Brands may vary by region; substitute a similar product.*

## Seasoned Grill Salmon and Alfredo Flatbread Pizza

Morey's

- 3 portions Morey's* Seasoned Grill Marinated Salmon
- 6 pieces Flatout Flatbread (11.2-ounce package)
- 2 cups Classico Alfredo sauce
- 1 large red onion, diced
- 6 tablespoons minced fresh chives
- 6 tablespoons Kirkland Signature Crumbled Bacon
- 3 cups shredded mozzarella cheese

Preheat oven to 375°F.

Cook salmon according to package directions. Remove the skin and slice the salmon.

Place flatbread pieces on several parchment-lined cookie sheets. Spread 1/3 cup Alfredo sauce to the edges of each flatbread. Top with salmon, onions, chives, bacon and mozzarella.

Bake for 10-12 minutes, or until the cheese is golden brown. The edges of the flatbread will begin to turn light golden brown, but the bread will still be soft and flexible. Remove from the oven and let sit for 1-2 minutes on the cookie sheets to crisp. Cut and serve immediately. Makes 6-12 servings.

**Variations:** Use your favorite pizza toppings, cheeses or veggies for variety. Substitute pizza crust for the flatbread.

** Brands may vary by region; substitute a similar product.*

# Burrata Cheese, Cherry Tomato and Pesto Appetizer

La Brea Bakery

- 4 1/2-inch-thick slices La Brea Bakery* Demi Baguette
- Olive oil
- 6 cherry tomatoes, quartered
- 1 tablespoon extra-virgin olive oil
- 2 tablespoons basil pesto
- 1 garlic clove, finely minced
- Sea salt
- 4 1/2-inch-thick slices burrata cheese (see note)

Preheat oven to 350°F.

Brush each slice of bread with olive oil on both sides. Place on a baking sheet and toast in the oven for 15-20 minutes, or until light golden brown.

In a medium bowl, combine tomatoes, extra-virgin olive oil, pesto and garlic. Mix and season to taste with salt.

Place a slice of burrata on each slice of bread. Top with the tomato mixture. Makes 4 servings.

**Note:** Burrata is a fresh Italian cheese made from mozzarella and cream. If it is not available, substitute fresh mozzarella.

** Brands may vary by region; substitute a similar product.*

## Grilled Mediterranean Shrimp

Kirkland Signature

- **2 pounds Kirkland Signature frozen easy-peel shrimp**
- **5 large garlic cloves, minced**
- **3/4 teaspoon sea salt**
- **1/4 teaspoon ground black pepper**
- **1/8 teaspoon crushed red pepper**
- **5 tablespoons fresh lemon juice**
- **3/4 cup extra-virgin olive oil**
- **1/4 cup finely chopped fresh oregano**
- **Lemon wedges, for serving**

Defrost shrimp and rinse under running water. Leave the shrimp in their shells and set aside in a bowl.

In another bowl, combine garlic, salt, both peppers, lemon juice, oil and oregano; whisk until emulsified. Pour 1/4 cup of the mixture over the shrimp and toss together. Marinate for 20-30 minutes.

Prepare the grill for cooking over direct heat with medium-hot charcoal or gas.

Grill the shrimp for about 3-4 minutes, then turn over and continue until cooked through, 7-8 minutes total.

Transfer to a platter with lemon wedges. Serve with the remaining dressing for dipping. Makes 6-8 servings.

## Crab Salad Stuffed Sweet Mini Peppers

Royal Flavor

- **1 pound fresh lump crabmeat**
- **1 cup finely chopped celery**
- **1 cup finely chopped carrots**
- **3/4 cup mayonnaise**
- **1/4 cup lemon or lime juice (optional)**
- **1/4 cup finely chopped canned jalapeños**
- **Salt and pepper**
- **1 cup olive oil**
- **2 pounds (about 40) Royal Flavor* sweet mini peppers**

Place crab in a bowl and gently break into small pieces. Add celery, carrots, mayonnaise, lemon juice and jalapeños. Season to taste with salt and pepper. Mix the ingredients well and then refrigerate for 30 minutes to let the flavors develop.

Heat oil slowly in a frying pan to 300°F (keep the temperature below 350°F to prevent bitterness). Add salt and pepper to taste. Sauté the mini peppers until tender and then place on paper towels to absorb the excess oil.

Once the peppers have cooled, make a small cut along the side and remove the seeds. Stuff with the crab mixture. Makes 13-14 servings.

** Brands may vary by region; substitute a similar product.*

# Campari Caesar Bruschetta with Grilled Bread

## Mastronardi Produce/SUNSET

- 1 pound SUNSET* Campari tomatoes,
- 1 small loaf rustic artisanal bread or baguette
- Olive oil, for brushing
- Kosher salt
- 1/4 cup chopped fresh basil
- 2 tablespoons finely diced red onion
- 2-3 teaspoons minced fresh garlic
- 3 tablespoons high-quality Caesar dressing
- Freshly grated Parmesan cheese and small fresh basil leaves, for garnish (optional)

Preheat the grill to medium-high.

Dice tomatoes into 1/4- to 1/2-inch pieces and set in a strainer to drain off excess juice.

Cut the bread with a serrated knife. If using a "fat" bread loaf, cut six 1/2-inch slices, then cut each piece in half crosswise, making 12 pieces. If using a baguette, cut twelve 1/2-inch diagonal slices from the loaf. (Use any remaining bread for another purpose.)

Lightly brush both sides of the bread slices with oil and grill on each side until lightly marked or toasted. Sprinkle the bread lightly with salt. Place on a platter.

In a medium bowl, toss together the drained tomatoes, basil, onion, garlic and Caesar dressing. Divide the tomato mixture among the grilled bread slices. Sprinkle with Parmesan and garnish with basil leaves if desired. Makes 6-12 servings.

** Brands may vary by region; substitute a similar product.*

Goodness Grown Naturally™

## Wine-Steamed Clams with Orange Cream Sauce

### Cedar Key Aquaculture Farms

**36 Cedar Key Sweets* farm-raised clams, scrubbed**
**2 cups white wine**
**1/2 cup dairy sour cream**
**3 tablespoons orange juice**
**1 teaspoon prepared horseradish**
**1 teaspoon grated orange peel**
**Orange slices, for garnish**

Place clams and wine in a large saucepan; simmer, covered, over medium heat until the clams open.

Remove the clams from the pan; let cool. With a knife or spoon, loosen the clam meat and leave in the shell.

In a small bowl, combine sour cream, orange juice, horseradish and grated orange peel; mix well.

Place 1/4 teaspoon of sauce on each clam and arrange on a serving tray. Set the tray in the refrigerator and chill for 1 hour.

Garnish with orange slices and serve. Makes 6 servings.

** Brands may vary by region; substitute a similar product.*

## Halibut Grapefruit Tangerine Ceviche

### Seald Sweet

**3/4 cup fresh tangerine juice (about 3 Seald Sweet* tangerines)**
**1 cup fresh lime juice**
**1 large tomato, diced**
**1 small red onion, diced**
**2 bunches cilantro, leaves roughly chopped**
**2 jalapeños, finely chopped**
**1 1/2 teaspoons salt**
**1/2 teaspoon crushed red pepper**
**1 1/2 pounds halibut, cut into 1/4-inch cubes**
**1 cup Seald Sweet* tangerine sections, diced**
**1 cup Seald Sweet* red grapefruit sections, diced**
**2 tablespoons extra-virgin olive oil**
**Sliced avocado, for serving**
**Tortilla chips or tostados, for serving**

In a bowl, combine tangerine juice, lime juice, tomatoes, onions, cilantro, jalapeños, salt and red pepper. Mix until well blended.

Add halibut to the mixture and toss gently. Stir in diced tangerine and grapefruit. Cover and refrigerate for at least 2 hours but no longer than 12 hours.

Serve in tall martini glasses with a sprinkle of olive oil on top. Place the glasses on a serving plate full of avocado slices and tortilla chips or tostados.
Makes 10-12 servings.

**Tip:** Tilapia, cod or other white fish can be used for this recipe.

** Brands may vary by region; substitute a similar product.*

## Spicy Mussels in Adobo Sauce
### North Coast Seafoods

- 2 tablespoons vegetable oil
- 1/2 cup diced onion
- 1/2 cup diced red bell pepper
- 1 tablespoon chopped garlic
- 1 7-ounce can chipotle peppers in adobo sauce
- 2 pounds North Coast Seafoods* PEI rope-grown mussels
- 1 cup white wine
- 2 tablespoons butter
- 1 tablespoon chopped fresh cilantro
- Salt and pepper

In a large pot, heat oil over medium-high heat. Add onions, bell peppers and garlic; cook for 3-4 minutes, or until soft.

Add some chopped chipotle peppers with the adobo sauce, the amount depending on how spicy you want the dish (1 pepper and 1 tablespoon of sauce will yield a spicy bowl of mussels). Cook for 2-3 minutes.

Add mussels and wine, stir everything together and cover the pot. Cook for about 4 minutes, or until the mussels have opened.

Add butter and cilantro, mix well and adjust seasoning with salt and pepper. Makes 6 servings.

** Brands may vary by region; substitute a similar product.*

## Bacon-Wrapped Mango Wedges

### Freska Produce

**2 ripe Freska* mangoes**

**1 teaspoon canned chipotle pepper**

**12 slices bacon**

**Salt and pepper**

**4 tablespoons olive oil, divided**

**2 cups baby arugula**

**1/2 cup thin red onion strips**

**1/2 cup thin red bell pepper strips**

Peel mangoes and cut into 12 wedges, saving the trimmings. Set aside.

Place the mango trimmings in a blender and add just enough water to cover. Process until pureed; measure 1/2 cup puree. Add chipotle pepper to the 1/2 cup puree and blend until very smooth. Set aside.

Wrap each mango wedge with bacon and season to taste with salt and pepper. Heat 2 tablespoons oil over medium heat in a sauté pan. Add the mango wedges and cook on each side for 1-2 minutes, or until the bacon is cooked through and crisp. (A toothpick can be used to hold the bacon in place while cooking.)

In a mixing bowl, combine arugula, red onion and bell pepper. Lightly season with salt and pepper, and toss with 2 tablespoons oil.

To serve, place some salad mixture on each plate. Place 3 cooked mango wedges on each salad and drizzle with the chipotle dressing. Makes 4 servings.

*Recipe courtesy of Chef Peter Edwards.*

** Brands may vary by region; substitute a similar product.*

## Grilled Tuscan-Style Skewers

### Dulcinea

**3/4 cup honey**

**1/4 cup limoncello (lemon liqueur)**

**2 tablespoons butter**

**1 tablespoon lemon juice**

**1 Dulcinea* Tuscan-Style cantaloupe, seeded and cubed**

**2 lemons, very thinly sliced**

**Grated lemon peel and small fresh mint leaves, for garnish**

Preheat the grill to high.

In a small saucepan, combine honey, liqueur, butter and lemon juice. Bring to a boil, then reduce heat to medium and keep the mixture at a full rolling boil for about 8 minutes, or until golden brown. Remove from the heat and let cool.

Thread cantaloupe cubes and lemon slices onto metal skewers.

Grill for a few minutes on each side to lightly char, brushing with a little caramel sauce during the last few minutes of grilling.

Place on a platter and drizzle with the warm (not hot) caramel sauce.

Dust with grated lemon peel and garnish with mint leaves. Makes 6-8 servings.

** Brands may vary by region; substitute a similar product.*

# Grilled Hot Italian Sausage, Vidalia Onion and Pineapple

Premio

$^{3}/_{4}$ cup pineapple juice
2 garlic cloves, chopped
1 cup basil leaves, coarsely chopped
Salt
Hot pepper sauce
2 pounds Premio* hot Italian sausages, split lengthwise
1 large Vidalia onion, quartered and separated into individual pieces
4-8 slices fresh pineapple, quartered
Wooden skewers, for serving

In a large bowl, mix pineapple juice, garlic and basil. Season to taste with salt and hot pepper sauce.

Add sausages, onions and pineapple to the bowl and toss to coat. Marinate for 30-60 minutes.

Prepare a charcoal or wood fire.

Grill sausages, onions and pineapple over a hot fire, brushing with marinade as they cook.

Arrange sausages, onions and pineapple on skewers to serve. Makes 6-8 servings.

** Brands may vary by region; substitute a similar product.*

## Fresh California Grape Salsa
Stevco

**2 cups coarsely chopped California seedless grapes**
**1/2 cup chopped green onions**
**1/2 cup diced fresh chiles (or diced canned Anaheim chiles)**
**2 tablespoons chopped fresh cilantro (or 1/4 cup chopped fresh basil)**
**2 tablespoons red wine vinegar**
**1 garlic clove, minced**
**1/2 teaspoon salt**
**1/8 teaspoon hot pepper sauce**

Combine all ingredients in a medium bowl and mix well.

Let stand for at least 1 hour.

Drain off excess liquid before serving.

Serve with tortilla chips. Makes 8 servings.

**Nutritional information:** Each serving has 38 calories, 0.6 g protein, 9 g carbohydrates, 0.3 g fat, 0 mg cholesterol, 0.7 g fiber, 147 mg sodium.

## Peach-Grape Salsa
Divine Flavor

**1/4 cup lime juice**
**1 tablespoon honey**
**1/2 teaspoon salt**
**2 cups Divine Flavor* red and green seedless grapes, chopped**
**2 cups peeled and chopped Divine Flavor* peaches**
**1/4 cup chopped fresh cilantro**
**1 tablespoon finely chopped green bell pepper**
**1 small jalapeño, seeded and finely chopped**

In a large bowl, mix lime juice, honey and salt. Add remaining ingredients and toss.

Cover and refrigerate for at least 1 hour to let the flavors blend.

Serve with oven-toasted quartered mini pitas or corn chips. Makes 4-6 servings.

*Recipe developed by Christine W. Jackson, food stylist.*
** Brands may vary by region; substitute a similar product.*

# Craveable Taco Dip
## Don Miguel Mexican Foods

- 1 8-ounce package cream cheese, softened
- 1 16-ounce can refried beans
- 1 8-ounce package shredded Cheddar cheese
- 1 8-ounce package shredded Monterey Jack cheese
- 1 6-ounce can pitted medium black olives, sliced
- 1 4-ounce can diced green chiles
- 1 12-ounce jar sliced jalapeños

Preheat oven to 375°F.

Spread cream cheese evenly over the bottom of a 13-by-9-inch casserole.

Top with a layer of refried beans.

Add a layer of Cheddar cheese, then Monterey Jack cheese, and then olives.

Top with diced green chiles.

Add a generous handful of jalapeños for garnish and heat.

Bake for 15-20 minutes, or until the cheese is bubbling. Serve immediately.

This dip is delicious with any of your favorite Don Miguel products, especially mini tacos. Makes 12 servings.

## Avocado Garlic Dip for French Fries

### Chilean Hass Avocados

**5 Hass avocados from Chile***
**1/2 cup plain yogurt**
**1/4 cup grated onion**
**2 tablespoons lemon juice**
**2 tablespoons sesame oil**
**2 tablespoons mayonnaise**
**1 large garlic clove, finely chopped**
**2 teaspoons grated horseradish**
**Salt and pepper**
**Hot french fries, for serving**

Rinse avocados. Cut in half and spoon out the pit. Spoon out the flesh into a medium bowl. Mash with a fork or masher.

Stir in yogurt, onion, lemon juice, oil, mayonnaise, garlic and horseradish. Season to taste with salt and pepper.

Serve as a dip for hot french fries. Makes 8 servings.

**Tip:** This can also be served with fresh vegetable dippers, chips or toasted pita.

** Brands may vary by region; substitute a similar product.*

## Fresh Roma Tomato and Cucumber Salsa

### Houweling's Hot House

**2 pounds Houweling's* Roma Tomatoes on the Vine, seeded and chopped into large chunks**
**2 cups diced Houweling's* mini cucumbers**
**1/2 cup finely chopped red onion**
**1 tablespoon chopped garlic**
**2 jalapeños, stemmed, seeded and chopped**
**1 tablespoon olive oil**
**1 tablespoon red wine vinegar**
**Juice of 1 lime**
**Coarse kosher salt**
**1/4 cup chopped fresh cilantro**
**Tortilla or pita chips, for serving**

In a medium bowl, combine tomatoes, cucumbers, onions, garlic and jalapeños.

In a small bowl, beat oil and vinegar with a whisk or fork until well emulsified. Add lime juice, salt to taste and cilantro.

Pour the dressing over the tomato mixture and toss thoroughly. Chill for 30 minutes before serving.

Serve with tortilla or pita chips. Makes 6-8 servings.

** Brands may vary by region; substitute a similar product.*

## Aztec Pyramid Avocado Dip
Raskas

- 3 California avocados, peeled
- 2 tablespoons lemon juice
- 1 cup Raskas cream cheese, softened
- 2 cups Raskas sour cream
- 1 packet (1 1/4 ounces) taco seasoning mix
- 2 cups shredded sharp Cheddar cheese
- 3 cups finely chopped fresh tomatoes
- 5 green onions, sliced
- 1/2 cup black olives, sliced
- Tortilla chips, bell peppers, jicama and/or lobster, for dipping

Mash avocados and blend in lemon juice, mixing well. Spread evenly in a bowl or on a serving plate to the edges of the dish.

Beat cream cheese until smooth and creamy. Add sour cream, mixing well, and blend in taco seasoning. Spread over the avocado layer.

Sprinkle Cheddar over the cream cheese mixture.

Distribute tomatoes over the Cheddar layer.

Spread green onions over the tomato layer.

Top with olives.

Serve at room temperature with tortilla chips, bell peppers, jicama and/or lobster. Makes 8 servings.

## Easy Sesame Hummus

### Sensible Portions

- 1 15-ounce can garbanzo beans
- 3 tablespoons lemon juice
- 1/2 cup sesame seeds
- 1 garlic clove
- Salt
- Chopped fresh parsley, for garnish
- Sensible Portions* Veggie Straws or Pita Bites, for serving

In a blender or food processor, combine beans, including the liquid from the can, lemon juice, sesame seeds and garlic. Cover and blend at high speed, stopping occasionally to scrape the sides. Continue until the hummus has the desired consistency. Season with salt to taste.

Spoon the hummus into a serving dish. Sprinkle with parsley.

Serve with Veggie Straws or Pita Bites. Makes 10-12 servings.

** Brands may vary by region; substitute a similar product.*

Sensible Portions

Quick &Easy

## Fried Stuffed Olives

### Lindsay Olives

- 2 tablespoons minced garlic
- 2 tablespoons anchovy paste
- 1 tablespoon finely shredded lemon peel
- 1/2 teaspoon chopped fresh thyme
- 1/2 teaspoon chopped fresh basil
- 20 Lindsay extra-large California pitted ripe olives
- 3/4 cup flour
- 2 eggs, beaten
- 3/4 cup plain or seasoned dry bread crumbs
- Olive oil, for frying

In a small bowl, combine garlic, anchovy paste, lemon peel, thyme and basil. Transfer the mixture to a small pastry bag fitted with a small plain tip. Stuff olives with the mixture.

Roll the stuffed olives in flour, dip in beaten eggs and then roll in bread crumbs.

Pour oil into a medium saucepan to the depth of 1 inch. Heat oil over medium heat to 275°F. Fry the olives in batches for 3-4 minutes, or until crisp and golden brown. Drain on a paper-towel-lined plate. Serve warm. Makes 4 servings.

**Variation:** Substitute 5-6 tablespoons prepared sun-dried tomato tapenade or basil pesto for the garlic and anchovy mixture; proceed as directed above.

**Nutritional information:** Each serving has 302 calories, 8 g protein, 33 g carbohydrates, 15 g fat, 70 mg cholesterol, 2 g fiber, 560 mg sodium.

# Focaccia Pizza with Rosemary and Grapes

Anthony Vineyards

1 pound pizza dough
2 tablespoons extra-virgin olive oil
Coarse sea salt
1 garlic clove, minced
1 shallot, sliced into thin rounds
1 tablespoon fresh rosemary leaves
1/2 cup green seedless grapes, halved
1/2 cup red seedless grapes, halved

Preheat oven to 400°F.

Roll pizza dough into a rectangle on a sheet of parchment paper. Transfer the dough on the parchment paper to a baking sheet.

Using a pastry brush, cover the top of the dough with olive oil. Sprinkle with sea salt. Sprinkle with garlic, shallot and rosemary. Arrange grapes on the pizza, pushing down into the dough.

Bake until golden brown, about 25 minutes. Cut into slices and serve. Makes 4-6 servings.

## Cayenne Coconut Crusted Chicken with Spicy Apricot Dipping Sauce

Mazola

- **1/2 cup cornstarch**
- **1 teaspoon cayenne pepper**
- **3/4 teaspoon salt**
- **1/2 teaspoon finely ground black pepper**
- **3 large egg whites**
- **2 cups sweetened shredded coconut**
- **1 1/2 pounds chicken tenders**
- **Mazola* corn oil, enough for deep-frying**

*SPICY APRICOT DIPPING SAUCE*

- **1 tablespoon red wine vinegar**
- **1 cup apricot preserves**
- **1 teaspoon crushed red pepper flakes**

Mix cornstarch, cayenne pepper, salt and black pepper in a shallow bowl. Set aside.

Beat egg whites in a medium mixing bowl until frothy.

Place coconut in a shallow bowl.

Dredge chicken tenders in the cornstarch mixture; shake off excess. Dip chicken in the egg whites, then press into the coconut, turning to coat both sides.

Heat oil in a heavy skillet (oil should be about 2 inches deep) or a deep-fat fryer to 350°F. Add chicken to the hot oil in batches. Fry until cooked through, about 2-3 minutes. Transfer to a paper-towel-lined plate.

To make the Spicy Apricot Dipping Sauce, place all ingredients in a small bowl and stir to mix thoroughly. Serve the chicken hot with the Spicy Apricot Dipping Sauce. Makes 8 appetizer or 4 entrée servings.

** Brands may vary by region; substitute a similar product.*

## Baja Cod Lettuce Wraps

Trident Seafoods

- **12 portions Trident Seafoods* Baja Style frozen cod**
- **12 leaves green leaf lettuce**
- **12 slices avocado**
- **12 slices red bell pepper**
- **24 cilantro sprigs**
- **Toothpicks**

*CHIPOTLE AIOLI SAUCE*

- **6 tablespoons mayonnaise**
- **6 tablespoons sour cream or plain yogurt**
- **1 tablespoon chopped garlic**
- **3 tablespoons Tabasco chipotle pepper sauce**

To prepare the sauce, mix all ingredients in a bowl. Let stand in the refrigerator for at least 20 minutes.

Preheat oven to 450°F.

Bake frozen cod portions on a lightly greased baking sheet for 17-20 minutes, turning the pieces halfway through.

In the center of each lettuce leaf, perpendicular to the stem, place avocado, bell pepper and cilantro sprigs. Top with cod and drizzle with a little sauce. Starting from the stem, roll up and secure with a toothpick through the stem.

Serve the remaining dressing on the side for dipping. Makes 6 servings.

** Brands may vary by region; substitute a similar product.*

# Kickin' Crabby Patties

## Kirkland Signature/Request Foods

When serving Kirkland Signature frozen lasagna, start the meal with this dish.

2 tablespoons Old Bay seasoning
$1/2$ teaspoon coarsely ground black pepper
3 tablespoons Dijon mustard
2 tablespoons Frank's Red Hot Sauce
4 tablespoons fresh lemon juice
$1/2$ cup Hellmann's (or Best Foods) light mayonnaise
3 large eggs
$1/2$ cup minced green onions
$1/2$ cup finely diced yellow onion
$1/2$ cup finely diced celery
$1/2$ cup finely diced yellow bell peppers
$1/2$ cup finely diced red bell peppers
3-3 $1/2$ cups dry bread crumbs, divided
$1/3$ cup Kirkland Signature Parmigiano Reggiano cheese
1 pound lump crabmeat
Olive oil

*CAPER SAUCE*

1 cup Hellmann's (or Best Foods) light mayonnaise
$1/2$ cup sour cream
4 tablespoons capers
2 tablespoons Frank's Red Hot Sauce
2 tablespoons fresh lemon juice
$1/4$ teaspoon coarsely ground black pepper

In a bowl, combine Old Bay seasoning, pepper, mustard, hot sauce, lemon juice, mayonnaise and eggs; mix until well blended. Stir in onions, celery and bell peppers. Stir in 1 $1/2$ cups bread crumbs and Parmesan. Gently fold crab into the mixture. Refrigerate for 1-2 hours.

To prepare the Caper Sauce, place all ingredients in a blender and puree.

Shape the crab mixture into 3-ounce patties. Gently coat the patties with the remaining bread crumbs.

In a sauté pan over medium heat, heat enough oil to generously coat the pan. Gently place the patties in the pan and cook for 4 minutes per side. Drain on paper towels. Serve with Caper Sauce. Makes 20 patties.

KIRKLAND Signature

# Southwest-Style Roasted Chicken Spread

## Sensible Portions

- 2 jalapeños, split and seeds removed
- 2 garlic cloves
- 1/4 cup fresh cilantro leaves
- 1 1/2 tablespoons lime juice
- 1/4 teaspoon cayenne pepper
- 1 teaspoon paprika
- 1 pound roasted chicken breast
- 3/4 cup sour cream
- 1/4 cup heavy cream
- Salt and pepper
- 1 20-ounce box Sensible Portions* Pita Bites–Sea Salt

In a food processer, combine jalapeños, garlic, cilantro, lime juice, cayenne pepper and paprika; chop well but do not puree.

Cut chicken into 1- to 2-inch pieces. Add to the food processor with sour cream and pulse slowly. Add heavy cream and pulse until the spread has the desired consistency. Season to taste with salt and pepper.

Spoon the spread into a serving dish. Serve with Pita Bites. Makes 10-12 servings.

**Tip:** If the spread is too thick, slowly add more heavy cream.

** Brands may vary by region; substitute a similar product.*

# Cherry Meatball Sliders

## Grant J. Hunt Company

- 1 pound lean ground beef
- 1 cup pitted and chopped Northwest* fresh sweet cherries
- 1 egg, lightly beaten
- 1/4 cup chopped onion
- 2 tablespoons chopped fresh parsley
- 1 tablespoon Dijon mustard
- 3/4 teaspoon garlic salt
- 1/2 teaspoon ground pepper
- 16 small lettuce leaves
- 16 dinner rolls, sliced in half

*CHERRY AVOCADO SALSA*

- 1 cup pitted and chopped Northwest* fresh sweet cherries
- 1 ripe avocado, pitted, peeled and coarsely mashed
- 1/4 cup finely chopped Anaheim chile
- 2 tablespoons chopped green onions
- 1 tablespoon balsamic vinegar
- 1/2 teaspoon garlic salt
- 1/4 teaspoon ground pepper

Preheat oven to 350°F.

In a bowl, mix ground beef, cherries, egg, onion, parsley, mustard, garlic salt and pepper. Form into 16 meatballs; place on a rack in a broiler pan. Bake for about 20 minutes, or until the juices run clear, turning the meatballs halfway through the baking time.

To prepare the salsa, combine all ingredients in a bowl and stir to blend.

Gently toss hot meatballs with 1/2 cup salsa, if desired. Place 1 meatball and 1 lettuce leaf on each roll. Serve the remaining salsa on the side. Makes 8-16 servings.

**Tip:** Substitute Blue Goose* Italian prune plums as a delicious alternative.

** Brands may vary by region; substitute a similar product.*

# Coconut Curry Trail Mix
## Kirkland Signature/Kerry

- 1 cup Kirkland Signature Cinnamon Pecan cereal
- 1/4 cup sweetened coconut
- 1/3 cup whole cashews
- 1/4 cup coconut milk
- 1 tablespoon canola oil
- 1 teaspoon curry powder
- 3 tablespoons brown sugar
- Dash of salt
- 1/3 cup golden raisins
- 1/3 cup diced dried mango
- 1/2 cup apple chips
- 1/3 cup sweet potato chips

Preheat oven to 350°F.

In a large mixing bowl, combine cereal, coconut and cashews.

In a small bowl, combine coconut milk, oil, curry powder, brown sugar and salt; mix well. Pour over the cereal mixture. Stir until evenly coated.

Spread the mixture evenly on a baking sheet lined with parchment paper or aluminum foil. Bake for 15 minutes, or until lightly browned. Remove from the oven and let cool.

Meanwhile, combine raisins, mango, apple chips and sweet potato chips in a large bowl. Once the cereal mixture has cooled, add to the fruit and stir to blend.

Store in an airtight container. Makes 11 servings.

KIRKLAND Signature KERRY

## Green Tea Holiday Punch

### Kirkland Signature/Ito En

- 10 Kirkland Signature/Ito En green tea bags
- 2 quarts water
- 4 cinnamon sticks, divided
- 8 whole cloves, plus more for garnish
- 4 peeled slices fresh ginger (about 1 by 2 inches), divided
- 1 apple
- 1 orange
- 1 quart unfiltered apple juice
- Cranberries, for garnish (optional)

Remove tea bags from individual packets. Tie the tea bag strings together.

Pour water into a large pitcher and lay a wooden spatula across the rim. Wrap the tea bag strings around the handle and immerse the tea bags in the water.

Add 2 cinnamon sticks, 8 cloves and 2 ginger slices to the water. Let steep at room temperature for 2 hours. Remove the tea bags and refrigerate the tea for up to 1 hour.

Wash, core and slice the apple; stud with cloves.

Wash the orange, then cut into thin slices.

To serve the punch, mix the steeped green tea, apple juice and 2 ginger slices. Stir well. Garnish with the sliced fruit, cinnamon sticks and cranberries.

Serve chilled. Makes 3 quarts (12 cups).

## Angel Punch

### Kirkland Signature/Newman's Own

- 1 cup simple syrup (see tip)
- 2 quarts Kirkland Signature/Newman's Own 100% Grape Juice
- 1 pint lemon juice
- 1 quart green tea
- 1 small block of ice
- 2 quarts club soda
- 1 lemon, sliced, for serving (optional)

Combine simple syrup, grape juice, lemon juice and green tea. Chill for 1-2 hours.

Place the block of ice in a large punch bowl. Pour the chilled punch over the ice. Add club soda.

Serve in punch cups with lemon slices.
Makes 14 servings.

**Tip:** To make your own simple syrup, mix one part sugar to one part water in a saucepan. Bring to a boil, then simmer until the sugar is dissolved. Let cool.

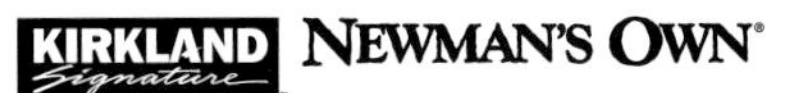

# Blackberry Margarita Duet
## Sun Belle

**Kosher salt**
**Lime wedges for coating rims of glasses**
**18 ounces Sun Belle* blackberries**
**8 toothpicks**
**$1/2$ cup lime juice**
**$1/2$ cup lemon juice**
**$1/2$ cup agave nectar**
**2 tablespoons Rose's sweetened lime juice**
**$1/2$ cup orange juice (or $1/2$ cup orange liqueur such as Cointreau)**
**Water (or 1 $1/2$ cups fine tequila)**
**Ice**

Spread a layer of salt in a saucer. Rub lime wedges on the rims of 8 glasses. Dip each rim in the salt.

Set aside 16 blackberries for garnish. Spear 2 blackberries on each toothpick.

In a blender, combine the remaining blackberries, lime juice and lemon juice. Blend until liquefied. Force the mixture through a strainer to remove the seeds.

For Virgin Margaritas, stir agave nectar, Rose's lime juice and orange juice into the blackberry mixture. Add enough water to make 3 cups.

For Spiked Margaritas, stir agave nectar, Rose's lime juice, orange liqueur and tequila into the blackberry mixture.

Pour into a chilled blender. Fill the blender with ice. Blend until smooth.

Pour the frozen drinks into the prepared glasses. Place a toothpick of blackberries in each glass. Makes 8 servings.

** Brands may vary by region; substitute a similar product.*

# Blueberry Sparkling Lemonade
## Naturipe Farms

**2 $1/4$ cups Naturipe Farms* fresh blueberries, divided**
**1 cup water**
**$1/2$ cup sugar**
**$3/4$ cup fresh lemon juice**
**1 cup ginger ale**
**Mint sprigs, for garnish**

In a blender, combine 2 cups blueberries, water, sugar and lemon juice; blend until very smooth. Strain through a fine-mesh strainer.

Fill 4 tall glasses with ice cubes. Top the ice cubes in each glass with 1 tablespoon of blueberries.

Fill the glasses with the lemonade mixture—about $3/4$ cup per glass. Top off with ginger ale. Garnish with mint sprigs. Makes 4 servings.

**Tip:** For an adult version, add 1 shot of vodka over the ice before pouring in the blueberry lemonade.

** Brands may vary by region; substitute a similar product.*

## Coffee Liqueur
### Kirkland Signature

- **3/4 cup sugar**
- **4 cups freshly brewed extra-strong Kirkland Signature whole bean coffee (see tips)**
- **4 cups Kirkland Signature or premium vodka**
- **2-2 1/2 tablespoons Kirkland Signature pure vanilla extract**

Add sugar to the hot coffee. Stir until dissolved.

Add vodka and vanilla. Mix together well.

Adjust the ingredients to taste. Let cool.

Pour into a resealable container or containers (nice liqueur bottles are available online). Store at room temperature. Makes approximately 8 cups (64 ounces).

**Tips:** Brew the coffee using fresh, cold water. If the water in your area doesn't taste very good, use bottled drinking water. For extra-strong coffee, use 1 1/2 times the amount of coffee you usually use. Try adding other ingredients for your own creation, such as 1/4 cup good-quality chocolate syrup. Serve it hot or over ice, or try it with coffee, cream, ice cream, chocolate or all of the above!

## Chocolate Peanut Butter Hot Cocoa
### ConAgra Foods

- **1 envelope (1 ounce) Swiss Miss Milk Chocolate Hot Cocoa Mix***
- **1 tablespoon Peter Pan Creamy Peanut Butter***
- **3/4 cup hot (not boiling) water**
- **Reddi-wip Original Whipped Light Cream*, for serving**
- **Grated chocolate, for serving (optional)**

Place cocoa mix in a cup. Add peanut butter. Gradually stir in hot water until blended.

Top with Reddi-wip. Add grated chocolate, if desired. Makes 1 serving.

** Brands may vary by region; substitute a similar product.*

# Salads and soups

## Storing your produce

Buying bulk-size amounts of fresh fruit and vegetables has many advantages. The downside is the threat of spoilage if you don't eat everything in time. Some simple storage tips can help ensure that your produce will stay fresh as long as possible.

**By the editors at America's Test Kitchen**

America's Test Kitchen, founded by Christopher Kimball (center), is home to *Cook's Illustrated* and *Cook's Country* magazines and a growing book-publishing program. The company also hosts the hit public-TV shows *America's Test Kitchen* and *Cook's Country*. Their latest book is *The America's Test Kitchen Healthy Family Cookbook.*

**Ethylene: the enemy of freshness**

As produce ripens, it emits small amounts of the ripening hormone ethylene. If ethylene is allowed to build up (in the closed environment of a plastic bag, for example, or a crisper), the gas will activate enzymes that break down and soften the cell walls of produce, speeding moisture loss and spoilage. Most storage techniques are designed to slow the production of ethylene or mitigate its impact.

**It's a wrap**

It's a good idea to look at whether you can store produce in the packaging in which it was sold. Sometimes ready-made packaging has a function beyond simple convenience and can actually help to preserve the contents. For example, though they appear solid, the bags in which some greens are sold are made of a polymer that allows ripening gases to pass through freely, staving off spoilage. Other types of packaging feature small perforations or other openings; here, too, the intent is to allow gases to escape while protecting the produce from the drying effects of air.

**Keep in the front of the fridge**

These items are sensitive to chill injury and should be placed in the front of the fridge, where the temperatures tend to be higher.

| | | |
|---|---|---|
| **Berries** | **Corn on the cob** | **Peas** |
| **Citrus** | **Melons** | |

**Best in the crisper**

These items do best in the humid environment of the refrigerator's crisper.

| | | |
|---|---|---|
| **Artichokes** | **Cucumbers** | **Peppers** |
| **Beets** | **Eggplant** | **Radishes** |
| **Broccoli** | **Fresh herbs** | **Scallions** |
| **Cabbage** | **Green beans** | **Summer squash** |
| **Carrots** | **Leafy greens** | **Turnips** |
| **Cauliflower** | **Leeks** | **Zucchini** |
| **Celery** | **Lettuce** | |
| **Chiles** | **Mushrooms** | |

**Chill anywhere**

These items are not prone to chill injury and can be stored anywhere in the fridge (including its coldest zones), provided the temperature doesn't freeze them.

| | | |
|---|---|---|
| **Apples** | **Grapes** | **Cherries** |

**On the counter**

Some produce is sensitive to chill injury and is subject to dehydration, internal browning and/or internal and external pitting if stored in the refrigerator.

| | | |
|---|---|---|
| **Avocados*** | **Mangoes** | **Peaches** |
| **Bananas** | **Nectarines** | **Pineapple** |
| **Kiwis*** | **Papayas** | **Tomatoes** |

*Once they've reached their peak ripeness, these fruits can be stored in the refrigerator to prevent overripening, but some discoloration may occur.

**In the pantry**

The following produce should be kept at cool room temperature and away from light to prevent sprouting (in the case of potatoes) and to prolong shelf life.

| | | |
|---|---|---|
| **Garlic** | **Potatoes** | **Sweet potatoes** |
| **Onions** | **Shallots** | **Winter squash** |

**When to wash**

It's a good idea to thoroughly wash all produce. It's best to wash produce just before you use it. Moisture promotes the growth of mold, which in turn causes spoilage. If you do wash ahead of time, make sure to dry the produce thoroughly before storing.

**Water your spears**

To keep asparagus tender and flavorful, trim the ends and store the spears upright in cool water in the fridge. Limp broccoli and celery benefit from the same treatment.

## Bella Chopped Prawn Salad
### FirstFruits

- **1 1/2 pounds tiger prawns, cooked and cut into bite-size pieces (3-4 pieces per prawn)**
- **3 cups chopped FirstFruits* Fuji apples (unpeeled)**
- **3 cups chopped celery**
- **1 1/2 cups halved red seedless grapes**
- **1/2 cup shredded Parmesan cheese**
- **4 cups butter lettuce torn into bite-size pieces**
- **1/4 cup shredded Cheddar cheese**

***DRESSING***

- **1 1/2 cups mayonnaise**
- **1/2 cup Heinz chili sauce**
- **1 1/2 tablespoons dried minced onion**
- **1/2 teaspoon garlic seasoning**
- **3 boiled eggs, minced**
- **2 tablespoons salad seasoning (Salad Elegance)**
- **Salt and pepper**

Blend all dressing ingredients and chill for at least 1 hour.

In a large bowl, combine prawns, apples, celery, grapes and Parmesan.

Add approximately 1 cup of the dressing to the salad and toss to coat.

Place lettuce in the bottom of a large bowl. Spoon dressed salad on top of the lettuce and sprinkle with Cheddar cheese.

Serve chilled, with the remaining dressing on the side. Makes 6-8 servings.

*Recipe created by Tracy Tudor, FirstFruits apple grower.*
** Brands may vary by region; substitute a similar product.*

## Summer Shrimp and Fresh Fruit Salad
### Bee Sweet/Premier Citrus Marketing/ Mas Melons & Grapes/Regatta Tropicals

- **8 ounces grilled/cooked peeled small shrimp (51-70 count)**
- **1 grapefruit, peeled and pithed**
- **1 small honeydew melon, halved, seeded, sliced and rind removed**
- **4 kiwifruit, peeled and cut in wedges**
- **1/2 cup fresh cilantro leaves, for garnish**

***DRESSING***

- **2 tablespoons Kirkland Signature extra virgin olive oil**
- **1/4 teaspoon toasted sesame oil**
- **3 tablespoons orange or grapefruit juice**
- **2-3 teaspoons minced shallot**
- **1 teaspoon soy sauce**
- **1 teaspoon honey**
- **1 teaspoon grated fresh ginger**

To prepare the dressing, combine all ingredients in a small bowl and whisk together.

Toss shrimp with 2 tablespoons of the dressing.

Cut grapefruit crosswise into 4 slices. Place a slice in the center of each of 4 serving plates. Place honeydew and kiwi slices around the grapefruit in pinwheel fashion.

Mound the shrimp on the grapefruit. Drizzle the remaining dressing over the fruit slices. Garnish with cilantro leaves. Makes 4 servings.

**Tip:** As a variation, cut the fruit into chunks and thread onto small skewers, alternating with the marinated shrimp. Brush with the remaining dressing. Serve as festive appetizers.

*Recipe developed by Amy Muzyka-McGuire, RD.*

# Provençal Salad

## Ready Pac

1 16-ounce bag Ready Pac* Grand Parisian Complete Salad

1 ripe Hass avocado

1/2 cup diced ripe tomatoes

4 4-ounce grilled boneless, skinless chicken breasts, cut into bite-size strips, or 12 ounces cooked shrimp (see note)

Remove the dressing packet, frosted almonds, dried cranberries and feta cheese from the salad bag. Chill the salad greens.

In a small bowl, mash half of the avocado with a fork. Slice remaining half of avocado and set aside. Stir mashed avocado into the dressing. Set aside.

To serve, place the chilled salad greens in a large bowl. Top with tomatoes, frosted almonds, dried cranberries, feta, sliced avocado and chicken strips or shrimp. Add the avocado dressing and toss. Makes 4-6 servings.

**Note:** Either purchase cooked chicken or shrimp, or cook them with 2 tablespoons olive oil seasoned with 1/2 teaspoon each salt and pepper. Grilling will add a wonderful flavor note, but the salad will still succeed if they are baked, broiled or even poached.

**Variations:** If you love avocados, use two: one for the dressing, one for the salad, sliced or diced. Use diced ripe heirloom tomatoes, peeled cucumbers or shaved fennel.

** Brands may vary by region; substitute a similar product.*

Quick &Easy

# Apple Crab Salad
## Yakima Fresh

1 pound fresh crabmeat
1 large Yakima Fresh* Red Delicious apple, cored and thinly sliced
1 cup whole pecans
1 cup red seedless grapes
Gorgonzola cheese, crumbled, to taste
3/4 cup mayonnaise
1 cup light sour cream
Red leaf lettuce, for serving
Parsley sprigs, for garnish

Combine crabmeat, apple, pecans, grapes and cheese in a bowl.

In another bowl, combine mayonnaise and sour cream; stir until well blended. Stir into the crab mixture. Chill at least 2 hours before serving.

Serve on a bed of red leaf lettuce, garnished with parsley sprigs. Makes 6-8 servings.

**Tip:** Lemon slices or wedges can also be added for garnish.

** Brands may vary by region; substitute a similar product.*

## Garden Chicken Salad

### Stemilt Growers

- **3 cups cubed roasted chicken (2 chicken breasts)**
- **1 cup sliced sugar snap peas**
- **3/4 cup diced celery**
- **1/2 cup chopped green onions**
- **1/3 cup chopped pecans**
- **1 Stemilt Pink Lady Brand* apple, diced**
- **12 leaves butter-leaf lettuce**
- **10 Stemilt dark sweet cherries (or Rainiers), quartered or halved**
- **1 large red onion, sliced**
- **1/2-1 cup fresh pea sprouts**

***DRESSING***

- **1/2 cup mayonnaise**
- **1 6-ounce container plain yogurt**
- **1/3 cup honey mustard**
- **2 tablespoons fresh lemon juice**
- **1 tablespoon apple cider vinegar**
- **1/4 teaspoon salt**
- **1/8 teaspoon ground black pepper**

In a large bowl, combine chicken, peas, celery, green onions, pecans and apple. Set aside.

In a separate bowl, combine all ingredients for the dressing. Whisk to completely incorporate.

Slowly add the dressing to the chicken mixture, a little at a time so as not to saturate the salad. Refrigerate the dressed chicken salad for at least 1 hour before serving. Refrigerate any remaining dressing in a covered container.

Serve the salad on lettuce, topped with cherries, red onions and pea sprouts. Makes 6 servings.

** Brands may vary by region; substitute a similar product.*

## Island Pineapple Chicken Salad

### Alpine Fresh

- **1 1/2 pounds (4 cups) diced cooked chicken breast**
- **2-3 cups (1 pound) diced Alpine Fresh* fresh cut pineapple**
- **2 cups diced celery**
- **1 bunch green onions, thinly sliced**
- **Salt and pepper**
- **1 head romaine or Bibb lettuce**
- **1/3 cup sliced almonds, toasted**
- **1/3 cup shredded coconut, toasted**

***DRESSING***

- **3/4 cup mayonnaise**
- **2 teaspoons Dijon mustard**
- **1 teaspoon curry powder**
- **1/2-1 teaspoon salt**
- **1/4 teaspoon ground pepper**
- **Grated peel and juice of 1 large lemon**

In a large bowl, combine chicken, pineapple, celery, onions, and salt and pepper to taste.

To prepare the dressing, combine all ingredients in a small bowl and blend.

Add dressing to the salad mixture and stir to coat well.

Serve on whole lettuce leaves. Garnish with almonds and coconut. Makes 6-8 servings.

*Recipe developed by Christine W. Jackson, food stylist.*

** Brands may vary by region; substitute a similar product.*

# Grape and Orange Chicken Salad in Lettuce Cups

Chilean Fresh Fruit Association

- 2 cups diced grilled chicken breast
- 1 cup red and green seedless Chilean* grapes, halved
- 1/2 cup thinly sliced celery
- 1/2 cup sliced almonds, toasted and coarsely chopped
- 2 tablespoons thinly sliced green onion
- 1/4 cup goat cheese (chèvre)
- 2 1/2 medium oranges, peeled, sectioned and cut into bite-size pieces
- 1 head butter lettuce
- Salt and pepper

*DRESSING*

- Juice of 1/2 medium orange
- 1 teaspoon chopped fresh Italian parsley
- 1/2 teaspoon Dijon mustard
- 1/2 teaspoon salt
- 1/4 teaspoon ground black pepper
- 2 tablespoons olive oil

In a medium bowl, combine chicken, grapes, celery, almonds, green onion, cheese and oranges.

To prepare the dressing, combine orange juice, parsley, mustard, salt and pepper in a small bowl. Gradually whisk in oil.

Add the dressing to the chicken mixture; toss to combine.

Remove 4-8 leaves from the lettuce head and divide equally among 4 plates. Top with the salad. Add salt and pepper to taste. Makes 4 servings.

** Brands may vary by region; substitute a similar product.*

## Persimmon-Chicken Salad

### Regatta Tropicals/Richard Bagdasarian

**2 cups (about 12 ounces) boneless, skinless chicken, baked or grilled and cut in bite-size strips**

**1 ripe persimmon, thinly sliced or cut in chunks**

**1 cup halved red or green seedless grapes**

**1/3 cup coarsely chopped toasted pecans**

**2-3 tablespoons sliced green onions**

**1 small head Bibb or Boston lettuce**

**Additional persimmon slices and small grape clusters, for garnish (optional)**

*DRESSING*

**1/3 cup mayonnaise**

**1 tablespoon seasoned rice vinegar**

**2 teaspoons minced fresh ginger**

**1 tablespoon chopped fresh herb of choice (or 1 teaspoon dried): tarragon, parsley, rosemary or thyme**

**1/4 teaspoon crushed red pepper**

**Sea salt to taste**

In a medium bowl, combine chicken, persimmon, grapes, pecans and green onions.

To prepare the dressing, combine all ingredients in a small bowl and stir to blend.

Gently stir the dressing into the chicken mixture.

Place 2-3 lettuce leaves on each of 4 plates. Top with a scoop of salad. Garnish with persimmon slices and a grape cluster. Makes 4 servings.

*Recipe developed by Amy Muzyka-McGuire, RD.*

## Summer Salad with Orange Dressing

### Kirkland Signature

**4 cups Kirkland Signature frozen Normandy-Style Vegetable Blend, thawed**

**3 cooked and seasoned chicken breasts, cut in bite-size pieces**

**1/4 cup Kirkland Signature extra virgin olive oil**

**3 tablespoons plain yogurt**

**4 tablespoons apple cider vinegar**

**Freshly squeezed juice of 1 orange**

**1 tablespoon orange marmalade**

**1/4 cup sweetened dried cranberries**

**1/4 cup cashews**

**1/2 red onion, cut in fine strips**

In a large bowl, combine thawed vegetable blend and chicken.

In a small bowl, combine oil, yogurt, vinegar, orange juice and marmalade; mix until well blended.

Pour the dressing over the chicken and vegetables. Stir in cranberries, cashews and onions.

Makes 4-6 servings.

# Tuscan Bread Salad
## Panné Provincio

7 slices Panné Provincio* roasted garlic bread, cut 1 inch thick
6 tablespoons olive oil, divided
1 5-ounce package baby spinach
12 ounces cooked boneless, skinless chicken breasts, cut into 3/4-inch cubes
1 cup grape tomatoes, halved
1/2 cup pitted Kalamata olives, halved
4 ounces fresh mozzarella, cut into 1/2-inch cubes
1/4 medium red onion, sliced into thin wedges
1/3 cup chopped fresh parsley
1/4 cup thinly sliced fresh basil leaves
1 cup prepared balsamic vinaigrette, divided

Cut bread slices into 1-inch cubes. Heat 3 tablespoons oil in a sauté pan over medium-high heat for 1-2 minutes, or until hot. Add half of the bread cubes and cook for 2-3 minutes, turning the cubes, or until golden brown. Transfer to a paper-towel-lined plate. Repeat with remaining 3 tablespoons oil and bread cubes.

Arrange spinach on a large platter. Top with bread cubes, chicken, tomatoes, olives, mozzarella and onions. Toss gently. Sprinkle with parsley and basil.

Drizzle 1/2 cup vinaigrette over the salad. Serve with the remaining vinaigrette on the side. Makes 8 servings.

**Tip:** Substitute 4 ounces of perlini (mini fresh mozzarella balls) for the cubed fresh mozzarella.

** Brands may vary by region; substitute a similar product.*

## Crunchy Asian Salad with Fish Sticks
### Trident Seafoods

- 3 cups shredded iceberg lettuce
- 3 cups shredded Napa cabbage
- 3 cups shredded purple cabbage
- 1/2 cup sliced water chestnuts
- Salt and pepper
- 12 Trident Seafoods* Ultimate Fish Sticks

*DRESSING*

- 4 tablespoons peanut oil
- 3 tablespoons toasted sesame oil
- 3 tablespoons seasoned rice vinegar
- 1 teaspoon sugar
- 1 tablespoon grated fresh ginger
- 2 garlic cloves, minced

*TOPPINGS*

- 1/4 cup sliced almonds
- 2 tablespoons toasted sesame seeds
- 1/2 cup chopped green onions

Preheat oven to 475°F.

To prepare the dressing, mix all ingredients in a large bowl.

Add lettuce, cabbages and water chestnuts to the dressing and toss to coat. Season to taste with salt and pepper.

Bake fish sticks for 11-13 minutes, turning the pieces halfway through.

Divide the salad among 4 plates or dinner bowls and top with the fish sticks. Sprinkle with sliced almonds, toasted sesame seeds and green onions. Makes 6 servings.

** Brands may vary by region; substitute a similar product.*

## Buffalo Grilled Chicken over Greens
### Perdue

- 3 tablespoons hot pepper sauce
- 3 tablespoons butter, melted
- Salt
- 4 Perdue* Individually Frozen Select Size Boneless, Skinless Chicken Breasts
- 1/2 cup light mayonnaise
- 1/4 cup plain low-fat yogurt
- 1/2 cup crumbled blue cheese (about 2 ounces)
- 1 garlic clove, finely chopped
- 8 cups salad greens

Preheat the grill or broiler to medium-high.

In a small bowl, combine hot pepper sauce, melted butter and salt to taste; mix until blended.

Grill or broil frozen chicken, turning occasionally and basting with the pepper sauce mixture, for 15 minutes, or until a meat thermometer inserted in the center registers 170°F. Note: Do not baste during the last 5 minutes of grilling.

Meanwhile, in a medium bowl, combine mayonnaise, yogurt, blue cheese and garlic until blended; refrigerate until ready to serve.

To serve, cut the chicken into strips and arrange over salad greens. Spoon garlic blue cheese dressing over the chicken and greens. Makes 4 servings.

** Brands may vary by region; substitute a similar product.*

## Asparagus, Grape Tomato and Crab Cake Salad with Chili-Lime Sauce

Alpine Fresh

**2 pounds Alpine Fresh* asparagus, trimmed**
**1 pound Alpine Fresh* grape tomatoes, halved**
**3 cups chopped romaine**
**Salt and pepper**

*CRAB CAKES*

**1 13-ounce can lump crabmeat (12-14 ounces fresh crabmeat)**
**2 tablespoons mayonnaise**
**1/4 cup grated Parmesan cheese**
**2 tablespoons chopped green onion**
**2 tablespoons chopped fresh cilantro**
**2 large eggs**
**1 cup panko bread crumbs**
**Salt and pepper**
**2 tablespoons vegetable oil**

*DRESSING*

**1/2 cup mayonnaise**
**1/2-1 tablespoon chili lime hot sauce or other hot sauce**
**2 tablespoons lime juice**
**2 tablespoons chopped fresh cilantro**

Cut asparagus into 1-inch pieces. Steam or blanch for 3 minutes in salted water, then drain and chill in iced water.

To prepare the crab cakes, combine crab, mayonnaise, Parmesan, green onion, cilantro, eggs, panko, and salt and pepper to taste in a bowl. Stir until well blended and form into 6 cakes.

Heat oil in a frying pan over medium heat. Add crab cakes and cook for about 3-4 minutes on each side, or until browned and heated through.

To prepare the dressing, whisk together all ingredients.

Combine asparagus, grape tomatoes and lettuce. Place 2 cups of the vegetables on each plate. Season to taste with salt and pepper.

Place 1 crab cake on top of each serving of vegetables and drizzle dressing over all. Makes 6 servings.

**Tip:** Garnish with chopped cilantro and lime wedges.

*Recipe developed by Christine W. Jackson, food stylist.*
** Brands may vary by region; substitute a similar product.*

## Black Olive Marinated Tuna Salad

Norpac Fisheries Export

**1/4 cup red wine vinegar**
**2 tablespoons minced shallot**
**1 teaspoon dry mustard**
**1 cup olive oil**
**1/4 cup chicken stock**
**1/4 cup black olives (your choice), pitted and finely chopped**
**Salt and pepper**
**4 6-ounce tuna steaks**

*SALAD*

**6 cups shredded romaine lettuce**
**16-24 green beans, blanched**
**4 hard-boiled eggs, quartered**
**12 olives**
**16 cherry tomatoes**
**Thinly shredded carrots**

In a medium bowl, combine vinegar, shallots and mustard. Whisk in oil and chicken stock slowly to emulsify. Stir in olives and season to taste with salt and pepper.

Using half of the vinaigrette, marinate the tuna for 1-2 hours.

Preheat a pan or grill. Add the tuna and sear over high heat for about 2 minutes per side.

To prepare the salad, place the romaine in a large bowl and toss with some of the remaining vinaigrette until lightly coated. Spread the romaine on a large platter.

Slice the tuna. Arrange the tuna and the other salad ingredients attractively on top of the romaine. Makes 4 servings.

## Winter Holiday Salad

Ann's House of Nuts/Harvest Manor Farms

2 heads romaine lettuce, cut into bite-size pieces (about 8 cups)

1/2 cup red seedless grapes, halved

1/2 cup green seedless grapes, halved

1/2 cup sweetened dried cranberries

1/2 cup purple onion cut into bite-size pieces

1/2 cup Kirkland Signature Whole Fancy Cashews

1/2 cup grated Jarlsberg cheese

1/2 cup sliced celery

1 apple, cored and cubed (not peeled)

1 cup raspberry vinaigrette dressing

In a large salad bowl, combine all ingredients except the dressing.

Just before serving, drizzle the dressing over the salad and toss. Makes 8-10 servings.

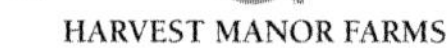


## Kid-Friendly Pancake Syrup Romaine Heart Salad

Andy Boy

***DRESSING***

2 tablespoons extra-virgin olive oil

1 tablespoon cider vinegar

2 tablespoons pure maple syrup

1 1/2 tablespoons Dijon mustard

Coarse salt and ground pepper

***SALAD***

2 heads Andy Boy* romaine hearts, chopped, washed and spun dry

4 celery stalks, thinly sliced

1 apple, halved, cored and thinly sliced

3 ounces crumbled blue cheese (such as Stilton)

1/2 cup candied walnuts

To prepare the dressing, whisk together oil, vinegar, maple syrup and mustard. Season to taste with salt and pepper.

To prepare the salad, combine romaine, celery and apples in a large bowl. Toss with the dressing.

Serve the salad sprinkled with blue cheese and candied walnuts. Makes 6 servings.

*Recipe courtesy of Chef Todd Fisher of Chef Todd Food Concepts and The Kitchen.*

** Brands may vary by region; substitute a similar product.*

# Spinach, Apple and Pecan Salad

## Boskovich Farms/Fresh Innovations

- 2 tablespoons olive oil
- 1 1/2 tablespoons cider vinegar
- 1 tablespoon prepared mustard
- 1 tablespoon sugar
- 1/2 teaspoon salt
- 1/4 teaspoon ground black pepper
- 1 bag Prize Slice* apple slices, cut into bite-size pieces
- 1/4 cup thinly sliced red onion
- 1 pound Boskovich Farms* Fresh 'n' Quick spinach, leaves torn
- 1/2 cup toasted pecans

In a large serving bowl, whisk together oil, vinegar, mustard, sugar, salt and pepper. Just before serving, add apples, onion, spinach and pecans. Toss until well coated with dressing. Makes 4 servings.

** Brands may vary by region; substitute a similar product.*

## Grilled Peach Salad
### I.M. Ripe

- 3 I.M. Ripe* peaches (white or yellow), pitted and cut into wedges
- 1 tablespoon olive oil
- 1 teaspoon salt
- 5 cups mixed spring greens
- 1/2 cup chopped glazed pecans (see tip)
- 1/3 cup crumbled feta cheese

*DRESSING*

- 3 tablespoons rice or white wine vinegar
- 1 tablespoon Dijon mustard
- 1/3 cup olive oil
- 1/2 teaspoon sugar
- 1/2 teaspoon salt

Preheat the grill to medium-high.

To prepare the dressing, combine vinegar and mustard in a small bowl. Slowly pour oil into the bowl, whisking constantly to emulsify. Stir in sugar and salt.

Place peaches in a bowl and drizzle with oil. Sprinkle with salt and toss well. Place on the grill and cook for 1-2 minutes on each side.

Place the spring greens in a large bowl. Add pecans, feta and grilled peaches.

Drizzle the salad with dressing and toss to coat. Makes 4 servings.

**Tip:** You can make your own glazed pecans, or substitute sweet pecans for a quick option.

** Brands may vary by region; substitute a similar product.*

## Strawberry-Mango Salad
### Babé Farms/Gold Coast Packing

- 1/2 cup sugar
- 3/4 cup extra-virgin olive oil
- 1 teaspoon salt
- 1/4 cup balsamic vinegar
- 8 cups Babé Farms* Organic Spring Mix Organic
- 4 cups Gold Coast* spinach
- 2 cups sweetened dried cranberries
- 1/2 pound fresh strawberries, trimmed and quartered
- 1 mango, peeled and cubed
- 1/2 cup chopped red onion
- 1 cup slivered almonds

Combine sugar, oil, salt and vinegar in a jar. Seal the jar and shake vigorously to mix.

In a large bowl, combine spring mix, spinach, cranberries, strawberries, mango and onion. Toss with the dressing and sprinkle with almonds. Makes 8-10 servings.

** Brands may vary by region; substitute a similar product.*

## Roasted Red Onion and Artisan Lettuce Salad

Tanimura & Antle

**1 Tanimura & Antle* Artisan Red Onion**

**1 tablespoon olive oil**

**Sea salt and freshly cracked black pepper**

**3 heads Tanimura & Antle* Artisan Lettuce**

**1/4 cup crumbled feta cheese**

**1/2 cup watermelon cut in 1/4-inch dice**

**1/4 cup walnuts, toasted**

**1/3 cup rice wine vinegar**

**1 teaspoon honey**

**1/3 cup walnut oil**

**1/4 cup canola oil**

Preheat oven to 325°F.

Cut red onion in quarters lengthwise. Toss with olive oil and season to taste with salt and freshly cracked pepper. Place on a pan and roast for 1 hour, or until translucent and lightly browned around the edges.

Wash lettuces; cut in half crosswise. Drain in a colander, then dry.

Place lettuce in a bowl with feta, watermelon, walnuts and half of the roasted onion, separated into leaves.

To prepare the dressing, place the remaining half of the roasted red onion in a blender with vinegar and honey; blend until smooth. Slowly add oil while blending on medium speed. Season to taste with salt and pepper.

Add dressing to the salad and toss to coat. Makes 2-4 servings.

** Brands may vary by region; substitute a similar product.*

## Pacheco Salad

Bravante Produce

**2 6-ounce cans water-packed albacore tuna, drained**

**1/2 cup sliced Bravante* green and/or red table grapes**

**1/3 cup chopped celery**

**1/3 cup chopped red onion**

**1/3 cup diced avocado**

**1/3 cup diced cherry tomatoes**

**1/3 cup chopped walnuts**

**1 tablespoon fresh lemon juice**

**2 teaspoons ground black pepper**

**2 teaspoons Lawry's seasoned salt**

**1/2 cup plain low-fat yogurt**

**1/3 cup reduced-fat mayonnaise**

**1/2 cup Dijon mustard**

**Lettuce or bread, for serving**

In a large bowl, combine tuna, grapes, celery, onion, avocado, tomatoes, walnuts, lemon juice and seasoning.

In a small bowl, combine yogurt, mayonnaise and mustard; stir to blend. Add to the tuna mixture and toss, making sure to coat everything.

Serve on a bed of lettuce or with your favorite bread, such as a croissant. Makes about 6 servings.

** Brands may vary by region; substitute a similar product.*

## Cocovanilla Fruit Salad

Del Monte Fresh Produce

- 1 cup halved Del Monte* strawberries
- 3/4 cup Del Monte* cantaloupe chunks
- 1 cup Del Monte* grapes, green or red
- 1 cup Del Monte* Gold Extra Sweet pineapple chunks
- 1 Del Monte* kiwifruit, peeled and sliced
- 1 Del Monte* banana, sliced
- 1/2 cup nonfat vanilla yogurt
- 2 tablespoons honey
- 1/2 cup shredded coconut
- 1/4 cup slivered almonds

Combine the fruit in a large mixing bowl.

In a small bowl, combine yogurt and honey; stir to blend. Stir into the fruit mixture. Refrigerate for 1 hour.

Just before serving, sprinkle the fruit salad with coconut and slivered almonds. Makes 6-8 servings.

** Brands may vary by region; substitute a similar product.*

Eat Healthy. Live Healthy.®

# Mandarin Salad
## Trinity Fruit

- 1 20-ounce can pineapple chunks in heavy syrup
- 2 tablespoons sugar
- 2 tablespoons apple cider vinegar
- 1 tablespoon butter
- 3 egg yolks, slightly beaten
- 7 fresh Trinity* mandarin oranges, peeled and sectioned
- 2 cups large marshmallows cut into quarters
- 1 cup whipping cream, whipped

Drain pineapple; reserve 2 tablespoons syrup.

In a saucepan, combine reserved pineapple syrup, sugar, vinegar, butter and egg yolks. Cook, stirring, over low heat for about 6 minutes, or until the custard thickens. Let cool to room temperature.

In a large bowl, combine mandarin oranges, pineapple chunks and marshmallows. Pour the custard into the bowl and stir gently.

Fold the whipped cream into the fruit mixture.

Place in a serving bowl, cover and chill for 24 hours. Makes 8 servings.

*Recipe created by Patricia White.*

** Brands may vary by region; substitute a similar product.*

## Five Fruit and Wild Rice Salad

### Fowler Packing

- 2 peaches, pitted and chopped
- 2 plums, pitted and chopped
- 2 apricots, pitted and chopped
- 1 1/2 cups green seedless grapes, rinsed and cut into quarters
- 2 tablespoons superfine sugar, divided
- 6 cups cooked wild rice, chilled
- Juice of 2 small limes
- 3 tablespoons canola oil
- 1/2 teaspoon salt

In a large bowl, combine peaches, plums, apricots and grapes. Add 1 tablespoon sugar and toss to blend. Add chilled wild rice and mix to combine.

In a small bowl, whisk lime juice, oil, salt and 1 tablespoon sugar. Pour over the rice and gently mix. Cover and chill until serving time. Makes 10-12 servings.

*Recipe developed by Kati Neville.*

## Grape Tomato and Sugar Snap Pea Pasta Salad

### Alpine Fresh

- 1 pound Alpine Fresh* sugar snap peas, stems and strings removed
- 1/2 pound dry orecchiette or gigli pasta
- 1 pound Alpine Fresh* grape tomatoes, halved
- 1 small container (3/4 ounce) fresh basil, leaves torn into bite-size pieces
- Freshly grated Parmesan cheese, for serving

*DRESSING*

- 1 tablespoon minced garlic
- 1/4 cup Kirkland Signature extra virgin olive oil
- 2 tablespoons lemon juice
- 2 teaspoons Dijon mustard
- 1/2 teaspoon sea salt
- 1/2 teaspoon freshly ground pepper
- 1 teaspoon soy sauce
- 1/2 teaspoon dried basil

Steam sugar snap peas in a steamer basket over salted boiling water for 3-4 minutes. Drain, chill in an ice-water bath, drain and set aside.

Cook pasta according to package directions. Drain, rinse and cool in cold water.

To prepare the dressing, combine all ingredients until well blended.

Drain pasta and place in a large bowl. Add sugar snap peas, grape tomatoes and basil. Toss with dressing.

Serve the salad topped with grated Parmesan. Makes 4 servings.

*Recipe developed by Christine W. Jackson, food stylist.*
** Brands may vary by region; substitute a similar product.*

## Broccoli and Cauliflower Salad with Chicken Salad Rollers

### Kirkland Signature

- 1 head of broccoli, cut into bite-size pieces (2 1/2 cups)
- 1 head of cauliflower, cut into bite-size pieces (3 cups)
- 1 cucumber, peeled, seeded and cut into bite-size pieces
- 2 cups grape tomatoes, halved
- 1 6-ounce can small pitted black olives, drained and halved
- 6 ounces feta cheese, crumbled
- 1 16-ounce bottle zesty Italian dressing

In a large bowl, combine broccoli, cauliflower, cucumber, tomatoes, olives and cheese. Add enough dressing to coat and toss.

Serve immediately or marinate in the refrigerator overnight.

Serve with Kirkland Signature Chicken Salad Rollers from your Costco deli. Makes 8 servings.

## Summer Broccoli Salad

### Wholesome Garden

- 1 pound Wholesome Garden Broccoli Florets
- 1/3 cup olive oil
- 2 garlic cloves, minced
- 1/2 teaspoon grated lemon peel
- Juice of 3 lemons
- 1 teaspoon honey
- 1/2 teaspoon fresh thyme, finely chopped
- Salt
- Freshly ground pepper
- 3 ounces prosciutto, finely chopped
- 2 ounces shaved Parmesan cheese
- 3 tablespoons pine nuts, toasted

In a deep saucepan, bring 1 inch of water to a boil. Place broccoli in a steamer basket, add to the saucepan, cover and steam for 5 minutes, or until tender but still crisp. Transfer broccoli to a large bowl and let cool.

In a small bowl, combine oil, garlic, lemon peel, lemon juice, honey and thyme. Add salt and pepper to taste.

Once the broccoli is cool, add the dressing, prosciutto, Parmesan and pine nuts; stir to combine. Makes 6 servings.

# Tomato, Pancetta, Bresse Blue and Arugula Salad

Windset Farms

4 slices pancetta
1/4 cup olive oil
1 small baguette, cut into 1-inch cubes
1 garlic clove, finely minced
1/4 teaspoon kosher salt
2 cups baby arugula
2 Windset Farms* Virtuoso beefsteak tomatoes, quartered
4 ounces Bresse blue cheese or Cambozola

*DRESSING*

1/4 cup rice vinegar
1 teaspoon Dijon mustard
1 small shallot, finely minced
1 garlic clove, finely minced
1/2 cup extra-virgin olive oil
1/2 teaspoon kosher salt
Ground pepper

Preheat oven to 375°F.

Place pancetta slices on a baking sheet topped with parchment paper. Bake for 10-12 minutes, or until crisp. Remove and drain on paper towels.

To prepare the dressing, whisk together vinegar, mustard, shallot and garlic in a small bowl. Slowly whisk in oil. Season to taste with salt and pepper. Set aside.

Pour the 1/4 cup of olive oil into a rimmed baking sheet. Place in the oven for 2 minutes, then carefully remove and place cubed bread in the oil. Return to the oven and toast for 3 minutes. Carefully remove from the oven, turn the croutons and return to the oven for 3 minutes. Transfer the croutons to a bowl and toss with garlic and salt.

To assemble the salad, arrange arugula and tomatoes on 4 plates. Drizzle with dressing and add a piece of pancetta to each serving. Break the cheese into pieces and sprinkle onto the salads. Top with the warm croutons. Makes 4 servings.

** Brands may vary by region; substitute a similar product.*

# Superhero Brussels Bites

## Eat Smart

**2 cups quartered Eat Smart* Brussels sprouts (6-7 ounces)**
**1/4 cup extra-virgin olive oil, divided**
**Salt and pepper**
**1/4 cup chopped or minced red onion**
**2 tablespoons sunflower kernels**
**2 tablespoons raisins**
**2 tablespoons grated Romano cheese**
**5 tablespoons red wine vinegar**

Preheat oven to 400°F.

Place Brussels sprouts in a roasting pan. Add 2 tablespoons oil and salt and pepper to taste; toss to coat. Roast for about 15 minutes, or until tender, turning occasionally. Remove from the oven and let cool for 5 minutes.

In a large bowl, combine sprouts, onion, sunflower kernels, raisins and cheese.

In a separate bowl, combine remaining olive oil, vinegar, and salt and pepper to taste.

Add the dressing to the sprouts mixture and toss to coat. Serve hot or cold. Makes 4-6 servings.

** Brands may vary by region; substitute a similar product.*

Eat Smart Apio, INC.

# Greek Yogurt Salad

## Foxy Vegetables

**1/2 Foxy* iceberg lettuce head, chopped**
**1 Foxy* romaine heart, chopped**
**2/3 cup pitted Kalamata olives**
**1/2 medium cucumber, stripe-peeled and sliced into rounds**
**1/2 yellow bell pepper, diced**
**1/2 medium red onion, thinly sliced**
**2 small tomatoes, sliced**
**3/4 cup crumbled feta cheese**

***DRESSING***

**2 tablespoons plain Greek-style yogurt**
**1/2 teaspoon Dijon mustard**
**1/2 teaspoon fresh lemon juice**
**1/4 teaspoon fresh crushed garlic**
**1/4 teaspoon dried oregano, rubbed between palms of hands**
**1/4 teaspoon dried dill**
**3 tablespoons white wine vinegar**
**Pinch of salt and black pepper**
**1/2 cup extra-virgin olive oil**

In a large bowl, combine lettuces, olives, cucumber, bell pepper, onion and tomatoes. Sprinkle with feta.

To prepare the dressing, combine yogurt, mustard, lemon juice, garlic, oregano, dill, vinegar, and salt and pepper in a small mixing bowl. Slowly whisk in oil until fully blended.

Pour the dressing over the salad and toss gently until well coated. Makes 4-8 servings.

** Brands may vary by region; substitute a similar product.*

## Blue-Ribbon Potato Salad
### Top Brass/Farm Fresh Direct

- **1 2/3 pounds (5 medium) potatoes, peeled or unpeeled, cut into 3/4-inch cubes**
- **1/4 cup olive oil**
- **1/4 cup lemon juice**
- **1/4 cup chopped fresh parsley**
- **2 garlic cloves, minced**
- **1 teaspoon salt**
- **1 teaspoon paprika**
- **1 teaspoon ground cumin**
- **2 medium tomatoes, cut in 3/4-inch cubes**
- **3/4 cup thinly sliced red onion**

In a heavy 3-quart saucepan, cook potatoes, covered, in 2 inches boiling water for 10-12 minutes, or until just tender.

Meanwhile, in a large bowl, whisk oil, lemon juice, parsley, garlic, salt, paprika and cumin. Mix in tomatoes and onion.

Drain the potatoes thoroughly and add to the bowl. Toss gently to coat completely. Serve warm or at room temperature. Makes 4 servings.

**Nutritional information:** Each serving has 282 calories, 6 g protein, 41 g carbohydrates, 14 g fat, 0 mg cholesterol, 5 g fiber, 596 mg sodium.

## California Rice Salad
### Dole

- **1 20-ounce can Dole* pineapple chunks**
- **4 cups cooked long-grain white rice**
- **1 1/2 cups packed arugula or spinach**
- **1/2 pound sliced bacon, cooked, drained and crumbled**
- **1/2 cup sliced red onion**
- **1/3 cup olive oil**
- **1 tablespoon Dijon mustard**
- **Salt and pepper**

Drain pineapple; reserve 1/4 cup juice.

In a large bowl, combine rice, pineapple chunks, arugula, bacon and onion.

In a small bowl, whisk together oil, reserved pineapple juice and mustard. Season to taste with salt and pepper. Pour over the rice mixture; toss to evenly coat. Makes 4-6 servings.

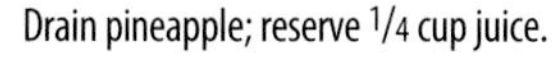
** Brands may vary by region; substitute a similar product.*

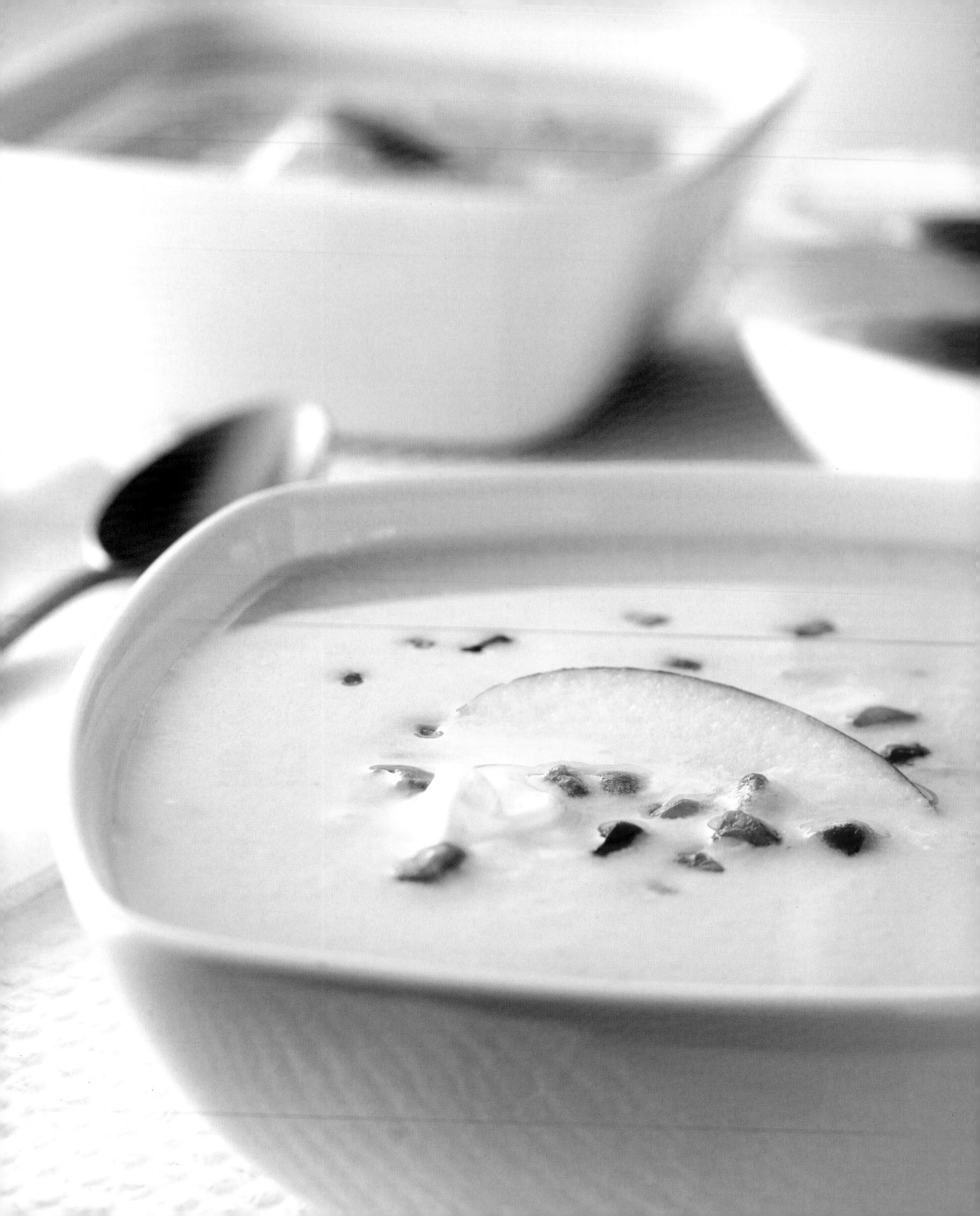

## Apple Squash Soup
Rainier Fruit Company

- **2 Rainier Fruit* Fuji or Cameo apples**
- **2 pounds winter squash such as butternut, kabocha or acorn**
- **1/2 cup chopped onion**
- **2 14-ounce cans chicken broth**
- **1/2 cup dry white wine**
- **1/2 teaspoon ground cinnamon**
- **1/4 teaspoon ground nutmeg**
- **1/4 teaspoon ground pepper**
- **Salt**
- **1 tablespoon olive oil**
- **1 cup half-and-half, at room temperature (see tip)**
- **1/2 cup dairy sour cream**
- **1/2 cup pomegranate seeds**

Reserve half an apple for garnish. Peel, core and dice the remaining 1 1/2 apples.

Peel and cut squash into 1- to 1 1/2-inch cubes.

Combine diced apples, squash, onions, chicken broth and wine in a large saucepan. Bring to a boil, then reduce the heat, cover and simmer for 30-40 minutes, or until all the ingredients are tender. Puree the mixture in a food processor or blender. Return the pureed mixture to the saucepan and add cinnamon, nutmeg, pepper and salt to taste. Bring the mixture to a boil, then simmer, uncovered, for 10 minutes to let the flavors blend.

Core the reserved apple and cut into thin wedges. Sauté in oil over medium heat until golden on both sides.

Stir half-and-half into the soup and heat thoroughly.

Ladle the soup into bowls and garnish each serving with an apple wedge, a dollop of sour cream and pomegranate seeds. Makes 4-6 servings.

**Tips:** Let the half-and-half stand at room temperature while the soup is being prepared to prevent it from curdling when it is added to the simmering soup.

**For squash:** To make it easier to remove the skin, halve squash and place cut-side down in a microwave-safe pan. Cover with plastic wrap and fold back one corner to vent. Microwave on high for 5-7 minutes, or until partially cooked.

**For pomegranate seeds:** To remove the seeds, cut a pomegranate in half vertically. Loosen and break the outer skin along the cut edges. Hold the fruit, cut-side down, over a bowl and tap the uncut surfaces with a wooden spoon. The seeds will loosen and fall into the bowl.

**Nutritional information:** Each serving has 311 calories, 6 g protein, 40 g carbohydrates, 15 g fat, 41 mg cholesterol, 6 g fiber, 840 mg sodium.

** Brands may vary by region; substitute a similar product.*

## Creamy Potato Soup with Poblano and Mushrooms
MountainKing Potatoes

- **2 teaspoons vegetable oil**
- **1 white onion, cut into 1/4-inch dice**
- **8 ounces mushrooms, sliced**
- **1 garlic clove, minced**
- **1 serrano pepper, minced**
- **2 poblano peppers, charred (under a broiler or over a gas flame), peeled, seeded and chopped into 1/4-inch dice**
- **3 small to medium MountainKing* Butter Golds, peeled and cut into 1/2-inch dice**
- **5 cups chicken broth**
- **1 cup whipping cream**
- **Salt and black pepper**

In a large saucepan, heat oil over medium-high heat. Add onions and sauté for 2-3 minutes.

Add mushrooms and sauté for 2-3 minutes.

Add garlic and peppers; sauté for another minute.

Now add potatoes and chicken broth. Reduce heat, cover and simmer for 15 minutes, or until the potatoes are tender. Add cream.

With a slotted spoon, scoop out about 1 1/2 cups of the soup vegetables and puree in a blender. Return the puree to the soup and stir well.

Reheat the soup to a simmer, season to taste with salt and pepper, and serve. Makes 6 servings.

** Brands may vary by region; substitute a similar product.*

## Ramen Olé Soup
### Top Ramen

- **4 cups water**
- **1 cup cubed cooked turkey or chicken**
- **1 3-ounce package Nissin Top Ramen Chicken Flavor**
- **1 cup shredded lettuce**
- **1/4 cup chopped green onions**
- **1/4 cup thinly sliced radishes**
- **1/2 cup chopped fresh tomatoes**
- **1/2 cup shredded Monterey Jack cheese**
- **Crushed dried oregano**
- **Hot sauce**
- **Warm tortillas or tortilla chips, for serving**

In a saucepan, bring water to a boil. Add turkey or chicken pieces.

Break noodles before opening the ramen package. Add noodles to the water and cook for 3 minutes. Add the flavor packet to the pan and stir.

Divide the soup between 2 bowls. To each serving add lettuce, green onions, radishes, tomatoes and cheese. Sprinkle lightly with crushed oregano and top with your favorite hot sauce.

Serve with warm tortillas or tortilla chips. Makes 2 servings.

## Mulligatawny Soup
### L&M Companies

- **1/4 cup butter**
- **1/2 cup chopped onion**
- **2 celery stalks, chopped**
- **1 carrot, diced**
- **1 1/2 tablespoons all-purpose flour**
- **1 14-ounce can coconut milk**
- **1 1/2 teaspoons curry paste**
- **4 cups chicken broth**
- **2 cups cored and chopped Nature's Delight* Fuji apples**
- **1/4 cup white rice**
- **1 skinless, boneless chicken breast half, cut into cubes**
- **Salt**
- **Ground black pepper**
- **1 pinch dried thyme**
- **1/2 cup heavy cream, heated**

Melt butter in a large soup pot over medium heat. Add onions, celery and carrots; sauté until the onions are translucent.

Add flour, coconut milk and curry paste; cook for 5 more minutes.

Add chicken broth, mix well and bring to a boil. Simmer, uncovered, for about 30 minutes.

Add apples, rice, chicken, salt and pepper to taste, and thyme. Simmer, uncovered, for 15-20 minutes, or until the rice is done.

When serving, add hot cream. Makes 10 servings.

** Brands may vary by region; substitute a similar product.*

# Tommy V's Roasted Campari Tomato Soup with Basil Pesto

## Eurofresh Farms

**2 pounds Eurofresh Farms* Campari tomatoes**

**6 ounces canola oil**

**1/4 cup peeled garlic cloves**

**2 medium shallots, peeled and cut in half**

**1 medium bunch of herbs – basil, thyme, oregano, flat-leaf parsley, tied together**

**Salt and pepper**

***BASIL PESTO***

**2 cups fresh basil leaves**

**1/4 cup pine nuts**

**1/4 cup freshly grated Parmesan cheese**

**1 garlic clove**

**2 tablespoons extra-virgin olive oil**

**Salt**

Preheat oven to 350°F.

In a large roasting pan, combine tomatoes, oil, garlic, shallots and herbs. Roast in the oven for 1 1/2 hours. Remove from the oven and discard the herbs.

To prepare the pesto, combine basil, pine nuts, Parmesan and garlic in a blender. Turn on the blender and slowly pour in the oil, blending until smooth. Season to taste with salt. Keep tightly wrapped in the refrigerator.

Carefully puree the soup in a blender. Season to taste with salt and pepper.

Serve the soup hot, garnished with basil pesto. Makes 4-5 servings.

*Recipe created by Chef Matt Alleshouse of Tommy V's Osteria Pizzeria in Phoenix.*

** Brands may vary by region; substitute a similar product.*

# The super foods

**Steven Pratt, M.D.**
Steven G. Pratt, M.D., is the author behind the *SuperFoods* series of books. His latest work is *SuperHealth: 6 Simple Steps, 6 Easy Weeks, 1 Longer, Healthier Life*. Dr. Pratt teaches that if your "tank" is filled with the right foods, you can increase your chances of living a longer, healthier life.

**By Steven Pratt, M.D.**

THE ENTRÉE USUALLY draws the most "oohs" and "ahhhs" in a meal, but side dishes play an important complementary role. When it comes to choosing a side dish, consider a healthy option using one or more of the 14 powerhouse foods that I call SuperFoods. These dishes can be as tasty as they are nutritious.

SuperFoods are rich in nutrients, yet smart in terms of calories. Research has shown that these foods can help prevent—and in some cases reverse—maladies such as cardiovascular disease, Type II diabetes, hypertension, certain cancers and even dementia. The good news is that they're not hard to find or necessarily expensive. I pick up most of them at my local Costco.

Here are some SuperFoods that can be used in side dishes, along with how many servings you should try to eat.

**Beans:** All legumes are super, but the most popular are pinto, navy, Great Northern, lima, garbanzo, lentils, green beans, sugar snap peas and green peas. Eat at least four 1/2-cup servings per week.

**Broccoli:** Sidekicks include Brussels sprouts, cabbage, kale, turnips, cauliflower, collards, bok choy, mustard greens and Swiss chard. Try 1/2 to 1 cup daily.

**Oats:** Oats themselves are usually associated with breakfast, but this category includes brown rice, barley, bulgur, quinoa, wild rice and couscous. Eat 10 to 20 grams of whole-grain fiber a day (check the label for help).

**Pumpkin:** It's popular in pie, but related foods are carrots, butternut squash, sweet potatoes and orange bell peppers. Try 1/2 cup most days.

**Spinach:** This is right at the top of SuperFood choices. Cousins include kale, collards, Swiss chard, turnip greens and romaine lettuce. Eat 1 cup steamed or 2 cups raw most days.

**Tomatoes:** These pack a nutritional wallop—and you can enjoy their benefits in tomato sauce and paste as well. Aim for multiple servings each week.

**Walnuts:** Nuts offer extraordinary health benefits, but must be eaten judiciously because they are high in calories. Sidekicks include almonds, pistachios, peanuts, sesame seeds, macadamia nuts and cashews. Eat 1 ounce, five times a week.

**Yogurt:** Yogurt helps the digestive system and is a good source of protein and minerals. But make sure to eat a brand that contains live active cultures (Kirkland Signature yogurt does). Eat 2 cups a day.

Other healthy foods I often pick up at Costco include wild Alaskan salmon, avocados, organic honey, fresh and frozen berries, organic peanut butter, Kirkland Signature green tea and Kirkland Signature soy milk. There's no excuse for not being able to pick out healthy food—while staying within your budget.

You're only as healthy as the food you put in your body. No matter what other healthy lifestyle choices you're making, without putting good fuel in your car, which is your body, you're not going to get years of service-free use.

# Couscous with California Avocado, Mango and Shrimp
## California Avocado Commission

- 24 large shrimp, peeled and deveined
- 1 tablespoon seafood grill seasoning
- 1 tablespoon olive oil, plus more for sautéing (optional)
- 2 cups water
- 1 10-ounce box plain couscous
- 1/2 teaspoon salt
- 2 fresh, ripe California Avocados, peeled, seeded and cut into 1-inch cubes
- 2 tablespoons fresh lemon juice
- 1 ripe mango, peeled, pitted and cut into 1-inch cubes
- 2 green onions, thinly sliced
- 1 cup cooked edamame (soybeans)

*MANGO-LIME DRESSING*

- 1 ripe mango, peeled, pitted and cut into 1-inch cubes
- 1/2 cup fresh lime juice
- 1/4 cup olive oil
- 2 garlic cloves, finely chopped
- 1 teaspoon Dijon-style mustard
- 1/2 teaspoon sea salt
- 1/4 teaspoon ground white pepper
- 1/4 teaspoon ground cumin
- 2 tablespoons snipped fresh mint leaves
- 2 tablespoons snipped fresh cilantro leaves

Toss shrimp with grill seasoning. Barbecue or sauté in olive oil for about 3 minutes, turning once. Remove to a plate. Set aside.

In a 2-quart saucepan, bring water to a boil. Stir in couscous, 1 tablespoon oil and salt. Remove from the heat, cover and let stand for 5 minutes. Remove the lid, fluff with a fork and let cool.

In a bowl, combine avocado and lemon juice. Set aside.

In a large bowl, combine couscous, avocado, mango, onions and edamame.

To prepare the dressing, combine mango, lime juice, oil, garlic, mustard, salt, pepper and cumin in a food processor and puree. Set aside. Stir in mint and cilantro just before using. Pour dressing to taste over the salad and toss to coat. Dressing makes 2 cups.

Serve the salad topped with shrimp. Makes 8 servings.

**Note:** Large avocados (about 8 ounces) are recommended. If using smaller or larger avocados, adjust quantity accordingly.

*Recipe provided by the California Avocado Commission.*

# Clementine Pilaf
## Duda Farm Fresh Foods

- 8-10 Dandy* clementines
- 1 tablespoon unsalted butter
- 1 tablespoon canola oil
- 1 large shallot, very finely chopped
- 1/2 red bell pepper, finely chopped
- 1 cup parboiled (converted) rice
- 1/2 cup frozen green peas
- Salt and ground black pepper

Halve the clementines crosswise and juice them, using an electric citrus juicer or squeezing over a bowl. Strain 1 cup of the juice into a measuring cup. Reserve the pulp from the strainer. Save any remaining juice for another use.

In a wide, large saucepan over medium-high heat, melt butter with oil. Add shallots and bell pepper; cook until shallots are soft, about 5 minutes, stirring often. Mix in rice, stirring until coated with butter. Pour in the clementine juice and 1 1/4 cups water. When the liquid boils, reduce the heat, cover and simmer for 15 minutes.

Stir in peas and the pulp from the clementines; cover and cook 5 minutes longer. Remove from the heat and let sit, covered, for 5 minutes. Fluff the pilaf with a fork and season to taste with salt and pepper. Serve hot. Makes 4 servings.

** Brands may vary by region; substitute a similar product.*

# Mashed Yams with Marshmallow Butter

## Rupari Foods

This dish is a delicious complement to Tony Roma's ribs.

**2 pounds yams**
**1/2 cup heavy cream**
**1/4 cup finely chopped fresh sage**
**1/4 cup maple syrup**
**3 tablespoons butter**
**Salt and pepper**
**Mini marshmallows, for garnish**

***MARSHMALLOW BUTTER***
**1 cup mini white marshmallows**
**1/2 cup chopped pecans**
**1/4 cup butter**
**2 tablespoons orange juice**
**Pinch of cayenne pepper**

Peel yams and cut into 3-inch chunks. Cook in a large pot of boiling salted water until tender, 20-25 minutes. Drain well, then return the pot to the stove over low heat for 1 minute to dry the yams.

Meanwhile, prepare the marshmallow butter: In a microwave-safe dish, combine marshmallows, pecans, butter, orange juice and cayenne pepper. Microwave on high for 1-2 minutes, or until the marshmallows have softened and the butter is melted. Stir the mixture to blend.

Mash the yams. Beat in cream, sage, maple syrup, butter, and salt and pepper to taste.

Top each serving of yams with a dollop or two of marshmallow butter. Garnish with mini marshmallows. Serve with Tony Roma's ribs. Makes 6 servings.

TONY ROMA'S
WORLD · FAMOUS · RIBS

# Almond Sausage Stuffing

## Paramount Farms

**1 one-pound loaf Pugliese or country-style bread, cut into 3/4-inch cubes**
**3 cups low-sodium chicken broth**
**1 pound Italian sausage, bulk or removed from casings**
**1 cup chopped onions**
**2 tart apples, cored and diced**
**2 teaspoons poultry seasoning**
**1/2 cup chopped fresh parsley**
**3/4 cup Almond Accents* Original Oven Roasted Flavored Sliced Almonds, divided**
**Salt and black pepper, as needed**

Preheat oven to 450°F.

In a large bowl, combine bread and chicken broth; mix gently to moisten the bread.

In a large skillet over high heat, cook sausage, breaking it up with a spoon into pieces no bigger than 1/2 inch, about 5 minutes or until lightly browned. Add onions, apples and poultry seasoning; cover and cook over medium-high heat, stirring occasionally, for 5 minutes, or until the onions are soft. Uncover, turn the heat to high and cook about 5 minutes more, stirring often, until the juices evaporate and the mixture begins to brown.

Add the sausage mixture, parsley and 1/2 cup Almond Accents to the bread; mix well and season to taste with salt and pepper.

Spoon the stuffing into a 13-by-9-inch casserole dish; sprinkle with remaining Almond Accents. Bake for about 25 minutes, or until lightly browned. Makes 8 servings.

**Nutritional information:** Each serving has 337 calories, 40 g carbohydrates, 12 g fat, 17 mg cholesterol, 5 g fiber, 601 mg sodium, 19 g protein.

** Brands may vary by region; substitute a similar product.*

# Wild Rice-Apple Pilaf
## Holtzinger Fruit

- $1/4$ cup uncooked wild rice
- 1 teaspoon olive oil
- 2 tablespoons chopped onion
- 2 $1/4$ cups fat-free, low-sodium chicken broth
- 1 cup peeled, diced Holtzinger* Fuji or Golden Delicious apple (about $1/4$ pound)
- $2/3$ cup uncooked long-grain brown rice
- 2 tablespoons chopped dried apple
- $1/2$ teaspoon salt

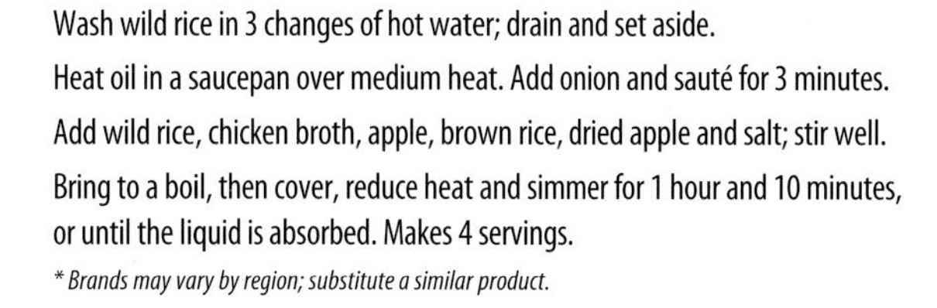

Wash wild rice in 3 changes of hot water; drain and set aside.

Heat oil in a saucepan over medium heat. Add onion and sauté for 3 minutes.

Add wild rice, chicken broth, apple, brown rice, dried apple and salt; stir well.

Bring to a boil, then cover, reduce heat and simmer for 1 hour and 10 minutes, or until the liquid is absorbed. Makes 4 servings.

** Brands may vary by region; substitute a similar product.*

## Portuguese-Style Crushed Potatoes

Festival

**3 pounds small yellow potatoes, washed**

**2/3 cup plus 2 tablespoons extra-virgin olive oil, divided**

**1 medium white onion, thinly sliced**

**2 tablespoons smoked paprika**

**1 1/2 tablespoons coarse sea salt**

**2 4-ounce cans Festival* sliced mushrooms, drained**

**3 11-ounce cans Festival whole mandarin oranges, drained**

**3 tablespoons chopped fresh parsley**

**3/4 cup pepitas (pumpkin seeds), toasted and salted**

Place potatoes in a large pot, cover with cold salted water and bring to a boil.

While the potatoes are cooking, heat 2 tablespoons oil in a sauté pan over low heat. Add onions and cook until soft and transparent.

When the potatoes are tender, drain. Return the potatoes to the pot and crush with a potato masher or the back of a fork and incorporate the rest of the oil, paprika and salt. Fold in the onions.

In the onion pan, sauté mushrooms over medium-high heat until they begin to brown. Remove from the heat and gently stir in oranges and parsley.

To serve, place the mushroom-mandarin mixture on top of the potatoes and sprinkle with pepitas. Makes 10 servings.

*Recipe developed by Chef Tyler Hefford-Anderson.*

** Brands may vary by region; substitute a similar product.*

## Lemon Chive Potatoes

Skagit Valley's Best Produce/ Wallace Farms/Valley Pride

**10-15 small Washington State* red potatoes (about 1 1/2 pounds)**

**1/2 teaspoon salt**

**2 tablespoons butter or margarine**

**1/2 teaspoon grated lemon peel**

**1 tablespoon fresh lemon juice**

**2 teaspoons chopped chives, plus more for garnish**

**1 teaspoon finely chopped fresh rosemary leaves**

**1 garlic clove, peeled and finely chopped**

**1/2 teaspoon salt**

**1/4 teaspoon lemon pepper**

Scrub potatoes with a vegetable brush under cold water. Cut in half.

Pour enough water into a large pot to just cover potatoes. Add the first 1/2 teaspoon salt. Add potato halves and turn the heat to high. When the water boils, turn the heat to medium, cover and simmer the potatoes until they are soft when poked with a fork, about 10-15 minutes.

While the potatoes are cooking, heat butter, lemon peel and juice, chives, rosemary, garlic and the seasonings just until bubbly, about 40 seconds in the microwave or a few minutes on medium-high heat.

Drain the cooked potatoes well.

Pour or spoon the potatoes into a serving dish. Pour on the lemon butter. Garnish with additional chives. Makes about 4 servings.

*This recipe was submitted by Skykomish Elementary School, Skykomish, Washington, for the Washington State Potato Commission* Kids Are Growing *competition.*

** Brands may vary by region; substitute a similar product.*

## Potato and Onion Gratin Pie
### Basin Gold Cooperative

**Nonstick cooking spray**
**2 teaspoons minced garlic**
**1 1/2 pounds Basin Gold* russet potatoes, peeled and thinly sliced**
**3/4 pound Basin Gold* yellow onions, halved and thinly sliced**
**Salt and pepper**
**1 cup grated Gruyère cheese, divided**
**2/3 cup whipping cream**

Preheat oven to 375°F. Coat a 9-inch glass pie dish with cooking spray.

Sprinkle half of the garlic over the bottom of the dish. Layer half of the potatoes in overlapping rows, followed by half of the sliced onions. Season with salt and pepper to taste. Sprinkle 1/3 cup of the cheese over the mixture. Repeat with the remaining garlic, potatoes, onions, and salt and pepper.

Pour cream evenly over the mixture. Sprinkle with the remaining 2/3 cup of cheese.

Cover with foil and bake for 30 minutes. Remove the foil and bake for another 30 minutes, or until the potatoes are tender when pierced with the tip of a knife. Remove from the oven and let stand for 10 minutes, then cut into pie-shaped wedges and serve. Makes 4-6 servings.

** Brands may vary by region; substitute a similar product.*

# Pear Relish

## Oneonta Starr Ranch Growers

1 6-pound bag Diamond Starr Growers* Red D'Anjou or Bosc pears, peeled, cored and cut into bite-size pieces
6 red bell peppers, seeded and chopped
6 yellow bell peppers, seeded and chopped
6 large sweet onions, chopped
2 cups sugar
1 cup white vinegar
2 tablespoons salt

Combine all ingredients in a large saucepan and simmer until the mixture thickens (about 1 hour), stirring often.

This is a wonderful garnish for chicken, fish or rice. Makes 3-4 pints.

**Tip:** To preserve the relish for future use, ladle into hot, sterilized pint jars, cover and process in a boiling bath for 15 minutes.

** Brands may vary by region; substitute a similar product.*

## Broccoli Florets with Toasted Garlic and Ginger Crumbs

Mann's

**1 1/2 pounds (half of 3-pound bag) Mann's Broccoli Florets***
**1/3 cup olive oil**
**4 garlic cloves, very thinly sliced**
**2 tablespoons grated fresh ginger**
**2/3 cup panko (Japanese bread crumbs) or regular bread crumbs**
**1 tablespoon low-sodium soy sauce**
**1/4 teaspoon ground black pepper**
**1/4 teaspoon salt**
**1 tablespoon grated lemon peel**

Put 1 inch of water in a heavy 5-quart pot, then put a steamer basket inside the pot and bring the water to a boil. Add broccoli and steam, covered, until just tender, 8-10 minutes.

Meanwhile, heat oil in a heavy 12-inch skillet over moderately low heat. Add garlic and ginger; cook, stirring occasionally, until pale golden, about 5 minutes. Stir in bread crumbs, soy sauce, pepper and salt, then increase the heat to moderate and cook, stirring occasionally, until the bread crumbs are golden, about 3 minutes. Remove from the heat and stir in grated lemon peel.

Transfer the broccoli with tongs to the crumb mixture in the skillet and toss to coat. Makes 6 servings.

** Brands may vary by region; substitute a similar product.*

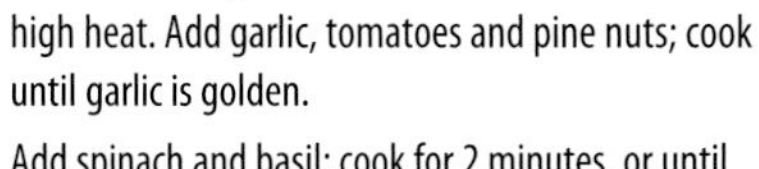


## Sautéed Spinach with Grape or Cherry Tomatoes

River Ranch Fresh Foods

**1/2 cup olive oil**
**2 garlic cloves, minced**
**1 pint basket grape or cherry tomatoes, halved**
**2-3 tablespoons pine nuts**
**1 40-ounce bag River Ranch* fresh spinach**
**2 tablespoons chopped fresh basil**
**Dash of salt**
**Dash of pepper**
**6 teaspoons crumbled feta cheese**

Heat oil in a large nonstick skillet over medium-high heat. Add garlic, tomatoes and pine nuts; cook until garlic is golden.

Add spinach and basil; cook for 2 minutes, or until the spinach is just wilted, stirring constantly. Season to taste with salt and pepper.

Serve topped with feta. Makes 6 servings.

** Brands may vary by region; substitute a similar product.*

# Sautéed Baby Carrot Mélange with Sun-Dried Tomatoes, Capers and Garlic

Grimmway Farms

- **4 tablespoons olive oil**
- **1 pound Grimmway Farms* Bunny Luv organic baby carrots** Organic
- **1 pound summer squash, sliced**
- **1 red bell pepper, cut into thin strips**
- **1 1/2 cups sugar snap peas**
- **2 garlic cloves, chopped fine**
- **3/4 cup water**
- **1/4 cup finely chopped sun-dried tomatoes**
- **2 tablespoons capers**
- **Coarse salt**
- **Freshly ground black pepper**

Heat oil in a large sauté pan over medium-high heat. Add carrots and sauté for 1 minute.

Stir in squash and sauté for 1 minute.

Add bell peppers, peas and garlic; sauté for 1 minute.

Pour in water and cook, stirring constantly, until the water evaporates and the vegetables are barely tender-crisp.

Stir in sun-dried tomatoes and capers.

Season to taste with salt and pepper.
Makes 6-8 servings.

**Tip:** You can use baby yellow or pattypan squash in place of summer squash in this recipe.

** Brands may vary by region; substitute a similar product.*

# French Green Beans with Mushrooms and Bacon

Alpine Fresh

- **1 tablespoon butter**
- **1 tablespoon olive oil**
- **1/4 cup chopped onion**
- **1 tablespoon minced garlic**
- **4 ounces sliced mushrooms**
- **1 pound Alpine Fresh* French green beans**
- **5 slices bacon, chopped, cooked until crisp and drained, divided**
- **Salt and pepper**
- **1/3 cup water**

In a large skillet (with a lid), melt butter with oil over medium heat. Add onions and sauté for 2 minutes. Then add garlic and mushrooms; sauté until tender.

Add green beans, half of the cooked bacon, salt and pepper to taste, and water to the skillet. Cover, lower the heat and simmer/steam for about 10 minutes, or until the beans are tender-crisp.

Serve with the remaining bacon on top.
Makes 6-8 servings.

*Recipe developed by Christine W. Jackson, food stylist.*
** Brands may vary by region; substitute a similar product.*

## Stuffed Portobello Mushrooms with Mashed Potatoes

Reser's Fine Foods

- 6 fresh portobello mushrooms
- 4 garlic cloves, chopped
- 4 tablespoons melted butter, divided
- 1 tablespoon olive oil
- 2 cups Reser's Mashed Potatoes*
- Pinch of black pepper
- Pinch of salt
- 1/2 teaspoon dried thyme
- 1/2 cup chopped chives
- 1/2 cup goat cheese
- 2 tablespoons grated Romano cheese
- 8 slices bacon, crisp cooked, crumbled
- 2 cups dry bread crumbs
- 1/4 cup grated Parmesan cheese
- 1/4 cup chopped fresh parsley

Preheat oven to 400°F.

Remove stems from mushrooms; set caps aside. Finely chop the stems.

In a skillet, sauté mushroom stems and garlic in 1 tablespoon butter over medium-high heat until tender.

Rub mushroom caps with oil and set in a greased baking pan.

In a bowl, combine mashed potatoes, pepper, salt, thyme, chives, goat cheese, Romano cheese, bacon and sautéed mushroom stems; mix until well blended. Stuff firmly into the mushroom caps.

In a separate bowl, combine the remaining melted butter, bread crumbs, Parmesan and parsley. Sprinkle over the stuffed mushroom caps.

Bake, uncovered, for 25 minutes, or until heated through. Serve warm. Makes 3-6 servings.

** Brands may vary by region; substitute a similar product.*

RESER'S FINE FOODS

## Fresh Mini Cucumber Pickles

Eurofresh Farms

- 1 2-pound bag Eurofresh Farms* mini cucumbers
- 1 teaspoon fennel seed
- 2 teaspoons coriander seed
- 3 teaspoons celery seed
- 2 teaspoons peppercorns
- 3 bay leaves
- 5 sprigs fresh thyme
- 2 tablespoons coarsely chopped fresh garlic
- 2 pounds sugar
- 3 teaspoons salt
- 48 ounces apple cider vinegar

Rinse cucumbers and cut in half lengthwise.

In a frying pan over low heat, lightly toast fennel, coriander, celery seed, peppercorns and bay leaves just until fragrant.

In a sauce pot, combine the toasted spices, thyme, garlic, sugar, salt and vinegar. Bring to a boil over high heat. Remove from the heat and let cool for about 5 minutes (should still be warm).

Dump the liquid over the cucumbers, cover and refrigerate for at least 24 hours. Makes 8-12 servings.

**Note:** These will keep in the refrigerator for a few weeks if the pickles are covered by the brine.

*Recipe created by Chef Clint Woods of the Fox Restaurant Group.*
** Brands may vary by region; substitute a similar product.*

# Chef's Choice

THE WORLD'S BEST CHEFS have the special ability to infuse dishes with their unique personalities. We asked several top chefs to do their magic with the products supplied by these great companies:

107

## Bruce Aidells

Bruce Aidells is America's "go-to guy" for all issues involving meat and meat cookery. Bruce founded Aidells Sausage Company in 1983, leaving it in 2002 to continue to pursue his food-writing career. The author of 11 cookbooks, he writes regularly for leading national newspapers and magazines; he's also a frequent guest on TV and radio shows. Bruce and his wife, Nancy Oakes, who is executive chef and co-owner of San Francisco's top-rated Boulevard Restaurant, live in the San Francisco Bay Area and the Sonoma wine country.

# Grilled Lamb Chops

The Lamb Cooperative

Recipes developed by Bruce Aidells

**8 Australian loin lamb chops (about 2 inches thick)**

**Chopped cilantro leaves, for garnish**

***MOROCCAN FRESH MINT AND LEMON MARINADE***

**2 small cloves garlic**

**1/2 cup cilantro leaves**

**2 tablespoons fresh mint**

**1/3 cup lemon juice**

**1 tablespoon olive oil**

**1 teaspoon salt**

**1 teaspoon freshly ground black pepper**

**1/2 teaspoon cayenne**

**2 teaspoons paprika**

**1 teaspoon ground cumin**

**1 teaspoon turmeric**

**1 teaspoon ground fennel seed**

**Pinch cinnamon**

***TAHINI SAUCE***

**2 tablespoons sesame paste (tahini paste)**

**3 tablespoons lemon juice**

**3 tablespoons olive oil**

**1 tablespoon or more water**

**Salt to taste**

To make the marinade, set up a food processor with a small bowl. With the motor running drop the garlic through the feed tube and process until chopped. Remove the lid and add the cilantro and mint. Pulse until the leaves are chopped. Add remaining ingredients and process to form a thick paste.

Rub the mixture all over chops and place on a plate. Cover with plastic wrap. Refrigerate for at least 2 hours or up to 16 hours. Turn chops from time to time. When ready to grill remove lamb from refrigerator and let rest at room temperature for 30 minutes.

Fire up a gas or charcoal grill to yield a medium hot fire. Remove chops from marinade and shake off excess. Sear the chops for 4 minutes per side, then over indirect heat for 8-10 minutes or until the internal temperature reaches 130°F-135°F for medium rare. Set chops aside for 5 minutes to rest.

While chops are resting, make the tahini sauce by combining sesame, lemon juice and oil in a food processor fit with a small bowl. Process until smooth. Add water 1 tablespoon at a time until the sauce is thin enough to drizzle. Taste for salt and set aside.

Arrange chops on a platter and drizzle tahini sauce over them. Garnish with cilantro leaves.

Makes 4 to 6 servings.

# Fresh Thyme and Fennel-Rubbed Roasted Rack of Lamb

The Lamb Cooperative

**1 frenched Australian rack of lamb (8 ribs)**

**1 teaspoon salt**

**1/2 teaspoon freshly ground black pepper**

**2 cloves garlic, finely chopped**

**2 tablespoons finely chopped fresh thyme**

**1 teaspoon fennel pollen or 1 teaspoon ground fennel seed**

**1 tablespoon olive oil**

Remove lamb from refrigerator and let rest at room temperature for 1 hour.

Preheat oven to 450°F.

Sprinkle lamb generously with salt and pepper all over. Heat a heavy 10-inch ovenproof skillet over high heat. Place rack in pan fat side down and sear for 1-2 minutes. Using meat tongs clasp lamb and sear meat with the bones vertical for another minute or 2. Then flip to the back bone side and sear 1-2 minutes more.

Make an herb paste by combining garlic, thyme, fennel and olive oil in the small work bowl of a food processor or simply combine the ingredients in a small mixing bowl. Smear the paste over the fat side and ends of the roast. Place rack bone side down. Cover the exposed part of the bones with foil and insert pan into oven.

Roast for 12 minutes for smaller racks and 15 minutes for larger rack. Check the internal temperature. When it reaches 130°F -135°F it is medium rare. If not yet done roast 5 minutes more and check again. Continue to check every 5 minutes. When done place rack on a cutting board, cover loosely with foil and let it rest for 5-7 minutes. Carve the roast between each bone.

Makes 2-4 servings.

# Butterflied Leg-Of-Lamb with a Provençal Olive Crust

## The Lamb Cooperative

*TAPENADE OLIVE PASTE*

**1/4 cup French black olive tapenade or 1/2 cup French Nyon or Greek Kalamata olives, pitted**

**2 cloves garlic**

**1 tablespoon grated lemon zest**

**1 tablespoon fresh savory**

**1 teaspoon freshly ground black pepper**

**1 tablespoon red wine vinegar**

**1 tablespoon, or more, extra virgin olive oil**

**1 Australian boneless leg of lamb (about 5 pounds), removed from the netting**

If starting with pitted olives, place them in a small bowl of a food processor and pulse several times to chop, then add the remaining ingredients. Otherwise, combine the jarred tapenade with the remaining ingredients in the food processor and pulse to form a soft paste. If too dry, add additional olive oil.

Spread out the lamb in a baking dish or shallow bowl and generously rub all the paste all over it. Cover with plastic wrap and marinate for 2 hours at room temperature or up to 24 hours in the refrigerator. If marinating the lamb in the refrigerator before cooking, remove the lamb from refrigerator and let rest at room temperature for 2 hours.

To grill, set up a charcoal or gas grill with fire on one side and the other side without fire. When the heat is medium hot, place the lamb, fat side down, directly over the fire (do not remove the olive coating) and sear for 5-7 minutes or until the meat begins to color and brown. Turn and repeat for the other side of the lamb.

Transfer to the area of the grill without fire, cover the grill and continue to grill fat side up for 40 minutes or until the internal temperature of the lamb reaches 135°F at the thickest part. This area will yield medium rare meat while thinner areas will be more done. (If you like rare lamb then remove it when it has an internal temperature of 125°F). After removing the lamb, transfer it to a platter and let it rest 10-15 minutes loosely tented with foil before carving. Slice into 1/4-inch slices and serve. Makes 6-8 servings.

**Tip:** Use leftovers in lamb sandwiches, or thinly slice the lamb and serve over salad greens with a lemony vinaigrette.

## Steven Raichlen

Multi-award-winning author, journalist, cooking teacher and TV host Steven Raichlen is the man behind the bestselling *Barbecue! Bible* cookbook series, with more than 4 million in print. Last year, he traveled to six continents to research his latest cookbook, *Planet Barbecue!* (Workman Publishing, 2010). All in all, Steven has written nearly 30 books on barbecuing.

Grilled Chicken Breasts under Bricks

## Grilled Chicken Breasts under Bricks

Foster Farms

Recipes developed by Steven Raichlen

- **4 boneless, skinless Foster Farms* chicken breast halves**
- **1 teaspoon coarse salt**
- **1 teaspoon cracked black peppercorns**
- **1/2-1 teaspoon hot red pepper flakes**
- **1 tablespoon chopped garlic**
- **1 tablespoon chopped fresh rosemary**
- **Juice of 1 lemon**
- **1/4 cup extra-virgin olive oil**
- **4 bricks, each wrapped in aluminum foil**

Rinse the chicken breasts under cold running water, then drain and blot dry with paper towels. Sprinkle the breasts on both sides with the salt, cracked black pepper and hot red pepper flakes. Sprinkle the breasts with the garlic and rosemary, patting them on with your fingers. Arrange the breasts in a nonreactive baking dish. Pour the lemon juice and oil over them and let marinate in the refrigerator, covered, for 30-60 minutes, turning several times.

Set up the grill for direct grilling and preheat to high. In the best of all worlds, you'd build your fire with oak chunks. Alternatively, use gas or charcoal, plus soaked wood chips for smoke. If using a gas grill, place all the wood chips in the smoker box or in a smoker pouch and preheat until you see smoke.

When ready to cook, brush and oil the grill grate. If using a charcoal grill, toss the wood chips on the coals. Arrange the chicken breasts on the hot grate, all facing the same direction, at a 45-degree angle to the bars of the grate.

Place a brick on top of each. Grill the breasts until cooked, 3-4 minutes per side, rotating the breasts 90 degrees after 2 minutes on each side to create an attractive crosshatch of grill marks.

To test for doneness, poke a breast in the thickest part with your finger. It should feel firm to the touch. Or use a meat thermometer; the internal temperature should be 165°F. Transfer the breasts to plates or a platter and serve at once. Makes 4 servings.

*Recipe from* How to Grill, *by Steven Raichlen (Workman Publishing, 2001).*

** Brands may vary by region; substitute a similar product.*

## Ground Turkey Shashlik with Onion and Dill

Foster Farms

- **2 pounds Foster Farms* fresh ground turkey**
- **1 garlic clove, minced**
- **1 1/2 teaspoons coarse salt (kosher or sea), or more to taste**
- **1/2 teaspoon freshly ground black pepper, or more to taste**
- **1/4 cup coarsely chopped sweet onion**
- **3 tablespoons chopped fresh dill**
- **Lavash or pita bread, for serving**

In a large bowl, combine the ground turkey with the garlic, salt, pepper, onion and dill until thoroughly blended. Cover the bowl and refrigerate it for 1-2 hours. This is optional, but it will make the turkey kebabs easier to form.

Divide the turkey mixture into 8 equal portions. Lightly oil your hands with vegetable oil, then mold the turkey mixture onto skewers to make kebabs that are about 1 inch in diameter and 5 inches long. Place the kebabs on a plate lined with plastic wrap and refrigerate them, covered, until you're ready to grill.

Set up the grill for direct grilling and preheat it to high.

When ready to cook, brush and generously oil the grill grate. Arrange the kebabs over the heat and grill them until golden brown and cooked through, 4-6 minutes per side. Using a piece of lavash or pita bread to protect your hands, slide the kebabs off the skewers onto a platter or plates. Serve at once. Makes 8 kebabs or 4 servings.

**Tips:** For the best results, make the kebabs 2-4 hours ahead to refrigerate until firm. Also, for a fattier version of this recipe, add 2 ounces of finely chopped fatty bacon to the ground turkey and spices. Serve with quartered and grilled tomatoes, onions and horn peppers, all brushed with olive oil and seasoned with salt and pepper.

*Recipe adapted from* Planet Barbecue!: 309 Recipes, 60 Countries, *by Steven Raichlen (Workman Publishing, 2010).*

** Brands may vary by region; substitute a similar product.*

# Chicken Wraps with Creamy Asian Peanut Sauce

## Foster Farms

1 pound Foster Farms* Frozen Grilled Chicken Breast Strips, thawed
4 leaves Napa cabbage, chopped (about 2 cups packed)
2 cups packed baby spinach
1 medium carrot, grated (about 1/2 cup)
3 medium radishes, sliced (about 1/3 cup)
2 tablespoons rice vinegar
1 tablespoon soy sauce
1 tablespoon canola oil
1 package 10-inch spinach wraps (6)

*CREAMY ASIAN PEANUT SAUCE*

2 tablespoons vegetable oil
1 small onion, finely chopped
2 garlic cloves, finely chopped
1 tablespoon minced peeled fresh ginger
3/4 cup smooth peanut butter
1 cup unsweetened coconut milk
1/4 cup chicken stock or water, or more as needed
1 tablespoon sugar, or more to taste
2 tablespoons soy sauce, or more to taste
1-2 teaspoons fish sauce (optional)
1 teaspoon Malaysian chili sauce, sambal oelek or other Asian chili paste
1/2 teaspoon freshly ground black pepper

Heat chicken strips in a 400°F oven for 10 minutes or microwave according to package directions.

Mix cabbage, spinach, carrot and radishes in a medium bowl.

In a small bowl, stir together rice vinegar, soy sauce and canola oil. Pour over the cabbage mixture. Let stand for 5 minutes.

To prepare the peanut sauce, heat oil in a saucepan over medium heat. Add onion, garlic and ginger; cook until lightly browned, about 3 minutes, stirring well. Whisk in peanut butter, coconut milk, chicken stock or water, sugar, soy sauce, fish sauce, if using, and chili sauce and pepper.

Let the sauce simmer until it is thick and richly flavored, about 5 minutes, stirring well. Add more chicken stock or water as needed—the sauce should be thick but pourable. Taste for seasoning, adding more sugar, soy sauce and/or chili sauce as necessary. The peanut sauce can be made up to 24 hours ahead and refrigerated, covered. Serve at room temperature.

Lay spinach wraps on a clean, flat surface. Divide the cabbage mixture evenly over the wraps. Top with chicken. Drizzle peanut sauce over the chicken, about 2 tablespoons for each wrap, or as much or little as desired. Fold in the edges, wrap and serve. Makes 6 servings.

*The Creamy Asian Peanut Sauce is from* Planet Barbecue!*; the wraps were developed by Lindsay Tkacsik.*
** Brands may vary by region; substitute a similar product.*

## Jill Davie

A graduate of the Culinary Institute of America, Chef Jill Davie was tapped by Sunkist to be their official spokesperson—the Sunkist Lemon Lady. She has appeared in several Food Network programs, highlighted by her victory in the *Hot Chefs: South Beach* competition in 2006, and was also a contestant on *The Next Iron Chef* in 2007. She has appeared on Recipe.TV and can be seen as a cohost of *Shopping with Chefs* on Fine Living Network.

## Orange Caprese Salad

Sunkist Growers

Recipes developed by Jill Davie

**1 medium red onion**
**4 medium Sunkist* navel oranges, divided**
**3 tablespoons red wine vinegar**
**Sea salt or any other larger-flake salt**
**Freshly ground black pepper**
**4 vine-ripe tomatoes**
**1 1-pound tub burrata cheese (buffalo mozzarella can be substituted)**
**1 small bunch of green basil, leaves picked (about 10 leaves)**
**1 small bunch of opal basil, leaves picked (optional)**
**6 tablespoons extra-virgin olive oil**

Peel onion. Using a sharp knife, slice it into approximately 1/8-inch rings and place in a shallow bowl. Squeeze the juice from 1 orange over the onion. Add vinegar and season to taste with salt and pepper. Let the onions marinate for 1 hour.

Using a sharp paring knife, remove the skin and pith from the remaining 3 oranges to expose the flesh. Slice horizontally into approximately 6 even wheels, 1/4 inch thick. Remove any seeds.

Leaving the stems intact, slice the tomatoes horizontally as you did the oranges, into approximately 6 even wheels, 1/4 inch thick.

Assemble each salad by alternating the orange, red onion and tomato slices on a plate and placing 1 large spoonful of cheese in between 2 layers.

Garnish the plates with basil leaves. Drizzle the salads with olive oil and season to taste with salt and pepper. Makes 4 servings.

**Note:** Opal basil is a variety with deep purple color and can be found at some farmer's markets and stores.

** Brands may vary by region; substitute a similar product.*

## Citrus Shrimp with Lemondaise Sauce

Sunkist Growers

**1/2 cup grapeseed oil**
**1 tablespoon grated Sunkist* lemon peel**
**1 tablespoon grated Sunkist* orange peel**
**1 teaspoon rosemary, chopped**
**1 teaspoon thyme, chopped**
**1 teaspoon oregano, chopped**
**2 pounds shrimp, peeled and deveined**
**Salt and pepper**

*LEMONDAISE SAUCE*

**3/4 cup white wine**
**2 tablespoons minced shallots**
**1 tablespoon grated Sunkist* lemon peel**
**1 cup heavy cream**
**1/4 teaspoon turmeric**
**1/2 teaspoon salt**
**1/2 teaspoon cornstarch mixed with 3 tablespoons cold water**
**Juice of 1/2 Sunkist lemon**

Mix grapeseed oil with lemon peel, orange peel and fresh herbs. Add shrimp and toss to coat. Marinate in the refrigerator for 3 hours. Season to taste with salt and pepper.

To prepare the Lemondaise Sauce, combine wine, shallots and lemon peel in a small saucepan. Cook over medium heat until reduced by half.

Whisk in cream, turmeric and salt; bring to a simmer while whisking.

Gradually whisk in the cornstarch and water mixture. Continue simmering to thicken, about 1 minute. Remove from the heat and mix in lemon juice.

Sauté the shrimp over medium heat until fully cooked. Serve with Lemondaise Sauce. Makes 4 servings.

**Tip:** This sauce is great over eggs Benedict, fish, asparagus and other recipes that call for hollandaise sauce.

** Brands may vary by region; substitute a similar product.*

## Ellie Krieger

Ellie Krieger is the host of Food Network's popular *Healthy Appetite* and author of the *New York Times* bestsellers *The Food You Crave* and *So Easy*. A registered dietitian, she has a master's degree in nutrition from Columbia University and completed her undergraduate work at Cornell University. Krieger is a regular columnist for *Fine Cooking* and *Food Network* magazines and lives in New York City.

# Spinach-Grape Salad

Delano Farms

Recipes developed by Ellie Krieger

- **1/3 cup walnut pieces**
- **2 tablespoons extra-virgin olive oil**
- **1 tablespoon cider vinegar**
- **1 teaspoon Dijon mustard**
- **Salt and freshly ground black pepper**
- **5 ounces baby spinach leaves (about 5 cups lightly packed)**
- **1 1/3 cups halved Delano Farms* seedless grapes**

Toast walnuts in a small dry skillet over medium-high heat until fragrant, about 2 minutes. Set aside.

In a small bowl, whisk together oil, vinegar and mustard. Season to taste with salt and pepper.

In a large bowl, toss spinach with the dressing until evenly coated. Divide the spinach among 4 serving plates.

Sprinkle 1/3 cup of grapes over each salad. Top with walnuts. Serve immediately. Makes 4 servings.

**Nutritional information:** Each serving (2 cups) has 170 calories, 3 g protein, 12 g carbohydrates, 13 g total fat, 0 mg cholesterol, 2 g fiber, 45 mg sodium.

** Brands may vary by region; substitute a similar product.*

# Curried Chicken Salad

Delano Farms

- **1/4 cup sliced almonds**
- **1/2 cup nonfat plain yogurt**
- **2 tablespoons mayonnaise**
- **1 teaspoon curry powder**
- **2 1/2 cups cubed cooked chicken breast (about 1 1/4 pounds)**
- **1 cup halved Delano Farms* red seedless grapes**
- **1/4 cup chopped fresh cilantro**
- **Salt and freshly ground black pepper**
- **5 ounces mixed greens (about 5 cups lightly packed)**
- **4 lemon wedges**
- **4 ounces pita chips**

Toast almonds in a small dry skillet over medium-high heat, stirring occasionally, until fragrant and beginning to turn golden, 2-3 minutes. Set aside.

In a large bowl, stir together yogurt, mayonnaise and curry powder. Fold in chicken, grapes and cilantro. Season to taste with salt and pepper. This salad will keep in an airtight container in the refrigerator for up to 3 days.

To serve, put a scoop of the chicken salad on a bed of greens on a plate or in a to-go container and sprinkle with the toasted almonds. Add a lemon wedge to squeeze over the greens just before eating. Serve with pita chips, stored in a separate container if packing. Makes 4 servings.

**Nutritional information:** Each serving (1 cup chicken salad, 1 1/4 cups mixed greens, 1 lemon wedge and 1 ounce pita chips) has 400 calories, 36 g protein, 26 g carbohydrates, 16 g total fat, 80 mg cholesterol, 4 g fiber, 460 mg sodium.

** Brands may vary by region; substitute a similar product.*

# Marinated Chicken and Grape Skewers with Garden Lentil Pilaf

Delano Farms

2 tablespoons olive oil
1 tablespoon fresh lemon juice
1/2 teaspoon finely grated lemon peel
2 garlic cloves, minced
1 teaspoon ground cumin
1/2 teaspoon ground coriander
1/2 teaspoon salt
1 pound boneless, skinless chicken breasts, cut into 3/4-inch cubes
8 10-inch skewers
1 1/2 cups Delano Farms* green seedless grapes (see tip)
Cooking spray
2 tablespoons chopped fresh mint leaves
1 lemon, cut into wedges

*GARDEN LENTIL PILAF*

1 cup green lentils
2 cups water
2 tablespoons olive oil
2 tablespoons diced shallots
3 cups baby spinach leaves (about 3 ounces)
1 cup halved grape tomatoes (about 1/2 pint)
1/4 cup chopped fresh basil leaves
1/4 cup chopped fresh mint leaves
1/4 cup chopped fresh parsley
2 tablespoons fresh lemon juice
1/2 teaspoon salt
1/4 teaspoon freshly ground black pepper

In a medium bowl, whisk together oil, lemon juice, grated lemon peel, garlic, cumin, coriander and salt. Add chicken to the marinade and toss to coat. Marinate in the refrigerator for at least 20 minutes and up to 4 hours. If you are using wooden skewers, soak them in water while the chicken is marinating.

To prepare the pilaf, place lentils in a pot with the water and bring to a boil. Reduce the heat, cover and simmer until the lentils are tender but still retain their shape, 30-35 minutes. Drain any excess water from the lentils and set them aside.

Heat oil in a large skillet over medium-high heat. Add shallots and cook, stirring, until softened, about 3 minutes. Add spinach and cook until just wilted, about 2 minutes. Add tomatoes, cooked lentils, basil, mint and parsley; stir to combine. Cook until warmed through, about 1 minute. Stir in lemon juice, salt and pepper.

Thread the chicken cubes onto the skewers, alternating them with grapes.

Spray a grill pan with cooking spray and preheat over medium-high heat, or prepare an outdoor grill.

Grill the chicken until cooked through, 3-4 minutes per side. Sprinkle with mint and serve with the pilaf and lemon wedges. Makes 4 servings.

**Tip:** Try using a combination of different grapes—green, red and black—for a multicolored take on these tasty skewers.

**Nutritional information:** Each serving (2 skewers, each with 4 pieces of chicken and 4 grapes, and 3/4 cup pilaf) has 440 calories, 35 g protein, 45 g carbohydrates, 16 g total fat, 65 mg cholesterol, 10 g fiber, 680 mg sodium.

** Brands may vary by region; substitute a similar product.*

## Matt Scialabba and Melissa Pellegrino

Matt Scialabba and Melissa Pellegrino are a husband-and-wife cooking and writing team who met while living and studying in Italy, where they learned the secrets of authentic regional cuisine. They are authors of *The Italian Farmer's Table* (Three Forks/Globe Pequot Press, 2010; *www.theitalianfarmerstable.com*). Melissa serves as a food editor at *Fine Cooking* magazine, and Matt works for an Italian wine importer representing small artisanal estates.

Sausage, Clam and Fennel Stew

## Sausage, Clam and Fennel Stew

Tarantino

Recipes developed by Matt Scialabba and Melissa Pellegrino

**2 tablespoons Kirkland Signature extra virgin olive oil, divided**

**4 links Tarantino* mild Italian sausage**

**2 medium shallots, thinly sliced**

**1 large fennel bulb, trimmed, halved lengthwise, cored and thinly sliced (reserve 1/4 cup of chopped fennel fronds)**

**Kosher salt**

**1/2 cup dry white wine**

**1 28-ounce can whole plum tomatoes**

**2 dozen littleneck clams**

**Freshly ground black pepper**

**1 cup Israeli couscous**

**1/4 cup chopped fresh parsley**

In a 12-inch skillet, heat 1 tablespoon oil over medium heat. Add sausages to the pan and cook until browned all over and almost cooked through, 4-6 minutes. Transfer to a cutting board and cut the sausages in half on a bias.

Add 1 tablespoon oil to the pan along with shallots, sliced fennel and a pinch of salt. Cover, reduce the heat to medium-low and cook until the fennel is tender, about 10 minutes. Increase the heat to medium-high, add wine and tomatoes, and bring to a boil.

Add clams and sausages to the pan, cover, reduce the heat to maintain a simmer, and cook until the clams open and the sausage is cooked through, 5-6 minutes. Transfer the clams to a large bowl. Season the broth with salt and pepper, and stir in the reserved fennel fronds.

Meanwhile, cook the couscous. In a large saucepan, bring 2 quarts well-salted water to a boil. In a medium skillet over medium heat, toast the couscous, stirring frequently, until lightly golden, about 4 minutes. Transfer to the pot of boiling water and cook until tender, about 10 minutes. Drain well.

Divide the couscous among 4 shallow dinner bowls. Top the couscous with the clams and then divide the sausages and broth among the bowls. Garnish with parsley. Makes 4 servings.

** Brands may vary by region; substitute a similar product.*

## Breakfast Sausage and Grape Skewers with Balsamic Glaze

Tarantino

**6 8-inch wooden skewers**

**1 1/2 cups halved red seedless grapes**

**1 tablespoon olive oil**

**Kosher salt and freshly ground black pepper**

**6 links Tarantino* breakfast sausage, cut into thirds**

**3/4 cup balsamic vinegar**

**2 sprigs of thyme**

**1 teaspoon honey**

Prepare a medium gas grill fire. Soak wooden skewers in water for at least 15 minutes.

In a medium bowl, toss grapes with oil and season to taste with salt and pepper.

Thread the grapes and sausages alternately onto the skewers, starting and ending with a grape half.

Meanwhile, in a small saucepan combine vinegar, thyme and honey. Bring to a boil over medium-high heat and cook until reduced by half, about 5 minutes. Remove from the heat. Season with a pinch of salt and pepper.

Grill the skewers, brushing all over with the balsamic glaze, until browned, about 4 minutes total. Makes 6 skewers.

** Brands may vary by region; substitute a similar product.*

# Baked Stuffed Artichokes with Sausage and Herbs

Tarantino

4 medium artichokes (about 10 ounces each)
Kosher salt
3 tablespoons Kirkland Signature extra virgin olive oil, divided
4 links (about 1 pound) Tarantino* mild Italian sausage, casings removed, crumbled
1 medium yellow onion, cut into fine dice
1 1/2 cups coarse fresh bread crumbs
2 tablespoons plus 1/2 cup cold water, divided
1/2 cup finely grated pecorino cheese
1/4 cup chopped flat-leaf parsley
1 tablespoon chopped fresh tarragon
2 teaspoons chopped fresh thyme
1 teaspoon grated lemon peel
Freshly ground black pepper
1/2 cup dry white wine
2 bay leaves
1/2 teaspoon black peppercorns

Position a rack in the center of the oven. Preheat oven to 425°F.

To prepare artichokes, cut off the stems with a paring knife (you'll need a flat bottom) and pull off any fibrous dark leaves around the base. Cut off the top ½ inch of the chokes and trim off the pointed tips of the remaining leaves with scissors.

In a 6-quart stockpot bring 2 cups of salted water to a boil over high heat. Put a steamer basket in the pot and arrange the artichokes bottom side down in the basket. Sprinkle with salt. Cover, reduce the heat to a gentle simmer and steam until completely tender, 35-40 minutes. Remove the artichokes and rinse under cold water. Pull out the inner leaves with your fingers and scrape out the choke with a spoon. Set aside.

In a 12-inch skillet, heat 1 tablespoon oil over medium-high heat. Add sausage and cook until browned, 5-7 minutes. Using a slotted spoon, transfer the sausage to a large bowl. Add another tablespoon of oil to the pan and the onions and cook over medium heat until tender and lightly browned, about 5 minutes. Transfer to the bowl with the sausage.

In a medium bowl, mix bread crumbs with 2 tablespoons cold water to dampen. Stir in pecorino, herbs and lemon peel. Transfer to the bowl of sausage and mix until combined. Season to taste with salt and pepper. Stuff each artichoke with about 1 cup of the sausage filling.

Add wine, bay leaves, black peppercorns and 1/2 cup water to a 3-quart roasting pan. Add the artichokes and cover with foil. Bake until the filling is heated through, 25-30 minutes. Remove the foil, raise the oven temperature to 450°F and bake until the stuffing is nicely browned, 6-8 minutes. Transfer the artichokes to a serving platter and drizzle with the remaining 1 tablespoon of oil. Makes 4 servings.

** Brands may vary by region; substitute a similar product.*

## Karine Bakhoum

Karine Bakhoum is a visionary of hospitality consulting, public relations and networking who has had a passion for cooking since childhood. She is the founder of KB Network News, a leading food consulting and PR firm. A frequent judge on *Iron Chef America*, Karine has entertained many luminaries of the food world with her own cooking over her 20-year career. In 2007, she became the only person to have her palate insured by Lloyd's of London. She lives in the Hamptons and is an avid Costco shopper.

# Roasted Rack of Pork

JBS Swift

Recipes developed by "Iron Palate" Karine Bakhoum

**1 5-pound rack of pork (8 ribs)**

**Salt and freshly ground black pepper**

**Rosemary sprigs, for garnish**

***MARINADE***

**1 cup Dijon mustard**

**1/2 cup Worcestershire sauce**

**1/4 cup finely chopped shallots**

**1/4 cup finely chopped garlic**

**1 cup finely chopped fresh rosemary**

**1/2 cup peach preserves**

**1 tablespoon ground ginger**

**1 teaspoon crushed red pepper**

**1 teaspoon Hungarian paprika**

**1 teaspoon grated nutmeg**

**Kosher salt and pepper to taste**

**1 tablespoon Kirkland Signature extra virgin olive oil**

***GRAVY***

**1 cup chicken stock**

**2 tablespoons top-quality unsalted butter**

Preheat oven to 450°F.

Rinse pork and cut off excess fat, then carefully cut the loin away from the ribs, about 1 inch deep, leaving them attached but partially separated. Slice the ribs about 1/2 inch deep from the bone down and pierce the meat with 6-8 holes, turning the knife a bit so the marinade can get inside. Season to taste with salt and pepper.

To prepare the marinade, place all ingredients in a bowl and mix until smooth and evenly blended.

Place the pork in a nonstick roasting pan and thoroughly rub with the marinade. Crisscross a string around the meat to keep the ribs and loin together and tie. Marinate for at least 30 minutes.

Place the pork in the oven with the ribs sticking up in the center of the pan. Roast for 20 minutes per pound (25 minutes if you like it well done). When the rack looks three-fourths cooked and the meat is still soft to the touch, remove from the oven and carefully cut off the string; place the rack on its side to finish cooking. Add a bit of chicken stock to the pan if it's sticky to begin making the gravy. Continue to cook until the meat is just a bit springy to the touch, longer for well done. Pork is best served medium (150°F), with a very pale pink color.

Remove the rack from the pan and cover loosely with foil.

Add more chicken stock and butter to the roasting pan and cook on the stovetop over low heat, stirring frequently, to make the gravy.

To serve, carve the ribs away from the loin and cut into 8 separate pieces. Place on a serving platter. Cut the loin into 1/4- or 1/2-inch slices and fan alongside the ribs. Spoon some of the gravy over the ribs and loin and garnish with rosemary. Serve the rest of the gravy on the side for mashed potatoes or gratin. Makes 6-8 servings.

# Pork Tenderloin à la Provençal

JBS Swift

**1 pork tenderloin**

**4 tablespoons Kirkland Signature extra virgin olive oil, plus more for coating the meat**

**4 tablespoons dried herbes de Provence, divided**

**Kosher salt and freshly ground black pepper**

**1 teaspoon Hungarian paprika**

**2 cups red grape tomatoes**

**1 Vidalia or sweet onion, cut in half and sliced vertically**

**6 garlic cloves, peeled**

**1 cup pitted Kalamata olives**

Preheat oven to 400°F.

Rinse and dry pork; remove any excess fat. Rub oil over the meat and season with 2 tablespoons herbes de Provence, salt and pepper to taste and paprika.

In a bowl, mix tomatoes, onion, garlic and olives with 4 tablespoons oil. Season with salt and pepper to taste and the remaining herbes de Provence.

In a sauté pan, sear the tenderloin over high heat until browned. Transfer to a roasting pan and surround with the tomato mixture. Roast for 15 minutes per pound, or until the pork is firm but still tender to the touch (internal temperature of 155°F). Remove from the oven and let rest for 8-10 minutes.

Slice the pork and serve on a platter with the tomato mixture on top and around. Serve with green salad and crusty country bread or with roasted fingerling or new potatoes. Makes 4 servings.

**Tip:** Use 2 pork tenderloins to serve 6 to 8 people.

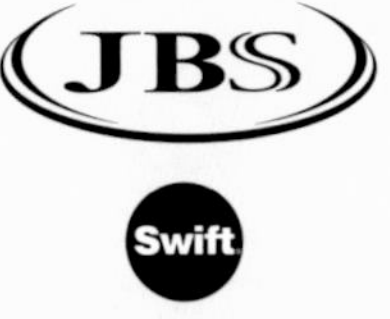

## Myra Goodman

Myra Goodman and her husband, Drew, founded Earthbound Farm in their Carmel Valley, California, backyard 26 years ago. Myra's cooking is inspired by the fresh, flavorful and healthy harvest of their organic farm, which led her to establish one of the country's first certified organic kitchens. Her latest cookbook is *The Earthbound Cook: Recipes for Delicious Food and a Healthy Planet* (Workman Publishing, 2010).

# Spring Mix Salad with Strawberries, Walnuts and Goat Cheese

Earthbound Farm

Recipes developed by Myra Goodman

Sweet-tart and succulent, strawberries are a true joy of spring and summer. This light and delicious salad uses spring mix as a beautiful and flavorful base for the delightful blending of sweet strawberries, creamy goat cheese and toasted walnuts. The flavors are melded perfectly by a quick-to-make balsamic vinaigrette that features toasted walnut oil.

**1 pint fresh strawberries, rinsed, dried and hulled**
**5 ounces prewashed Earthbound Farm* Organic Spring Mix** Organic
**1/2 cup walnut pieces, toasted**
**1/2 cup (about 2 ounces) crumbled goat cheese**

***WALNUT BALSAMIC VINAIGRETTE***

**2 tablespoons balsamic vinegar**
**1/2 teaspoon Dijon mustard**
**3 tablespoons toasted walnut oil**
**2 tablespoons extra-virgin olive oil**
**Salt and freshly ground black pepper**

To prepare the vinaigrette, combine vinegar, mustard and both oils in a glass jar and seal the lid tightly. Shake the jar vigorously to combine. Season the vinaigrette with salt and pepper to taste. (The vinaigrette can be refrigerated, covered, for up to 1 month. Let it return to room temperature and shake vigorously before using.)

Cut strawberries in quarters, place in a small bowl and toss with about 2 tablespoons of the vinaigrette. Set aside.

Place all of the spring mix in a large bowl and add 3 tablespoons of the vinaigrette. Toss to lightly coat the leaves; then taste and add more vinaigrette if needed.

Transfer the lettuce to individual salad plates. Top the lettuce with the strawberries, toasted walnuts and crumbled goat cheese. Serve immediately. Makes 4 servings.

**Tip:** This vinaigrette is also light enough to dress delicate baby spinach, mâche or baby greens.

** Brands may vary by region; substitute a similar product.*

*Food to live by.*

# Healthy Apple Crisp

Earthbound Farm

My family loves apple desserts, and we especially love ones that are healthy as well as delicious. This crisp uses just a little canola oil instead of lots of butter, as well as whole wheat flour and nutritious nuts. It's yummy, quick and easy to make, and a guilt-free pleasure. Great on its own, it's even better when served with a bit of vanilla frozen yogurt or ice cream.

**2 6-ounce bags Earthbound Farm* organic apple slices** Organic
**Juice of 1 lemon**
**1 cup old-fashioned rolled oats**
**3/4 cup chopped pecans or walnuts**
**1/2 cup packed light brown sugar**
**2 tablespoons whole wheat pastry flour**
**1 tablespoon ground cinnamon**
**1/4 cup canola oil, plus more if needed**

Position a rack in the middle of the oven and preheat the oven to 375°F.

Place apple slices in a large bowl, add lemon juice and toss to coat with the juice.

To make the topping, combine oats, pecans, brown sugar, pastry flour and cinnamon in a bowl, and stir to blend. Add 1/4 cup oil and stir again. If the mixture seems too dry (it should clump together when you squeeze it), add another teaspoon or two of oil.

Transfer the apples to a 9-inch-square baking dish. Add the topping, spreading it evenly over the apples; do not pack it down.

Bake until the apples are tender and the topping is golden, 45-50 minutes. Serve warm. Makes 6 servings.

** Brands may vary by region; substitute a similar product.*

## Mario Batali

Mario Batali shares his passion for the authentic spirit of Italian food through his restaurants, cookbooks, television shows and products. His latest cookbook is *Molto Gusto: Easy Italian Cooking*, published by ecco, an imprint of HarperCollins. Mario focuses on simple and seasonal dishes and less on protein-heavy main courses.

# Spaghetti all'Amatriciana

Garofalo

Recipes developed by Mario Batali

These recipes represent the actual pasta dishes Italians eat at home every day, often twice a day. Less is always more. It's more important for the sauce and pasta to be one, a sum greater than its parts.

**Kosher salt**
**1/4 cup extra-virgin olive oil**
**4 ounces sliced guanciale or pancetta (see note), or good American bacon, cut into 1/2-inch-wide strips**
**1 medium red onion, halved lengthwise, ends trimmed, and cut lengthwise into 1/4-inch-wide slices**
**1/4 cup tomato paste**
**1 1/2-2 teaspoons hot red pepper flakes**
**1/4 cup Mario Batali Pasta Sauce–Arrabiata***
**1 pound Garofalo* spaghetti**
**1/2 cup freshly grated Parmigiano-Reggiano, plus extra for serving**
**1/2 cup grated pecorino romano**
**1/3 cup coarsely chopped fresh Italian parsley**

Bring 6 quarts of water to a boil in a large pot and add 3 tablespoons kosher salt.

Meanwhile, combine the oil, guanciale and onion in another large pot and cook over medium-high heat, stirring frequently, until the guanciale is lightly browned and the onion is softened, about 7 minutes. Stir in the tomato paste and red pepper flakes and cook, stirring, until fragrant, about 1 minute. Stir in the pasta sauce and remove from the heat.

Drop the pasta into the boiling water and cook until just al dente. Drain, reserving about 1/2 cup of the pasta water.

Add the pasta and 1/4 cup of the reserved pasta water to the guanciale and stir and toss over medium heat until the pasta is well coated (add a splash or two more of the reserved pasta water if necessary to loosen the sauce). Stir in the cheeses and parsley and serve immediately, with additional grated Parmigiano on the side. Makes 6 servings.

**Note:** Guanciale and pancetta are thinly sliced, flavorful Italian meats, commonly called Italian bacon.

**Tip:** Substitute Garofalo organic whole wheat spaghetti for a healthful option.

*Recipe excerpted from* Molto Gusto: Easy Italian Cooking, *by Mario Batali and Mark Ladner, courtesy of ecco, an imprint of HarperCollins (2010).*

** Brands may vary by region; substitute a similar product.*

# Penne all'Arrabiata

Garofalo

**Kosher salt**
**1/4 cup tomato paste**
**1 tablespoon hot red pepper flakes**
**1/2 cup Mario Batali Pasta Sauce–Arrabiata***
**1 pound Garofalo* organic penne Organic**
**Maldon or other flaky sea salt**
**1/4 cup extra-virgin olive oil**
**Freshly grated Parmigiano-Reggiano for serving**

Bring 6 quarts of water to a boil in a large pot and add 3 tablespoons kosher salt.

Meanwhile, combine the tomato paste and pepper flakes in a large pot and stir over low heat just until fragrant. Stir in the pasta sauce and remove from the heat.

Drop the pasta into the boiling water and cook until just al dente. Drain the pasta, reserving 3/4 cup of the pasta water.

Add the pasta and the reserved pasta water to the pasta sauce and stir and toss over medium heat until the pasta is well coated. Season with salt if necessary, then add the oil, tossing well. Serve immediately, with grated Parmigiano on the side. Makes 6 servings.

*Recipe excerpted from* Molto Gusto: Easy Italian Cooking, *by Mario Batali and Mark Ladner, courtesy of ecco, an imprint of HarperCollins (2010).*

** Brands may vary by region; substitute a similar product.*

Garofalo

## Anne Byrn

Anne Byrn is an award-winning food writer and author of the *New York Times* bestselling "The Cake Mix Doctor" series of cookbooks, which have more than 3 million copies in print. Anne's latest work is *The Cake Mix Doctor Returns* (Workman Publishing, 2009). You can see her blog at *www.cakemixdoctor.com*.

# Peppermint Bark Magic Brownies

Kirkland Signature/Puratos

Recipes developed by Anne Byrn, The Cake Mix Doctor

**Vegetable oil spray**
**Parchment paper**
**8 tablespoons (1 stick) unsalted butter**
**1 20-ounce package brownie mix**
**1 cup sweetened flaked coconut**
**2 cups finely chopped Kirkland Signature peppermint bark**
**1 heaping cup chopped pecans**
**1 14-ounce can sweetened condensed milk**

Preheat oven to 350°F.

Lightly mist the bottom of a 13-by-9-inch pan with vegetable oil spray. Line the bottom and the long sides of the pan with parchment paper, extending the ends 3-4 inches beyond the edges of the pan.

Place butter on the parchment paper and set the pan in the center of the oven until the butter melts, 4-5 minutes.

Remove the pan from the oven to a wire rack. Sprinkle brownie mix evenly over the melted butter. Scatter coconut evenly over the brownie mix. Layer peppermint bark evenly over the coconut. Scatter pecans evenly on top. Drizzle sweetened condensed milk evenly over the pecans.

Bake until the brownies bubble and the edges are lightly browned, 30-35 minutes. Remove from the oven and let cool in the pan on a wire rack for 30 minutes. Run a sharp knife around the edges of the pan to loosen the brownies, then carefully lift the parchment paper and brownies onto a cutting board. Slice into squares and serve warm, or let cool for another 30 minutes to room temperature, slice, and then store. Makes about 3 dozen brownies.

# Peppermint Bark Fudge Chewies

Kirkland Signature/Puratos

**1 20-ounce package brownie mix**
**2 tablespoons all-purpose flour**
**8 tablespoons (1 stick) unsalted butter, melted**
**2 large eggs**
**2 cups finely chopped (1/4-inch pieces) Kirkland Signature peppermint bark, divided**

Preheat oven to 350°F. Set aside 2 ungreased baking sheets.

In a large mixing bowl, combine brownie mix, flour, melted butter and eggs with a wooden spoon until the ingredients are just combined, about 30 seconds. Fold in 1 cup of the peppermint bark.

Using a small scoop or spoon, drop cookie dough by generous tablespoonfuls or 1-inch balls about 2 inches apart on the baking sheets. Press 1/2 teaspoon peppermint bark onto the top of each ball of batter.

Place the baking sheets one at a time into the oven. Bake until the cookies are firm around the edges but still soft in the center, 10-12 minutes. Remove from the oven and let the cookies cool on the sheets for 2-3 minutes. Using a metal spatula, transfer the cookies to wire racks.

Serve warm or let cool for 20 minutes before storing. Makes 4 dozen cookies.

**Tips:** To make scooping easier, chill the dough first and place the bowl of dough in the refrigerator between batches. You can use any brownie mix that is about 20 ounces, but my favorite brand is Ghirardelli.

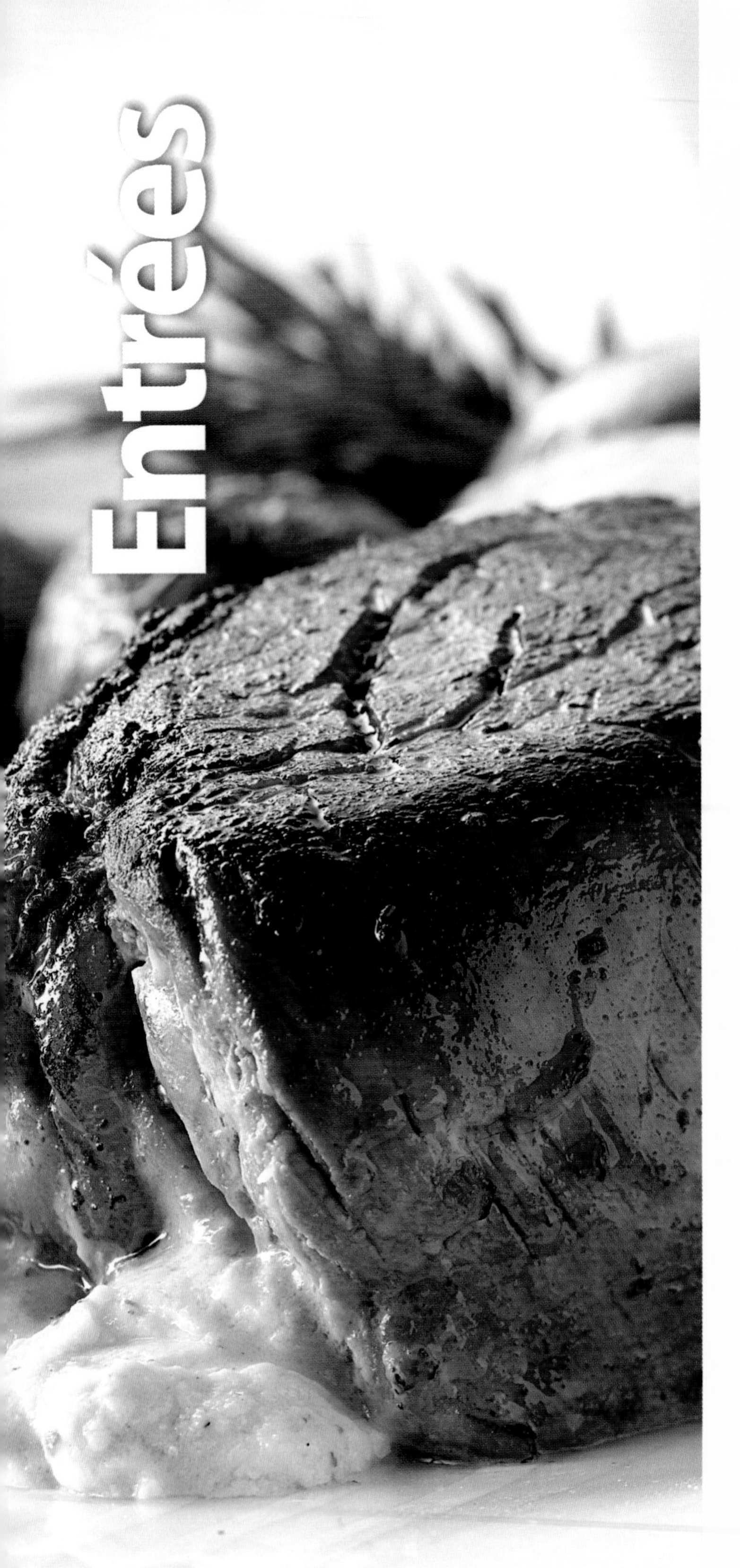


# Grilling a perfect steak

**Jamie Purviance**

Jamie Purviance is a national grilling expert, a 2010 James Beard Award nominee and the author of *Weber's Way to Grill* and this year's companion cookbooks *Weber's On the Grill: Steak & Sides* and *Weber's On the Grill: Chicken & Sides*.

**By Jamie Purviance**

MANY THINK THAT grilling the perfect meal is easy. It can be, but there is an art to it, and certain techniques make a huge difference.

The heart of grilling lies in the fire, within the grill itself, and what separates the master grillers from the masses is that the master grillers understand how the fire flavors the food. They know what kind of heat is right for each meat, fish and vegetable. They know how to control the fire and sear the food to create rich tastes and textures. They know how to capture the aromatic smoke that develops when juices and fats drip into the grill.

Keep the following techniques in mind as you grill your next steak. They can help make your steak taste sublime.

**Give it a rest.** Allow your steak to stand at room temperature for 15-30 minutes after you remove it from the refrigerator. A properly rested steak will cook faster than a cold one, which means it will be juicier in the end.

**Trim it down.** You want to leave a small layer of fat around the edges of your steak to add flavor, but don't overdo it. Trim all but 1/4 inch of fat around the edges. Any more than that could lead to flare-ups—which means unevenly cooked and sometimes burned meat.

**Sprinkle on the salt and oil it up.** Give the steak a light coating of olive oil to help prevent sticking, and salt it 15-30 minutes before it goes on the grill. The salt mingles with the meat juices, which helps to develop a delicious crust when the steak's on the grill. But don't salt too early—it can draw out too much moisture.

**Add some smoke.** Anyone with half a taste bud will tell you that wood smoke can flavor the meat as well as any seasoning mix or sauce. Consider tossing some wood chips or wood chunks (soaked for 30 minutes and drained first) onto the burning charcoal or a gas grill's smoker box.

**Keep the lid down.** Keep the grill lid down and open it only to flip the steak. You want to trap the smoke in the grill and surround your steak with those wonderful aromatic flavors.

**Forgo the fork.** Use tongs instead to flip steaks. Poking the meat with a fork will cause precious juices to escape.

**Getting it done, just right.** Because steaks get firmer as they grill, one way to check their doneness is to press the surface of a steak with your fingertip. For medium-rare, look for a firmness similar to that of the tip of your nose.

**Give it a rest ... again.** After it's removed from the grill, let your steak rest for 3-5 minutes. This allows the juices that were pushed to the center by the heat of the grill to migrate back to all parts of the steak so it's juicy throughout.

## Rafael's Honey Ginger Salmon
### Kirkland Signature/Marine Harvest

**4 Kirkland Signature frozen salmon portions, thawed**

***MARINADE***

**2 tablespoons soy sauce**

**1 tablespoon minced fresh ginger**

**1 tablespoon white wine**

**1 tablespoon lemon juice**

**2 tablespoons honey**

**Pinch of salt and pepper**

***GLAZE***

**4 tablespoons butter**

**1/4 cup packed light brown sugar**

To prepare the marinade, combine all ingredients.

Place the thawed salmon in a medium bowl and pour the marinade over the fish. Refrigerate for 2 hours.

Preheat oven to 375°F.

Transfer the salmon to a baking pan and place in the oven for 15 minutes.

To prepare the glaze, melt butter and mix with brown sugar. Spoon the sauce over the salmon and then set it directly under the broiler for 5 minutes, or until glazed. Makes 4 servings.

marineharvest
excellence in seafood

## Fresh Salmon with Quinoa
### True North Salmon

**1/2 cup dry quinoa**

**Salt and pepper**

**4 5-ounce True North* Atlantic salmon portions, or cut 4 portions from a fillet**

**Olive oil**

**1/2 red onion, cut into wedges**

**8 garlic cloves, peeled**

**2 tomatoes, cut into cubes**

**1 tablespoon capers, drained**

**8 pitted Kalamata olives**

**3 ounces arugula**

**1 teaspoon finely cut chives, for garnish**

Prepare quinoa according to package directions. Season to taste with salt and pepper. Keep warm.

Season salmon on both sides with salt and pepper to taste. Heat a nonstick sauté pan with just enough oil to coat over medium heat. Add salmon and cook on one side until golden brown, about 3 minutes. Turn the portions carefully with a spatula and cook for another 3 minutes.

In a separate pan, heat 1 tablespoon oil over medium heat. Add onions and sauté along with garlic and tomatoes until semi-soft. Add capers, olives and arugula. Toss until the leaves are wilted. Season to taste with salt and pepper.

Place the quinoa in the center of 4 plates, set the salmon on top and distribute the tomato-arugula mixture evenly next to the portions. Garnish with chives. Makes 4 servings.

** Brands may vary by region; substitute a similar product.*

## Cedar-Planked Salmon with Lemon Garlic Cilantro Sauce

Multiexport Foods

- 1 cedar grilling plank (about 15 by 7 inches)
- 1 bunch green onions (about 8)
- 1 bunch cilantro (1 ounce)
- 1 Multiexport Foods* fresh Atlantic or steelhead salmon fillet

*LEMON GARLIC CILANTRO SAUCE*

- 1/4 cup mayonnaise
- 1 large garlic clove, peeled
- 1/4 teaspoon Kirkland Signature pure sea salt
- 1/2 cup Kirkland Signature extra virgin olive oil
- 1 teaspoon grated lemon peel
- 1/4 cup fresh lemon juice
- 1/4 teaspoon Kirkland Signature fine ground Malabar black pepper
- 1/4 cup loosely packed cilantro leaves

Soak cedar plank in water for at least 20 minutes.

To prepare the sauce, place mayonnaise, garlic and salt in a blender; pulse several times to combine. On medium-high speed, add oil in a thin, steady stream. Blend for 30-40 seconds, or until smooth. Add lemon peel, lemon juice and pepper; blend until combined, about 10 seconds. Add cilantro and pulse until blended.

Preheat the grill to 300°F.

Spread green onions and cilantro on the cedar plank. Lay salmon on top. Set planked salmon on the grill, close and grill for 20-30 minutes, or until the fish flakes easily with a fork. Use a spray bottle of water to put out any flames.

Serve salmon with the sauce. Makes 6 servings.

*Recipe developed by Lindsay Tkacsik.*

** Brands may vary by region; substitute a similar product.*

Multiexport Foods

## Lemon Pepper Wild Alaska Salmon

Kirkland Signature/Copper River Seafoods

- 1/4 cup butter, at room temperature
- 5 Kirkland Signature Copper River Seafoods* Alaska sockeye portions, skin on, thawed
- 2 teaspoons lemon pepper seasoning
- Garlic salt

Preheat the grill or a skillet on medium heat.

Spread butter over the meat side of fish and place skin-side down on the grill or in the skillet. Sprinkle with lemon pepper and garlic salt to taste.

Cover the fish with a lid or foil and cook for about 5 minutes, or until cooked through and the fish flakes easily with a fork. Be sure to move the fish around a little on the grill to prevent sticking. Makes 5 servings.

** Brands may vary by region; substitute a similar product.*

KIRKLAND Signature

Quick & Easy

# Pan-Roasted Salmon with Clementine and Radish Salsa

Duda Farm Fresh Foods

- 5 Dandy* clementines
- 3 large radishes, finely chopped
- 1 large green onion, chopped (both green and white parts)
- 1 small serrano chile, seeded and finely chopped
- 1/2 green bell pepper, finely chopped
- 1 tablespoon fresh lime juice
- 1/2 teaspoon salt
- 1/8 teaspoon ground black pepper
- 1/2 cup lightly packed cilantro leaves, chopped
- 1 teaspoon canola oil
- 1 1/2 pounds salmon fillet with skin, cut in 4 pieces

Preheat oven to 425°F.

Peel 2 clementines and cut each section into 4 or 5 pieces; place in a mixing bowl. Halve the remaining 3 clementines crosswise and juice them, using an electric citrus juicer or squeezing them over a bowl. Strain the juice, about 1/3 cup, and add it to the chopped fruit.

Add radishes, green onion, chile, bell pepper and lime juice to the clementines. Mix in salt and pepper, then cilantro. Let the salsa sit for 20 minutes to allow the flavors to blend.

Heat oil over medium heat in an ovenproof skillet. When a drop of water dances on the surface of the pan, place the pieces of fish in it, skin-side up. Cook until the salmon is seared and has a golden crust, about 3 minutes. Using tongs, turn the fish skin-side down. Place the skillet in the oven and roast until the fish is translucent just in the center, about 8 minutes for a 1-inch-thick fillet. Transfer the salmon to individual dinner plates. Add 1/4 cup of the salsa to each plate. Makes 4 servings.

** Brands may vary by region; substitute a similar product.*

# Salmon with Vanilla Bean Ginger Sauce

## Kirkland Signature/Rodelle Vanilla

- 1 tablespoon olive oil
- 6 salmon fillets
- Salt and pepper
- 1/4 teaspoon Kirkland Signature vanilla extract
- 1 teaspoon extra-virgin olive oil
- 1 shallot, chopped
- 1 tablespoon chopped garlic
- 1 tablespoon chopped fresh ginger
- 1 Kirkland Signature Rodelle* vanilla bean, split lengthwise
- 1/4 cup brandy
- 1 1/2 cups white wine
- 1/4 cup heavy whipping cream
- 1/4 cup unsalted butter

Preheat oven to 350°F.

Drizzle oil on salmon fillets, coating both sides. Sprinkle with salt and pepper to taste and vanilla extract. Place salmon in a roasting pan and bake for 10-12 minutes, or until cooked to taste.

Heat extra-virgin olive oil in a saucepan over medium heat. Add shallot, garlic and ginger; sauté until soft. Scrape vanilla bean seeds into the pan and add the pod, brandy and wine. Bring to a boil and cook until reduced by half.

Lower the heat and add cream; cook until reduced by half.

Remove from the heat and add cold butter slowly, whisking into the sauce. Strain the sauce. Season to taste with salt and pepper. Keep warm.

To serve, place a spoonful of sauce in the center of each plate and place a salmon fillet on top. Drizzle with more sauce. Makes 6 servings.

** Brands may vary by region; substitute a similar product.*

RODELLE
A FAMILY OF FINE VANILLAS

# Eddy's Brown Sugar and Honey Grilled Wild Salmon

## Icicle Seafoods

- 2 cups water
- 3/4 cup lightly packed light brown sugar
- 1/3 cup kosher salt
- 4 tablespoons honey
- 1/4 cup chopped fresh dill
- 1 pound skin-on wild salmon fillet
- 1 tablespoon canola or other neutral cooking oil

In a saucepan, combine water, brown sugar, salt and honey. Boil until the sugar has dissolved. Remove from the heat, stir in chopped dill and let cool completely. Transfer to a baking dish that will accommodate the liquid and the salmon.

Place salmon fillet in the brine skin-side up and marinate in the refrigerator for no longer than 1 hour.

Preheat the grill to 350-400°F.

Remove salmon from the brine and pat dry. Rub oil on the skin side only to prevent sticking. Transfer the salmon, skin-side up, to the grill and grill for about 8 minutes, then flip and continue cooking for an additional 5 minutes, or until cooked to taste (the fish should flake easily with a fork). Makes 2 servings.

# Honey and Walnut Crusted Salmon
## California Walnuts

- Nonstick cooking spray
- 1 1/2 pounds salmon fillet
- Freshly ground sea salt and pepper
- 2 tablespoons stone-ground mustard
- 2 tablespoons honey
- 2 teaspoons finely chopped fresh basil or tarragon
- 2 garlic cloves, minced
- 1/2 cup finely chopped Kirkland Signature walnuts
- 4 cups baby arugula or spring mix greens
- 2 tablespoons extra-virgin olive oil
- 2 tablespoons balsamic vinegar

Preheat oven to 400°F. Coat a baking sheet with cooking spray.

Remove skin from salmon and cut into 4 pieces. Place on the baking sheet and season to taste with salt and pepper.

In a small bowl, stir together mustard, honey, herbs and garlic. Spread over the top and sides of the salmon.

Sprinkle 2 tablespoons walnuts over each piece of salmon.

Bake for 10-15 minutes, or until the surface of the salmon flakes easily with a fork.

Place salad greens in a bowl and toss with oil and vinegar. Season to taste with salt and pepper.

Divide the salad among 4 plates and top with salmon. Makes 4 servings.

# Orange-Glazed Salmon Fillets with Peach Salsa

## Booth Ranches/Pride Packing/ Sequoia Enterprises

4 6- to 8-ounce salmon fillets
1 tablespoon ancho chile powder
2 teaspoons kosher salt
2 cups juice from Booth Ranches* California oranges
1/2 cup Grand Marnier
2 tablespoons olive oil
Orange and peach slices, for garnish

*PEACH SALSA*

3-4 ripe but firm Mary's Pride* peaches, peeled and diced
1/3 cup finely diced red bell pepper
1/3 cup finely diced orange bell pepper
1/3 cup finely diced red onion
1/3 cup sliced green onions
1/3 cup chopped fresh cilantro
1 jalapeño, minced (remove seeds for milder flavor)
1 cup apricot preserves

To prepare the salsa, combine all ingredients in a bowl. Chill for 1-2 hours.

Season salmon on one side with ancho chile powder and salt.

In a saucepan, combine orange juice and Grand Marnier; bring to a boil and cook until reduced to 1/2 cup.

Heat oil in a large sauté pan until very hot. Add salmon, seasoned side down, cover and cook for 4-5 minutes over medium heat. Turn and cook an additional 4-5 minutes. Add orange juice mixture during the last minute of cooking.

Remove salmon and sauce to serving plates and top with peach salsa. Garnish with orange and Mary's Pride peach slices. Makes 4 servings.

**Tip:** The peach salsa is also excellent with other kinds of fish, chicken and pork.

*Recipe by Chef Bill Hassett, Booth Ranches, LLC.*
** Brands may vary by region; substitute a similar product.*

## Santana's Favorite Steelhead

True Nature Seafood

- 8 6- to 8-ounce True Nature Seafood* steelhead fillet portions
- 1/3 cup extra-virgin olive oil
- 1 teaspoon sesame oil
- 5 tablespoons soy sauce
- 4 tablespoons balsamic vinegar
- 3 tablespoons honey
- 1 tablespoon brown sugar
- 1 1/2 teaspoons ground ginger
- 1 teaspoon crushed red pepper, or to taste
- 1/2 teaspoon salt (optional)
- 2 green onions, chopped
- 3 garlic cloves, minced

Place steelhead fillets in a large resealable plastic bag.

In a medium bowl, combine the remaining ingredients. Whisk together well, and pour over the fish in the plastic bag. Remove the air from the bag and seal tightly. Marinate in the refrigerator for 8 hours or overnight.

Preheat the grill to medium-high.

Place each fillet on a piece of foil coated with nonstick cooking spray and wrap tightly.

Lightly oil the grill grates. Grill the steelhead for 15 minutes per inch of thickness, or until it just flakes with a fork, turning it over halfway through grilling. Makes 8 servings.

** Brands may vary by region; substitute a similar product.*

## Sautéed Alaskan Fish

Alaska Glacier Seafoods

- 3 pounds fresh Alaska Glacier Seafoods* skinless halibut fillets or salmon fillets, cut into 6 portions
- 1/2 cup flour
- 2 tablespoons olive oil
- 1/2 cup thinly sliced red onion
- 1/2 cup thinly sliced celery
- 2 tablespoons capers, drained
- 2 garlic cloves, crushed
- 1 tablespoon red wine vinegar
- 1/2 cup dry white wine (chardonnay)
- 2 tablespoons butter
- 3 cups hot cooked rice

Lightly dust fish with flour and set aside.

Heat oil in a large sauté pan over medium-high heat. Place as many pieces of fish as will fit comfortably into the pan and cook until lightly browned, but not cooked through. Remove the fish and keep warm while you cook the remaining pieces.

Add onion, celery, capers, garlic, vinegar and wine to the pan. Reduce the heat to low. Place the fish on top, cover and simmer very gently until the fish is cooked through and flakes easily.

Transfer the fish to a warm serving platter. Increase the heat to high, add butter to the pan and cook, stirring, until the butter melts.

Top the fish with the vegetables and sauce and serve immediately with rice. Makes 6 servings.

** Brands may vary by region; substitute a similar product.*

## Sweet Onion and Quinoa with Baked Halibut

Keystone

- 2 cups quinoa
- 2 tablespoons olive oil
- 2 Keystone* Certified Sweet Onions, diced
- 1 orange bell pepper, diced
- 1 jalapeño, seeded and diced
- 1 15-ounce can black beans, drained
- 2 cups corn kernels
- 1 1/2 pounds halibut fillets
- 1 avocado, peeled and sliced
- 2 plum tomatoes, sliced
- Juice of 1 lime
- 1 cup fresh cilantro leaves, chopped
- 1 ounce goat cheese, or more to taste

*VINAIGRETTE*

- 1/4 cup olive oil
- Juice of 2 limes
- 2 tablespoons ground cumin
- 1 tablespoon Dijon mustard
- 2 garlic cloves, minced
- Salt and pepper to taste

*SPICE BLEND*

- 1 tablespoon ground cumin
- 1 teaspoon salt
- 1 teaspoon ground black pepper

Cook quinoa according to package directions.

Preheat oven to 350°F.

Heat oil in a large skillet over medium-high heat. Add onions, bell pepper and jalapeño; cook for 5 minutes. Add beans and corn; cook for 5 minutes. Stir in quinoa. Keep warm.

To prepare the vinaigrette, combine all ingredients and blend well.

Place halibut in a greased baking dish. Mix the spice blend ingredients; sprinkle over the halibut. Bake for about 20 minutes, or until just cooked through.

Stir the vinaigrette into the quinoa mixture; transfer to a platter. Top with the fish, avocado and tomatoes. Sprinkle with lime juice, cilantro and cheese.
Makes 4-5 servings.

** Brands may vary by region; substitute a similar product.*

Keystone

## Roasted Halibut with Pine Nut and Parmesan Crust

S. M. Products (BC) Ltd.

- 1/2 cup pine nuts, coarsely chopped
- 1/2 cup freshly grated Parmesan cheese
- 2 tablespoons finely chopped fresh basil
- 1 garlic clove, minced
- 2 tablespoons olive oil
- 4 6-ounce halibut fillets
- Sea salt

Preheat oven to 425°F.

In a small bowl, combine pine nuts, Parmesan, basil, garlic and oil; stir to blend.

Place halibut fillets on a baking sheet and season to taste with salt. Pat the pine nut mixture onto the halibut, pressing lightly to make it stick.

Bake in the center of the oven for 10-15 minutes, or until the fish is opaque all the way through.
Makes 4 servings.

## Catfish Etouffée

### Consolidated Catfish Producers

- **3 tablespoons olive oil, divided**
- **1 cup diced onion**
- **1/2 cup diced bell pepper**
- **1/2 cup diced celery**
- **2 tablespoons chopped fresh garlic**
- **2 cups prepared étouffée sauce (see note)**
- **1 tomato, coarsely chopped**
- **2 fresh U.S. Farm-Raised Catfish fillets**
- **2 teaspoons Cajun seasoning**
- **1 cup rice, cooked**

Heat 2 tablespoons oil in a sauté pan over high heat. Add onions, bell pepper, celery and garlic; sauté until the onions are soft. Add étouffée sauce and tomatoes. Reduce the heat to a simmer.

In another skillet, heat 1 tablespoon oil over medium heat. Sprinkle catfish fillets with Cajun seasoning. Place in the skillet and sauté for about 4 minutes on each side.

Pour the sauce over the fillets in the skillet. Reduce the heat to low and simmer for about 5 minutes, or until the fish flakes easily when tested with a fork.

Serve over rice. Makes 2 servings.

**Note:** Etouffée is from the French word for smothered. This spicy sauce, such as Tony Chachere's, is a Cajun favorite.

## Catfish with Tangy Orange Sauce

### Heartland Catfish

- **1/4 cup orange juice**
- **2 tablespoons vegetable oil**
- **2 tablespoons light soy sauce**
- **1 tablespoon lemon juice**
- **1 garlic clove, minced**
- **1/8 teaspoon pepper**
- **4 pounds Heartland Catfish* U.S. farm-raised catfish fillets**

Prepare a grill or preheat the broiler.

In a bowl, mix orange juice, oil, soy sauce, lemon juice, garlic and pepper. Brush catfish fillets with the sauce mixture.

Place the fillets on an oiled grill rack or broiler pan rack. Grill or broil about 4 inches from the heat for 5 minutes on each side, brushing frequently with the sauce, or until the fish flakes easily when tested with a fork. Makes 8 servings.

** Brands may vary by region; substitute a similar product.*

# Citrus Sole

## Cecelia Packing/Kings River Packing

- 2 Cecelia Packing* Cara Cara oranges
- 1 Kings River* lemon
- 1 tablespoon olive oil
- 4 6-ounce fillets of sole
- 1/2 cup water
- 2 tablespoons honey
- 2 teaspoons cornstarch
- 1/2 teaspoon salt
- 1/8 teaspoon white pepper
- 2 tablespoons chopped fresh chives, divided

Grate the zest of oranges and lemon. Remove the peel and pith from the fruit, then cut the segments away from the membrane, saving the juices in a bowl.

Heat oil in a large skillet over medium heat. Add fish to the skillet and sprinkle with about 1 tablespoon of the orange and lemon juice, reserving the rest for the sauce, which you can start preparing while the fish is cooking. Cook for 5-7 minutes, or until the fish flakes easily with a fork. Remove from the heat and cover the skillet while you finish the sauce.

In the bowl with the citrus juices, stir in water, honey, cornstarch, salt and pepper. Transfer to a small saucepan and cook over medium heat until it thickens. Gently stir in the citrus segments and 1 tablespoon *each* of zest and chives.

Spoon the sauce over the fish and garnish with the remaining zest and chives. Makes 4 servings.

**Tips:** Cod, pollack or other whitefish can be used in this recipe. You can also use navel oranges instead of Cara Cara.

*Recipe developed by Christine W. Jackson, food stylist.*

** Brands may vary by region; substitute a similar product.*

# Venetian Tilapia with Mini Peppers

## Master's Touch

- 16 ounces tilapia
- Salt and pepper
- Flour
- Olive oil
- Mashed potatoes

*VENETIAN SALSA*

- 2 large green onion bulbs, chopped
- 2 tablespoons chopped Master's Touch* mini cucumber
- 6 Master's Touch* vine sweet mini peppers, 2 of each color, chopped
- 2 tablespoons chopped fresh cilantro
- 1 serrano chile, minced
- 1/4 teaspoon salt
- 1/8 teaspoon pepper
- Juice of 2 medium limes
- 2 tablespoons extra-virgin olive oil
- 2 tablespoons chopped avocado

*MINI PEPPER SAUCE*

- 4 Master's Touch* vine sweet mini peppers
- 4 tablespoons extra-virgin olive oil
- Salt and pepper

Preheat oven to 325°F.

Season tilapia with salt and pepper to taste. Dust with flour.

Heat oil in an ovenproof frying pan over high heat. Sear both sides of fish, then transfer to the oven for 10 minutes, or until just cooked through.

To prepare the salsa, combine onions, cucumber, mini peppers, cilantro and chile. Add salt, pepper, lime juice and oil; toss to blend. Stir in avocado.

To prepare the pepper sauce, boil mini peppers for 3 minutes, or until tender. Puree in a blender with oil, salt and pepper.

To serve, top the fish with salsa. Pour the pepper sauce over mashed potatoes. Makes 2 servings.

** Brands may vary by region; substitute a similar product.*

# Tilapia with Olives, Capers and Chilies

## Tropical Aquaculture

- 2 cups tomato sauce
- 1/2 cup green Sicilian olives
- 2 tablespoons capers
- 1 teaspoon dried red chili flakes
- 1 cup white wine
- 1/4 cup white wine vinegar
- 1 teaspoon sugar
- 2 fresh Tropical Brand* tilapia fillets
- Salt and pepper
- Extra-virgin olive oil
- Crusty bread, for serving

Preheat oven to 450°F.

In a saucepan, combine tomato sauce, olives, capers, chili flakes, wine, vinegar and sugar. Bring to a boil, and then turn off the heat.

Season fresh tilapia fillets with salt and pepper to taste. Place in a baking dish and spoon all the sauce over them.

Bake for 8-10 minutes, or until the fish is cooked through.

Serve on a warm platter with a drizzle of good olive oil and some crusty bread. Makes 2 servings.

** Brands may vary by region; substitute a similar product.*

## Tilapia with Tropical Fruit Sauce

Slade Gorton

*TROPICAL FRUIT SAUCE*

- 1/2 cup orange marmalade
- 1/4 teaspoon minced fresh ginger
- 1/3 cup coconut cream
- 1 tablespoon light rum
- 1/4 cup plus 2 tablespoons pineapple juice
- 1 tablespoon diced red onion
- 1 tablespoon diced red bell pepper
- 1 tablespoon cornstarch
- 1/4 cup diced pineapple
- 1/4 cup diced mango
- 1/2 teaspoon dried parsley
- 1/4 teaspoon salt
- 1/8 teaspoon ground black pepper
- 4 fillets Slade Gorton* Toasted Crumb Tilapia

Preheat oven to 375°F.

To prepare sauce, combine marmalade, ginger, coconut cream, rum, 1/4 cup pineapple juice, onion and bell pepper in a medium saucepan. Heat to a simmer, whisking. Mix cornstarch with 2 tablespoons pineapple juice; add to sauce and simmer until thickened. Add pineapple, mango, parsley, salt and pepper. Let cool.

Lightly coat tilapia with cooking spray. Bake until flaky (8-10 minutes). Cut each fillet into 2-3 pieces and place on top of your favorite salad. Top with sauce. Makes 4 servings.

**Tip:** A salad made of spinach, julienned red onion, diced mango and diced tomato, topped with a light dressing, complements the tilapia.

** Brands may vary by region; substitute a similar product.*

## Orange and Ginger Marinated Tilapia with Roasted Veggies

Rain Forest Aquaculture

- 3/4 cup orange juice
- 1 tablespoon grated fresh ginger
- Salt and freshly ground pepper
- 4 Rain Forest Aquaculture* fresh tilapia fillets
- 2 eggplants
- 1 red bell pepper
- 1 yellow bell pepper
- 2 zucchini
- 1 large onion
- 1/2 cup olive oil
- 2 tablespoons shredded orange peel, for garnish

In a glass pan, combine orange juice, ginger, and salt and pepper to taste. Add tilapia fillets and marinate, refrigerated, for 60 minutes.

Preheat oven to 400°F.

Chop the veggies into medium-size chunks and place in a roasting pan. Add oil and toss to coat. Season to taste with salt and pepper. Roast for 30 minutes, or until tender. Keep warm.

Place the tilapia in a baking pan and pour the marinade over it. Bake for 15 minutes, or until just opaque in the center.

Serve the tilapia with the veggies and garnish with shredded orange peel. Makes 4 servings.

** Brands may vary by region; substitute a similar product.*

# Lemon Butter Tilapia

## Kirkland Signature/Regal Springs

- 4 Kirkland Signature/Regal Springs frozen tilapia loins or fillets
- 1 tablespoon finely chopped fresh parsley
- 1/2 teaspoon ground paprika
- 1/2 teaspoon crushed red pepper
- 4 tablespoons butter
- 2 garlic cloves, finely chopped
- 2 tablespoons olive oil
- 1 lemon, peel grated, quartered

Thaw tilapia in the refrigerator, overnight or for 8 hours.

Preheat oven to 375°F. Lightly butter the bottom of a shallow baking dish.

In a small bowl, combine parsley, paprika and red pepper.

Melt butter in a small pan over medium heat. Add garlic and oil, then remove from the heat.

Place tilapia in the baking dish. Baste with half of the butter/garlic/olive oil mixture. Sprinkle with half of the parsley/paprika/pepper mixture.

Bake for 8 minutes. Remove from the oven and baste the tilapia with the remaining butter/garlic/olive oil mixture. Sprinkle with the remaining spice mixture. Return to the oven and bake for 6-8 minutes, or until the fish flakes easily with a fork.

Place on a serving platter, squeeze lemon juice over the tilapia and garnish with grated lemon peel. Makes 4 servings.

## Wild Pacific Cod with Green Curry

Kirkland Signature/Copper River Seafoods

- 2 pounds Kirkland Signature Copper River Seafoods wild Pacific cod portions, thawed
- 1 13 1/2-ounce can coconut milk
- 2 tablespoons green curry paste
- 1 cup chopped onions
- 1 1/2 cups water
- 2-3 stems sweet Thai basil
- Cooked rice, for serving (optional)

Cut cod into bite-size pieces.

In a large saucepan, heat coconut milk over medium heat until it boils and thickens. Stir in curry paste and onions; simmer for 5 minutes.

Mix in water and bring to a boil. Add the cod, cover and cook over high heat for 10 minutes, or just until the fish begins to break apart.

Place the basil leaves in the pan and cover.

To serve, place rice in soup bowls, top with fish and add some cooking liquid. Garnish with basil leaves. Makes 5-6 servings.

**Tip:** For a sweeter-tasting curry, add an extra 1/2 cup chopped onions.

## New Zealand Ling Cod Stew with Fennel and Sweet Potatoes

Quality Ocean International

- 2 large fennel bulbs
- 2 large sweet potatoes
- 6 tablespoons butter
- 1 onion, sliced
- 1 teaspoon paprika
- 1/2 cup flour
- 1 cup dry white wine
- 2 pounds New Zealand* ling cod, cut into bite-size pieces
- 2 bay leaves
- 1 cup heavy cream

*COURT BOUILLON*

- 2 cups dry white wine
- 6 cups water
- 1 cup white vinegar
- 3 celery stalks, roughly chopped
- 1 carrot, roughly chopped
- 1 leek, roughly chopped
- 1 yellow onion, roughly chopped
- 2 garlic cloves
- 1 fennel bulb, trimmed and chopped

To prepare the court bouillon, combine all ingredients in a large pot. Slowly bring to a boil, then boil slowly for 30 minutes. Strain.

Trim fennel and peel sweet potatoes, then cut into similar-size pieces. Cook in boiling water for about 5 minutes, until half cooked, then drain.

In a deep-sided sauté pan, heat butter over medium heat. Add onions and paprika; sauté until translucent. Add flour and cook, stirring constantly, for 2 minutes. Whisk in 1 3/4 cups court bouillon and wine; bring to a boil, stirring constantly.

Add the sweet potatoes, fennel, ling cod and bay leaves; simmer for 10 minutes. Add cream and simmer for 10 minutes. Makes 4 servings.

** Brands may vary by region; substitute a similar product.*

QUALITY OCEAN INTERNATIONAL

# Pistachio-Crusted New England Flounder

North Coast Seafoods

- 1 cup roasted pistachio nuts
- 1 cup plain dry bread crumbs
- 2 teaspoons chopped garlic
- 2 tablespoons chopped fresh parsley
- 2 teaspoons freshly cracked pepper
- 2 teaspoons kosher salt
- 4 eggs
- Olive oil
- 8 2- to 4-ounce fresh North Coast Seafoods* flounder fillets
- 1 cup all-purpose flour
- 1 lemon, cut into wedges

Combine the first 6 ingredients in a food processor and pulse until incorporated and the nuts are chopped. Transfer to a shallow bowl.

Place eggs in a shallow bowl and beat.

Heat oil in a cast-iron skillet over medium heat.

Dredge each fillet in flour, then in the egg and then in the bread crumb mixture. Make sure the fish has a nice coating of bread crumbs. Discard any leftover bread crumb mixture.

Place the fillets in the skillet and cook until crispy, about 3 minutes per side.

Serve with lemon wedges. Makes 4 servings.

** Brands may vary by region; substitute a similar product.*

# Coconut-Crusted Haddock

North Coast Seafoods

- 1/2 cup flour
- 2 eggs
- 1/2 cup coconut, toasted
- 1/2 cup panko bread crumbs
- 2 tablespoons chopped fresh parsley
- 1 tablespoon minced garlic
- Salt and pepper
- 4 8-ounce North Coast Seafoods* skinless haddock fillets
- 3 tablespoons olive oil
- Fruit salsa, for serving

Place flour in a shallow bowl.

Place eggs in another shallow bowl and beat lightly.

In a third shallow bowl, combine coconut, panko, parsley, garlic, and salt and pepper to taste.

Dredge haddock fillets in the flour, shake off excess and then dip in the egg. Place haddock in the coconut mixture and turn to coat.

Heat a sauté pan over medium-high heat. Add oil. Carefully place haddock in the pan and cook until golden brown, then turn and brown on the other side, about 3-4 minutes per side.

Serve with fruit salsa. Makes 4 servings.

** Brands may vary by region; substitute a similar product.*

## Pan-Roasted Tuna with Grapefruit and Leeks

alli

**1 teaspoon fennel seeds, crushed (see note)**
**1/4 teaspoon ground black pepper**
**4 6-ounce tuna steaks**
**Nonstick cooking spray**
**1 teaspoon olive oil**
**2 leeks (white ends only), halved, rinsed and thinly sliced (1 cup)**
**1 tablespoon chopped fresh ginger**
**1 teaspoon finely chopped jalapeño**
**1 medium grapefruit, segments removed and cut in half (about 1 cup)**
**1 teaspoon sugar**

In a small bowl, combine fennel seeds and black pepper. Rub onto the tuna.

Lightly coat a large nonstick skillet with cooking spray and heat over medium-high heat. Add tuna and cook for 10 minutes, or until it flakes easily when tested with a fork, turning once. Remove to a serving plate and keep warm.

Heat olive oil in the same skillet over medium heat. Add leeks, ginger and jalapeño; cook, stirring, for 3 minutes. Remove from the heat and stir in grapefruit and sugar. Pour over the tuna and serve. Makes 4 servings.

**Note:** To crush the fennel seeds, use a mortar and pestle or place in a resealable plastic bag and press very firmly with a heavy skillet.

**Tip:** Serve with 1 pound frozen steak fries, baked, and 1 pound green beans, steamed.

**Nutritional information:** Each serving has 482 calories, 44 g protein, 46 g carbohydrates, 14 g total fat, 123 calories from fat, 26% calories from fat, 63 mg cholesterol, 10 g fiber, 9 g sugars, 99 mg sodium.

*alli is the only FDA-approved, over-the-counter weight loss aid. It is proven to help boost your weight loss by 50% more than dieting alone.*

alli

## Ahi Tuna with Mango Salsa

Western United Fish Company

**1/3 cup light soy sauce**
**1 tablespoon honey**
**1 tablespoon cumin seeds**
**Juice of 1 fresh lemon**
**2 8-ounce Western United* ahi tuna steaks**
**1 teaspoon sea salt**
**1 tablespoon olive oil**
**1 whole habanero chile, seeded and minced (optional)**

***MANGO SALSA***

**1 fresh whole mango, cut into small cubes**
**1/3 cup minced radish**
**1/3 cup minced red onion**
**1/2 cup fresh cilantro, minced**
**Juice of 2 fresh limes**
**Sea salt**
**2 tablespoons capers**

Mix together soy sauce, honey, cumin seeds and lemon juice. Sprinkle tuna with sea salt. Pour the soy sauce mixture over the tuna. Marinate in the refrigerator for 1-2 hours.

To prepare the salsa, combine mango, radish, onion, cilantro and lime juice. Once well blended, season to taste with salt and add the capers. Let it sit for about 30 minutes for the flavors to meld.

Heat oil in a nonstick skillet over medium heat. Add the tuna and cook for about 1-2 minutes on each side, until just slightly browned but still reddish pink on the inside. Remove the tuna steaks to plates.

Top each serving with a large scoop of mango salsa. For an extra spicy taste, sprinkle with habanero chile. Serve immediately. Makes 2 servings.

** Brands may vary by region; substitute a similar product.*

*Your Direct Source*

# Mediterranean Grilled Shrimp
## Kirkland Signature

30 extra-jumbo (16-20/pound) frozen shrimp, thawed

6 wooden skewers, soaked in water for at least 30 minutes

Olive oil

Kirkland Signature garlic salt

Kirkland Signature ground black pepper

*SAUCE*

1 cup fresh mint leaves

1 cup fresh cilantro leaves

4 1/2 teaspoons Kirkland Signature dried chopped onion

1/2 teaspoon Kirkland Signature granulated garlic

1 cup coarsely chopped plum tomatoes

1 1/2 teaspoons Dijon mustard

1 tablespoon lemon juice

3 tablespoons olive oil

1 tablespoon red wine vinegar

1/2 teaspoon salt

1/8 teaspoon Kirkland Signature ground black pepper

Preheat the grill to high.

To prepare the sauce, combine all ingredients in a food processor. Blend on high until smooth. Set aside.

Thread 5 shrimp onto each skewer. Place on a parchment-lined sheet pan and drizzle with oil, garlic salt and pepper to taste.

Place the skewers on the hot grill. Grill on each side until pink.

Remove the shrimp from the skewers and drizzle with the sauce. Serve immediately. Makes 6 servings.

## Grilled Sea Scallops with Arugula, Watermelon and Feta Salad

### Atlantic Capes Fisheries

**1 1/2 pounds Atlantic Capes* sea scallops, thawed**

**1 teaspoon olive oil**

**1 teaspoon garlic powder**

**Salt and pepper**

**1/2 cup chopped fresh mint leaves (optional)**

***DRESSING***

**1 tablespoon honey**

**1 teaspoon Dijon mustard**

**1/4 cup freshly squeezed lemon juice (about 2 lemons)**

**1/4 cup freshly squeezed orange juice**

**1 large shallot, minced**

**1 teaspoon salt**

**Pinch of ground black pepper**

**1/2 cup extra-virgin olive oil**

***SALAD***

**6-8 cups cubed seedless watermelon**

**12 ounces good feta cheese, cut into cubes**

**1 small red onion, sliced (optional)**

**3-4 cups arugula, washed**

Preheat the grill to medium-high.

To prepare the dressing, whisk together honey and mustard. Add lemon and orange juices, shallot, salt and pepper. Slowly add oil, whisking constantly to form an emulsion. Set aside.

To prepare the salad, combine watermelon cubes, feta and red onion slices in a large bowl. Drizzle with enough of the dressing to just coat the mixture.

In another bowl, toss arugula with enough dressing to lightly coat. Make a bed of arugula on a large serving plate. Top with the watermelon mixture.

Toss scallops with oil, garlic powder, and salt and pepper to taste. Place scallops on the grill and cook for 2-3 minutes per side, or until translucent in the center and lightly browned on the outside. Do not overcook.

To serve, place the scallops around the watermelon salad. If desired, garnish the plate with mint. Drizzle any remaining dressing on the scallops. Makes 4-6 servings.

** Brands may vary by region; substitute a similar product.*

## Sweet and Sour Grilled Scallops

### American Pride Seafoods

**Olive oil**

**12 American Pride Seafoods* sea scallops**

**4 wooden skewers, soaked in water for 1 hour**

**1/4 cup light brown sugar**

**1/4 cup ketchup**

**1/4 cup chicken broth**

**2 garlic cloves, minced**

**2 tablespoons rice wine vinegar**

**2 tablespoons soy sauce**

**1 teaspoon cornstarch**

**2 tablespoons honey**

**1 teaspoon toasted sesame oil**

**2 tablespoons minced fresh ginger**

**1/4 teaspoon crushed red pepper**

**Green onions, for garnish**

Preheat the grill to medium and brush the grate with olive oil.

Thread 3 scallops onto each skewer and brush with olive oil to prevent sticking. Grill scallops for 2-3 minutes on each side, or until internal temperature is 145°F.

Meanwhile, combine all remaining ingredients except green onions in a saucepan. Whisk until well combined. Bring to a boil over medium-high heat, whisking occasionally. Remove from the heat and set aside.

When the scallops are done, brush with sauce immediately. Serve over rice with the remaining sauce. Garnish with green onions. Makes 4 servings.

** Brands may vary by region; substitute a similar product.*

## Stir-Fry with Scallops and Asparagus

Jacobs Malcolm & Burtt/Gourmet Trading/ NewStar Fresh Foods

- **3/4 pound fresh asparagus**
- **3/4 cup reduced-sodium chicken broth**
- **1 tablespoon cornstarch**
- **1 teaspoon light soy sauce**
- **1 teaspoon sesame oil**
- **3/4 pound sea scallops, cut in half horizontally**
- **1 cup sliced button mushrooms or 3-4 ounces oyster mushrooms**
- **1 medium garlic clove, minced**
- **1 cup halved cherry tomatoes**
- **2-3 green onions, thinly sliced**
- **Freshly ground black pepper**
- **2 cups hot cooked rice (no salt added)**

Trim or break off asparagus spears at the tender point; rinse and cut into 2-inch diagonal pieces. Cook in a large pan of boiling salted water until crisp-tender, about 3-5 minutes. Do not overcook. Drain and rinse under cold water.

In a small bowl, combine chicken broth, cornstarch and soy sauce. Set aside.

Heat oil in a large nonstick skillet over medium heat. Add scallops, mushrooms and garlic; stir-fry until scallops are just cooked through, about 4 minutes.

Add the cornstarch mixture and cook, stirring, until the sauce thickens. Add the drained asparagus, tomatoes and green onions; cook just until heated. Add pepper to taste.

Serve over rice. Makes 4 servings.

**Nutritional information:** Each serving has 282 calories, 25 g protein, 39 g carbohydrates, 3 g fat, 0.5 grams saturated fat, 27 mg cholesterol, 296 mg sodium.

JACOBS MALCOLM & BURTT

## Spaghetti Vongole (Cockles)

Quality Ocean International

- **16 ounces fresh spaghetti**
- **1/2 cup extra-virgin olive oil, divided**
- **5 pounds New Zealand* cockles (littleneck clams)**
- **3 large garlic cloves, crushed and peeled**
- **1/2 cup chopped fresh parsley**
- **1/2 cup snipped chives**
- **Grated peel of 1 lemon**
- **Generous splash of dry white wine**
- **Salt and freshly ground black pepper**

Cook spaghetti in a large pot of boiling salted water. Drain, reserving a tablespoon of the cooking water.

Heat 2-4 tablespoons oil in a deep frying pan over high heat. Add clams, cover and cook until they open. Drain, reserving the juices.

In the pan with the reserved pasta water, combine garlic, parsley, chives, grated lemon peel, wine, 4 tablespoons oil and reserved clam juices. Cook over medium heat, whisking until the sauce is emulsified. Add the clams.

Fold in the spaghetti and mix thoroughly. Season to taste with salt and pepper.

Serve hot. Makes 4 servings.

** Brands may vary by region; substitute a similar product.*

QUALITY OCEAN INTERNATIONAL

# Sautéed Garlic Prawns

## Johnny's

- **1-2 pounds prawns, peeled and deveined**
- **1 1/2 tablespoons Johnny's* Great Caesar Garlic Spread and Seasoning**
- **1 tablespoon lemon juice**
- **1/2 teaspoon ground black pepper (optional)**
- **1 tablespoon white wine (optional)**
- **1/2 cup butter or margarine**
- **Cooked pasta or rice, for serving**

In a glass bowl, combine prawns with Johnny's Garlic Spread, lemon juice, pepper and wine. Cover and refrigerate for 1 hour.

Melt butter in a large nonstick pan over medium-high heat. Transfer the prawns to the hot pan and cook for 2 minutes on each side, or until bright pink and opaque.

Serve the prawns over pasta or rice. Makes 2-4 servings.

** Brands may vary by region; substitute a similar product.*

# Cajun-Style King Crab

## Harbor Seafood

- **2 1/2 pounds frozen king crab legs and claws, thawed and drained**
- **1/2 cup mayonnaise**
- **1 teaspoon Cajun seasoning, or to taste**
- **1 teaspoon lemon pepper**
- **1 teaspoon minced garlic**
- **1 teaspoon dry vermouth**
- **Cooked pasta or rice, for serving**

Carefully slice thawed crab legs/claws lengthwise and remove crabmeat from the shell. Spread the crabmeat on a plate or in a flat dish.

In a small bowl, combine mayonnaise, Cajun seasoning, lemon pepper, garlic and vermouth; mix well. Spread the mixture over the crabmeat. Cover and marinate in the refrigerator for 30 minutes.

In a large nonstick skillet, carefully cook the crab over medium-high heat, turning frequently. Cook until browned and heated thoroughly. Serve with your favorite pasta or rice. Makes 2-4 servings.

# Grilled Chicken with Chimichurri Sauce

Kirkland Signature

- 6 skinless, boneless chicken breast halves
- 1 teaspoon olive oil
- 1/4 teaspoon Kirkland Signature garlic salt
- 1/8 teaspoon Kirkland Signature ground black pepper

*CHIMICHURRI SAUCE*

- 2 cups fresh parsley leaves
- 1 tablespoon Kirkland Signature granulated garlic
- 1/4 cup olive oil
- 3 tablespoons red wine vinegar
- 1 teaspoon Kirkland Signature pure sea salt
- 1/8 teaspoon Kirkland Signature ground black pepper

Preheat the grill to high.

In a food processor, combine all sauce ingredients. Blend on high until smooth.

In a bowl, combine chicken, oil, garlic salt and pepper. Toss to coat evenly.

Grill the chicken on both sides until the internal temperature is 165°F.

Drizzle the sauce over the chicken. Serve immediately. Makes 6 servings.

**Tip:** To serve as an appetizer, cut the grilled chicken into pieces and use the sauce as a dip.

## Imperial Orange Chicken

### Harvest Foods

- **24 ounces TastyWok All Natural Chicken**
- **9 ounces TastyWok All Natural Orange Sauce**
- **1/2 cup red bell pepper cut in 1-inch squares**
- **1/2 cup yellow bell pepper cut in 1-inch squares**
- **1/2 cup green bell pepper cut in 1-inch squares**
- **1/2 cup yellow onion cut in 1-inch squares**
- **3/4 teaspoon chopped green onion**
- **Sesame seeds**
- **Chili oil (optional)**
- **Cooked rice, for serving**

Prepare chicken according to package directions. Set aside.

Thaw orange sauce under warm water. Set aside.

Blanch bell peppers and onions in boiling water for 10 seconds, remove and put into iced water to chill. Drain and set aside.

Heat the orange sauce in a skillet over medium-high heat. Add the chicken and stir for 1 minute. Add all blanched vegetables and stir for an additional minute. Transfer to a serving plate. Sprinkle with green onions and sesame seeds.

For additional heat, add chili oil to the finished dish. Serve with rice. Makes 8 servings.

**Variation:** After cooking in the skillet, thread the chicken and vegetables on skewers.

## Southeast Asian Glazed Chicken Breasts with Green Papaya Salad

### Kirkland Signature/Tyson

- **4 Kirkland Signature boneless, skinless chicken breasts**
- **1 lemongrass stalk, crushed**
- **1 2-inch piece of fresh ginger, peeled and sliced**
- **3 garlic cloves, thinly sliced**
- **2 fresh basil leaves**
- **1 1/2 cups chicken stock**
- **Salt and pepper**
- **Peanut oil**
- **6 ounces Thai sweet chili sauce**

*GREEN PAPAYA SALAD*

- **1 medium green papaya (about 1 1/2 pounds), julienned (see note)**
- **1 large carrot, julienned**
- **1 tablespoon grated fresh ginger**
- **2 garlic cloves, minced**
- **2 mint sprigs, chopped**
- **10 fresh cilantro sprigs, leaves only**
- **Juice of 2 limes**
- **3 tablespoons fish sauce (optional)**
- **1/4 cup sugar**
- **5 tablespoons rice wine vinegar**

Pierce holes in chicken with a fork. Place chicken in a large resealable bag. Add lemongrass, ginger, garlic, basil and chicken stock. Refrigerate for at least 3 hours or overnight.

To prepare the salad, combine all ingredients in a bowl. Refrigerate for at least 30 minutes.

Preheat oven to 375°F.

Remove chicken breasts from the marinade. Season to taste with salt and pepper. In a well-oiled skillet over medium-high heat, sear chicken 1-2 minutes per side.

Transfer to an ovenproof pan. Spread chili sauce over the chicken and place in the oven. Cook until the internal temperature is 165°F at the thickest point, about 15-20 minutes.

Serve with Green Papaya Salad. Makes 4 servings.

**Note:** The unripe, green papaya gives this recipe a distinct, zesty taste.

## Ginger Apple Stir-Fry
### Chelan Fresh Marketing

- 2 teaspoons sesame oil
- 2 garlic cloves, minced
- 2 tablespoons minced ginger
- 1 pound boneless, skinless chicken breast, cut into strips
- 4 green onions, sliced
- 1/3 pound sugar snap peas or snow peas
- 1 small red or orange bell pepper, cut into strips
- 10 shiitake and/or white mushrooms, sliced
- 1/4 teaspoon ground black pepper
- 1/3 cup unsweetened applesauce
- 2 tablespoons soy sauce
- 2 tablespoons apple cider vinegar
- 1 tablespoon cornstarch
- 1/3 cup chicken broth or water
- 2 medium apples, cored and sliced (Granny Smiths or other variety)
- Steamed brown rice, for serving

Heat oil in a nonstick skillet or wok over medium heat. Add garlic and ginger, and stir for approximately 30 seconds.

Add chicken and cook in hot oil until no longer pink in the center. Remove from the skillet.

Add vegetables to the pan and cook, stirring, until tender-crisp. Sprinkle with pepper.

In a bowl, combine applesauce, soy sauce, vinegar, cornstarch and chicken broth or water.

Add chicken to the vegetables, stir in the applesauce mixture, and cook until the sauce is thickened and clear. Stir in apples during the last 5 minutes.

Serve over steamed brown rice. Makes 4 servings.

**Nutritional information:** Each stir-fry serving has 340 calories, 25 g protein, 25 g carbohydrates, 16 g fat, 5 g saturated fat, 70 mg cholesterol, 5 g fiber, 670 mg sodium.

*Recipe courtesy of U.S. Apple Association.*

## Chef Allen's Pan BBQ Chicken Mojo

### Chestnut Hill Farms/Legend Produce

- 1 teaspoon ground cumin
- 1 teaspoon ground black pepper
- 1 tablespoon salt
- 8 6-ounce boneless, skinless chicken breasts
- 4 tablespoons olive oil, divided
- 1/2 cup diced sweet onion
- 2 tablespoons minced garlic
- 1 whole ripe pineapple, peeled and diced
- 1 whole ripe cantaloupe, peeled and diced
- 1 cup orange juice
- 1/4 cup rice wine vinegar
- 1/4 cup light rum, divided
- 2 tablespoons fresh cilantro, for garnish

Combine cumin, pepper and salt. Season the chicken and drizzle with 2 tablespoons olive oil.

In a sauce pot, combine 2 tablespoons olive oil, onion and garlic. Stir in pineapple, cantaloupe, orange juice and vinegar. Simmer for 5 minutes, then carefully add half of the rum to the tropical mojo.

In a large sauté pan over medium-high heat, brown the chicken breasts well on one side for 3-4 minutes. Then turn them over and add the remaining rum. Cook for another 4-5 minutes, or until a meat thermometer inserted in the center registers 170°F.

Serve the chicken with the tropical mojo and garnish with cilantro. Makes 8 servings.

*Recipe courtesy of Chef Allen Susser.*

## Grilled Chicken with Cashew Dipping Sauce

### Ann's House of Nuts/Harvest Manor Farms

- 1/2 cup Kirkland Signature Whole Fancy Cashews, minced
- 1 1/3 cups cilantro leaves, chopped
- 4 garlic cloves, minced
- 4 green onions, chopped
- 2 tablespoons sugar
- 2 teaspoons ground pepper
- 2 teaspoons ground cumin
- 2 1/2 tablespoons white vinegar
- 2 teaspoons balsamic vinegar
- 1 cup honey
- 1 teaspoon mashed prune
- Pinch of ground saffron
- 1/2 cup olive oil
- 4 boneless, skinless chicken breast halves

Preheat the grill to medium.

In a blender, combine cashews, cilantro, garlic, green onions, sugar, pepper and cumin. Mix with short bursts until well blended.

In a microwave-safe bowl, combine vinegars, honey, prune and saffron. Microwave for 1 minute. Stir, then pour into the blender with the cashew mixture and mix with short bursts until well combined (about 20 seconds). Pour the blended sauce into a bowl. Add oil and stir by hand.

Refrigerate 1 cup of the sauce for dipping. Brush chicken with the remaining sauce.

Grill the chicken for 4-5 minutes on each side, or until or until a meat thermometer inserted in the center registers 170°F. Serve with the cashew sauce on the side for dipping. Makes 4 servings.

HARVEST MANOR FARMS

## Grilled Yogurt Ranch Chicken Satay with Mediterranean Couscous

### Rikki Rikki/Sandridge Foods/Kirkland Signature

- **3 pounds Kirkland Signature chicken tenderloins**
- **2 1/2 cups Rikki's* Gourmet Yogurt Ranch Dressing, divided**
- **16 bamboo skewers, soaked in cold water**
- **1 fresh lemon, cut in half**
- **1/4 cup chopped fresh parsley or other herbs**
- **1 1 1/2-pound container Kirkland Signature/ Sandridge Foods* Shrimp Couscous Salad**

Flatten chicken tenderloins slightly with a mallet or small frying pan. Marinate the chicken in 1 1/2 cups of the dressing in the refrigerator for 2-4 hours. Set aside the remaining cup of dressing.

Preheat the grill to medium-high.

Carefully thread the chicken tenderloins onto the bamboo skewers (about 3 ounces of chicken per skewer). Grill the skewers evenly on all sides for 4-6 minutes, or until the internal temperature is 165°F. As you grill, brush the skewers with the remaining 1 cup of dressing.

Squeeze lemon over the skewers and sprinkle with parsley. Serve each person 2 skewers accompanied with 1/2 cup couscous salad. Makes 8 servings.

** Brands may vary by region; substitute a similar product.*

RIKKI RIKKI

SANDRIDGE Food Corporation
WWW.SANDRIDGE.COM MEDINA, OHIO

KIRKLAND Signature

## Mediterranean Chicken

### Kirkland Signature/Perdue

- **1 tablespoon olive oil**
- **4 Kirkland Signature/ Perdue* Fit & Easy Boneless, Skinless Chicken Breasts**
- **2 cups chopped fresh tomatoes**
- **1 teaspoon dried basil**
- **1 teaspoon dried oregano**
- **Salt and ground pepper**
- **1/2 cup shredded Italian cheese blend or mozzarella cheese (optional)**
- **1/3 cup chopped pitted Italian olives**
- **Pasta, for serving (optional)**

Heat oil in a large nonstick skillet over medium heat. Add chicken and cook for 3-4 minutes per side, until browned. Add tomatoes, basil, oregano, and salt and pepper to taste. Reduce the heat to medium-low, cover and simmer for 10-15 minutes, or until a meat thermometer inserted in the center registers 165°F.

To serve, sprinkle with cheese and olives. Serve with pasta, if desired. Makes 4 servings.

** Brands may vary by region; substitute a similar product.*

# Italian Chicken with Mushroom Marsala Sauce

## Cardile Brothers/Giorgio Fresh/ Monterey Mushrooms

- **4 boneless, skinless chicken breast halves (about 6 ounces each)**
- **1/2 teaspoon salt**
- **1/2 teaspoon ground black pepper**
- **1/4 cup flour**
- **4 tablespoons olive oil, divided**
- **1 pound small fresh white and/ or crimini mushrooms, sliced (about 6 cups)**
- **1/2 cup chopped onion**
- **1 cup Marsala or red wine**
- **1 cup chicken broth**

Season chicken breasts with salt and pepper. Lightly coat both sides of chicken with flour.

In a large skillet, heat 2 tablespoons of the oil over medium-high heat. Add chicken and cook until golden, about 2 minutes on each side. Transfer to a plate.

Reduce the heat to medium. Add remaining 2 tablespoons oil to the skillet. Add mushrooms and onions; cook and stir until tender, about 7 minutes.

Stir in Marsala and chicken broth. Return the chicken to the pan and simmer, covered, until no pink remains in the center, 10-12 minutes, or until a meat thermometer inserted in the center registers 170°F. Makes 4 servings.

# Sweet Pear Chicken with Dates

## California Pear Advisory Board/ Bard Valley Medjool Date Growers

1 teaspoon vegetable oil
4 boneless, skinless chicken breasts
11.5 ounces pear nectar, divided
1 teaspoon cornstarch
1/4 teaspoon ground cloves
1/4 teaspoon ground nutmeg
Dash of ground allspice
Dash of ground white pepper
3 ripe California Bartlett pears, peeled, halved and cored
6 fresh Bard Valley Medjool Date Growers Medjool dates, cut in half and pitted
1/2 cup sliced green onions

Heat oil in a large nonstick skillet over medium-high heat. Add chicken and brown well on both sides, about 10-12 minutes. Drain off any excess fat.

Stir 1/4 cup pear nectar into cornstarch; set aside. Pour remaining nectar into the skillet with the chicken. Add spices and pepper. Cover and cook over low heat for 10 minutes.

Add pear halves, cut-side down, and continue cooking, covered, for 10-15 minutes or until a meat thermometer inserted in the center of the chicken registers 165°F and the pears are tender. Remove the chicken and pears to a serving platter.

Add cornstarch mixture, dates and green onions to the pan; heat, stirring, until the sauce thickens. Spoon some sauce over the chicken, and serve the remainder on the side. Makes 4 servings.

**Tip:** The fresh fruits in this low-fat recipe provide a shot of fiber and antioxidants to a main course. Enjoy the sweet flavor.

# Turkey Meatloaf with Prune Glaze

Kirkland Signature/Sunsweet

- 2 tablespoons olive oil
- 1 yellow onion, finely chopped
- 2 celery stalks, finely chopped
- 2 carrots, finely chopped
- 3 garlic cloves, minced
- 3 slices white bread, crusts removed
- 1/2 cup low-fat milk
- 2 eggs
- 1-2 tablespoons salt
- 1/2 teaspoon *each* ground black pepper, dried thyme and garlic powder
- 1/4 cup fresh parsley, chopped
- 1 cup chopped Kirkland Signature/ Sunsweet* pitted dried plums
- 1/4 cup fresh bread crumbs
- 3 pounds ground turkey

*GLAZE*

- 1/2 cup Kirkland Signature/ Sunsweet* pitted dried plums
- 3/4 cup Sunsweet prune juice
- 2 tablespoons Dijon mustard
- 2 tablespoons packed light brown sugar
- 1/4 cup chicken broth

Preheat oven to 350°F.

Heat oil in a skillet over medium-high heat. Add onions, celery, carrots and garlic; cook for 5 minutes, or until softened. Remove from the heat and let cool.

Soak bread in milk until both sides are moist, about 15 seconds.

In a large bowl, whisk eggs with salt, pepper, thyme, garlic powder and parsley. Add soaked bread, cooled vegetables, dried plums, bread crumbs and ground turkey. Fold all the ingredients together until well combined. Put the meatloaf in a 9-by-5-inch loaf pan.

To prepare the glaze, combine all ingredients in a saucepan and cook over medium heat for 10 minutes. Let cool and then puree. Set aside.

Bake the meatloaf for 45 minutes. Baste with glaze and bake for another 45 minutes, or until the internal temperature is 170°F, basting with glaze every 10 minutes. Makes 6-8 servings.

** Brands may vary by region; substitute a similar product.*

## Marsala-Rosemary Roast Tenderloin

Kirkland Signature/Tyson

**1 Kirkland Signature center-cut beef tenderloin roast (about 2 pounds), trimmed**

**Salt and pepper**

**2 teaspoons *each* minced fresh rosemary and parsley, mixed**

**2 tablespoons olive oil**

**4 medium shallots, minced (about 1/4 cup)**

**4 garlic cloves, sliced**

**1 1/2 cups Marsala wine**

**3 tablespoons butter**

**1 teaspoon coarse-ground mustard**

**1 14-ounce can beef broth**

Preheat oven to 425°F. Season tenderloin with salt and pepper to taste and the herb mixture.

Heat oil in a large skillet over medium heat. Add beef and brown evenly, about 4 minutes. Place the beef on a rack in a shallow roasting pan.

Add shallots and garlic to the skillet; cook and stir for 1-2 minutes. Add Marsala and cook, stirring, for 5-6 minutes. Add butter, mustard and beef broth; bring to a boil. Pour into the roasting pan; brush the roast with the broth mixture.

Roast, uncovered, for 25-30 minutes for medium-rare (135°F), 35-40 minutes for medium (150°F). Remove the roast and transfer to a carving board; cover. Let stand for 10 minutes, then cut into 4 portions.

Drizzle with Marsala sauce from the roasting pan and serve. Makes 4 servings.

## Steak Alfresco

Lea & Perrins

**1/2 cup Lea & Perrins Worcestershire sauce**

**2 tablespoons olive oil**

**2 tablespoons lemon juice**

**2 tablespoons chopped fresh basil, oregano, cilantro or parsley**

**1/4 teaspoon salt**

**2 pounds steak (boneless strip or ribeye, or T-bone)**

In a bowl, combine Worcestershire sauce, oil, lemon juice, herbs and salt; stir to blend.

Place the steaks in a large, shallow nonreactive baking dish or a resealable plastic bag. Pour 1/2 cup of marinade over the steaks, turning to coat. Marinate in the refrigerator for at least 30 minutes. Refrigerate the remaining marinade separately.

Remove the steaks from the refrigerator; discard the marinade. Grill or broil the steaks, brushing frequently with the reserved marinade. Makes 4 servings.

## Boursin-Stuffed Beef Fillets with Roasted Root Vegetables

Cargill Meat Solutions

**1 pound Red Bliss potatoes**
**2 pounds whole peeled carrots**
**1 yellow onion, thickly sliced**
**3 tablespoons Kirkland Signature canola oil, divided**
**4 10-ounce beef tenderloin steaks**
**1 5.2-ounce package Boursin cheese**
**Salt**
**Black pepper**

Preheat oven to 425°F.

Place vegetables in a roasting pan. Add 2 tablespoons oil and toss to coat. Season to taste with salt and pepper. Roast for 35 minutes, or until tender.

Make a 1-inch incision halfway up each steak to create a pocket for stuffing. Divide the Boursin into 4 portions and stuff the steaks. Season to taste with salt and pepper. You can use a toothpick to secure the pocket.

Heat 1 tablespoon oil in an ovenproof sauté pan over medium-high heat. Add steaks and sear until they are a rich mahogany brown on each side.

Transfer the steaks in the sauté pan to the oven with the vegetables for the last 10 minutes, or until the steaks' internal temperature is 130°F (medium-rare). Let the steaks rest for 10 minutes. Makes 4 servings.

## Garlic and Sage Basted Beef Tenderloin Roast

National Beef

**1 pound unsalted butter**
**3 garlic cloves, crushed**
**1 bunch sage, stems and all**
**1 beef tenderloin roast (about 5 pounds)**
**Salt and pepper**

Preheat oven to 400°F.

In a heavy saucepan, melt butter over medium heat. Add garlic and sage; continue to cook until the butter is a brownish caramel color and has a wonderful nutty aroma. Turn the heat to low and keep the butter warm.

Sprinkle beef with salt and pepper to taste. In a heavy-bottomed ovenproof pan, sear the roast on all sides over medium-high heat. Use a spoon to liberally baste with the brown butter.

Transfer the meat in the pan to the oven and roast, basting with pan juices every 4-5 minutes, for about 45 minutes, or until the internal temperature is 130°F (medium-rare). Remove from the oven and let rest for 10-15 minutes.

Slice the beef and serve with a little of the brown butter on each plate. Makes 12-16 servings.

**Tip:** Watch the meat carefully as it roasts, as the brown butter may smoke.

# Beef Stir-Fry with Vegetables
## Eat Smart

This recipe is one delicious way to use vegetables from an Eat Smart vegetable tray.

- **1/3 cup peanut butter or hoisin sauce**
- **2 tablespoons rice vinegar**
- **2 tablespoons honey**
- **2 tablespoons soy sauce**
- **1 teaspoon toasted sesame oil**
- **8 ounces linguine**
- **5 cups vegetables of your choice from an Eat Smart* vegetable tray**
- **1 tablespoon vegetable oil**
- **2 garlic cloves, peeled and sliced**
- **8 ounces top sirloin, cut into thin slices**
- **1/4 cup sesame seeds (optional)**

In a medium bowl, whisk together peanut butter (or hoisin sauce), vinegar, honey, soy sauce and sesame oil. Set aside.

Bring a large pot of salted water to a boil. Add linguine and cook according to package directions. Add carrots, snap peas and broccoli during the last 2 minutes of cooking. Drain, reserving 1/3 cup of the cooking water, and rinse under hot water.

Meanwhile, heat vegetable oil in a large nonstick skillet over medium-high heat. Add garlic and sirloin; stir-fry for 3-4 minutes, or until almost cooked. Add grape tomatoes and continue to stir-fry for 1-2 minutes, or until the meat is cooked. Pour the sauce mixture over the top to warm.

Return the linguine and vegetables to the pasta pot and stir in the meat/sauce mixture. Thin with the reserved cooking water if necessary. Garnish with sesame seeds. Makes 4 servings.

**Tip:** Leftover party trays make great salad toppers, soups and stews. Or mix with light olive oil, garlic, salt and pepper to taste and roast in the oven (400°F).

** Brands may vary by region; substitute a similar product.*

Eat Smart Apio, INC.

## Grilled Steak Fajitas

### Horizon International

- 1 pound flank or round steak
- 2 teaspoons olive oil
- 1/2 large red onion, sliced
- 1 yellow or red bell pepper, thinly sliced
- 2 portobello mushrooms, thinly sliced
- 2 tablespoons fajita seasoning mix
- 8-12 flour tortillas
- 3 cups salad greens
- 2 large tomatoes, chopped
- 1/4 cup nonfat sour cream
- 1/3 cup salsa

Preheat the grill to medium.

Grill steak for about 15 minutes, or until cooked to taste.

Heat oil in a sauté pan over medium heat. Add onions and peppers; sauté until the onions are caramelized. Transfer to a bowl.

Add mushrooms to the pan and cook until tender. Add to the onions and peppers. Add fajita seasoning to the vegetables and toss.

Warm the tortillas.

Slice the steak into 1/4-inch strips.

Fill the tortillas with sliced steak, the mushroom mixture and salad greens. Top with tomatoes, sour cream and salsa. Makes 4-6 servings.

## Tri-Tip Tacos

### Cargill Meat Solutions

- 1 2- to 4-pound Morton's of Omaha* Tri-Tip Roast (premarinated)
- 1 cup cilantro leaves
- 3 cups shredded romaine
- 3 cups shredded green cabbage
- 1/2 cup sliced green onions
- 1/2 cup chopped yellow onion
- 1/4 cup fresh lime juice
- Salt and pepper
- Flour or corn tortillas, for serving

*TOPPINGS*

- Mexican cream or sour cream
- Guacamole
- Salsa

Preheat oven to 425°F.

Place beef in a roasting pan fat side up. Roast in the oven for 1 hour, or until the internal temperature is 145°F, for medium. Remove from the oven and let rest for 10-15 minutes.

In a bowl, mix cilantro leaves, romaine, cabbage, green onions, yellow onion and lime juice until coated. Season to taste with salt and pepper.

Warm the tortillas.

Slice the beef across the grain. Place on the tortillas and top with the lettuce mixture.

Serve with toppings. Makes 6-8 servings.

**Tip:** Coleslaw mix can be substituted for the shredded cabbage.

** Brands may vary by region; substitute a similar product.*

## Yoshida's Meatloaf

### Mr. Yoshida's

**2 pounds lean ground beef**
**1 cup plain dry bread crumbs**
**$^1/_4$ cup chopped onion**
**2 eggs, lightly beaten**
**1 cup Mr. Yoshida's* Original Gourmet Marinade & Cooking Sauce, divided**

Preheat oven to 375°F.

In a large bowl, mix together beef, bread crumbs, onion, eggs and $^1/_2$ cup Original Gourmet Sauce. Form into a loaf shape and place in a 13-by-9-inch baking dish.

Bake for 45 minutes. Brush the top and sides of the meatloaf with the remaining $^1/_2$ cup Original Gourmet Sauce. Bake for another 15 minutes, or until cooked through. Let rest for 5 minutes before slicing. Makes 8 servings.

**Tip:** If desired, add 2 cups of assorted chopped fresh vegetables to the baking dish surrounding the meatloaf. Brush with Original Gourmet Sauce when brushing the meatloaf.

** Brands may vary by region; substitute a similar product.*

## Cuban-Style Pot Roast

### Cargill Meat Solutions

**2 tablespoons Kirkland Signature canola oil**
**1 tablespoon chopped garlic**
**1 cup sliced yellow onions**
**1 teaspoon dried oregano**
**1 teaspoon ground cumin**
**1 14 $^1/_2$-ounce can diced tomatoes, drained**
**$^1/_4$ cup sliced pimiento-stuffed green olives**
**2 $^1/_2$ tablespoons red wine vinegar**
**$^1/_4$ cup raisins (optional)**
**1 tablespoon chopped capers (optional)**
**1 2- to 4-pound Morton's of Omaha* Beef Pot Roast with Gravy**
**5 cups cooked white rice, for serving**

Preheat oven to 400°F.

In a large ovenproof skillet, heat oil over medium heat. Add garlic and onions; sauté for 2 minutes.

Add oregano, cumin, tomatoes, olives, vinegar, raisins and capers to the skillet; cook for 4 minutes.

Add pot roast to the skillet, cover and cook in the oven for 25 minutes, or until hot.

Serve over rice. Makes about 6 servings.

** Brands may vary by region; substitute a similar product.*

# Osso Buco
## Plume De Veau

4 Plume De Veau* veal shanks
1 cup all-purpose flour
2 teaspoons kosher salt
1 teaspoon ground black pepper
1/4 cup olive oil
1 medium carrot, finely chopped
1 medium onion, finely chopped
1 celery stalk, finely chopped
1/2 cup ruby Port
4 cups reduced veal stock
3 tablespoons finely chopped flat-leaf parsley
1 tablespoon grated lemon peel
1 tablespoon grated orange peel
Mashed potatoes, for serving (optional)

Preheat oven to 375°F.

Tie each veal shank to the bone with kitchen twine.

Combine flour, salt and pepper in a shallow dish. Dip veal in the flour.

Heat oil over high heat in a large, deep heavy-duty skillet or Dutch oven. Add veal and brown on all sides. Remove and set aside.

Add carrots, onions and celery to the skillet and cook, stirring, for 5 minutes, or until tender. Reduce heat to medium, stir in Port and stock, and cook for 2 minutes. Bring to a boil over high heat, then remove from the heat.

Arrange veal in a heavy 13-by-9-inch roasting pan. Pour sauce over veal. Cover with foil and bake for 90 minutes, or until tender.

Combine parsley with lemon and orange peel.

Serve veal with sauce on potatoes. Sprinkle with parsley mixture. Makes 4 servings.

*Recipe created by Chef John Halligan of The Park Steakhouse.*
** Brands may vary by region; substitute a similar product.*

# Hunter-Style Grilled Veal Chops
## Plume De Veau

- 4 Plume De Veau* veal chops (rib or loin)
- 2 teaspoons kosher salt
- 1 teaspoon ground black pepper
- 1/4 cup olive oil
- 2 tablespoons butter
- 3 ounces sliced fresh morel mushrooms
- 3 ounces smoked chorizo sausage, diced
- 2 fresh plum tomatoes, chopped
- 1 medium carrot, finely chopped
- 1 medium onion, finely chopped
- 1 celery stalk, finely chopped
- 2 cups reduced veal stock
- 1/2 cup heavy cream
- 3 tablespoons finely chopped flat-leaf parsley

Preheat grill to 400°F. Preheat oven to 350°F.

Season chops with salt and pepper. Place on the grill and sear, about 2 minutes per side. Transfer to a roasting pan and roast in the oven for 12-14 minutes for medium-rare (130°F). Remove from the oven and let rest for a couple of minutes before serving.

In a large sauce pot, heat oil and butter over high heat until melted. Add mushrooms, chorizo, tomatoes, carrots, onions and celery. Cook, stirring, until the vegetables are tender.

Stir in stock and cream. Bring to a boil and cook until reduced slightly. Add salt and pepper if necessary.

To serve, place the veal chops on plates and spoon the sauce over the top. Sprinkle with parsley. Makes 4 servings.

*Recipe created by Chef John Halligan of The Park Steakhouse.*
** Brands may vary by region; substitute a similar product.*

# Veal Cutlets Parmigiana
## Plume De Veau

- **2 cups Italian-flavored dry bread crumbs**
- **2 tablespoons grated Parmigiano-Reggiano cheese, plus more for topping**
- **2 eggs**
- **1/2 cup flour**
- **1/4 teaspoon salt**
- **1/8 teaspoon pepper**
- **8 Plume De Veau* veal cutlets**
- **Extra-virgin olive oil**
- **1 pound mozzarella cheese, cut into 8 slices**
- **16 ounces marinara sauce**
- **Pasta and garlic bread, for serving**

Preheat oven to 350°F.

In a large bowl, mix bread crumbs with Parmigiano-Reggiano.

In a shallow bowl, beat eggs.

On a large plate, mix flour with salt and pepper.

Pound cutlets between sheets of plastic wrap to 1/4 inch thickness. Coat the cutlets evenly with flour, shaking off excess. Dip into the eggs. Coat evenly with bread crumbs. Set on waxed paper.

In a nonstick skillet, heat 1/4 inch of oil to 350°F. Place single cutlets in the skillet and sauté for 2 minutes on one side, 1 minute more on the other side. Remove with a slotted spatula and drain on paper towels.

Place sautéed cutlets in a baking dish and cover each cutlet with 1 slice of mozzarella and marinara sauce. Sprinkle with Parmigiano-Reggiano. Bake for 10-15 minutes, or until the sauce and cheese start to bubble.

Serve with pasta and garlic bread. Makes 8 servings.

** Brands may vary by region; substitute a similar product.*

# Grilled Pork Chops with Mango Tequila Sauce

## Farmland Foods

- 1/2 tablespoon olive oil
- 1/4 cup chopped sweet yellow onions
- 1/3 cup chopped yellow bell pepper
- 1 tablespoon sugar
- Half of a 24-ounce jar mangoes in extra light syrup, drained
- 1 tablespoon tequila
- 1 tablespoon key lime juice, divided
- 1 large jalapeño, seeded and finely minced
- 1 tablespoon minced fresh cilantro
- Salt
- 4 slices Kirkland Signature hickory-smoked bacon
- 4 Farmland* boneless center-cut pork chops (about 1 1/2 inches thick)

To prepare the sauce, heat oil in a sauté pan over medium heat. Add onions and sauté until tender and slightly browned on the edges. Add bell pepper and sauté until heated through. Add sugar and cook, stirring, until dissolved; remove from the heat.

Combine mangoes, tequila, 1/2 tablespoon key lime juice and the onion mixture in a blender and puree.

In a small bowl, combine jalapeño, cilantro and remaining 1/2 tablespoon key lime juice; add salt to taste. Let stand until ready to serve.

Heat a charcoal or gas grill to medium-high.

Wrap 1 bacon slice around the outside edge of each pork chop; secure with a wooden pick. Grill the chops for 13-18 minutes, turning every 5 minutes, or until the internal temperature is 155°F.

To serve, spoon some Mango Tequila Sauce onto each plate; top with a pork chop. Garnish with the minced jalapeño mixture. Makes 4 servings.

** Brands may vary by region; substitute a similar product.*

## Braised Pork Chops with Tangerines

### Diversified Citrus Marketing/Noble Worldwide

- 4 boneless center-cut pork chops, 1 inch thick
- Flour, for dusting
- 2 tablespoons unsalted butter
- 1 tablespoon vegetable oil
- 2 small onions, sliced horizontally and separated into rings
- 3 fresh pears, cored and quartered
- 1/2 cup water
- 1 teaspoon dried marjoram
- 1/4 teaspoon ground cinnamon
- 3 Florida tangerines, peeled and sectioned

Dust pork chops liberally with flour on both sides.

In a large skillet, heat butter and oil over medium-high heat. Add pork chops and brown on both sides; remove from the pan.

Add onion rings to the pan and sauté briefly.

Return the pork chops to the pan. Add pears and water. Sprinkle with marjoram and cinnamon. Cook, uncovered, over low heat for 1 hour and 15 minutes, or until the chops are tender and the sauce has thickened.

Add tangerine sections to the pan and heat briefly. Serve immediately. Makes 4 servings.

## Asparagus Tart

### Dole

- Pastry dough for single-crust 9-inch pie
- 1 pound Dole* asparagus, trimmed and cut into 1-inch pieces
- 1-2 tablespoons olive oil
- 2/3 cup half-and-half
- 2 large eggs, lightly beaten
- 1 teaspoon Dijon mustard
- 1/2 cup shredded Gruyère cheese
- Dash of cayenne pepper
- 1/4 teaspoon salt
- 1/4 teaspoon freshly ground black pepper

*BALSAMIC BERRIES*

- 1/4 cup strawberry jam
- 2 tablespoons balsamic vinegar
- 20 Dole* strawberries, hulled and quartered
- Freshly ground pepper

Preheat oven to 450°F.

Place pastry dough in a 9-inch tart pan with a removable bottom; fold the edges over to create a thicker crust. Pierce all over with a fork.

Toss asparagus pieces with a small amount of oil; place on a rimmed baking sheet.

Place pastry and asparagus in the oven and bake for 5 minutes. Remove the asparagus. Bake the pastry 3 minutes longer and remove.

Reduce oven temperature to 375°F.

In a bowl, stir together half-and-half, eggs, mustard, cheese, cayenne pepper, salt and black pepper.

Place the asparagus in the crust. Pour in the egg mixture. Place on a foil-lined pan. Bake for 35 minutes, or until puffy and brown. Let stand for 10 minutes before slicing.

To prepare the berries, whisk together jam and vinegar in a large bowl. Add strawberries and toss to coat. Season to taste with pepper.

Serve the tart with Balsamic Berries. Makes 6-8 servings.

** Brands may vary by region; substitute a similar product.*

# Ham with Lemon Mustard Glaze

## Farmland Foods

- 1 Kirkland Signature/Carando spiral-sliced hickory-smoked half ham
- 1/2 cup butter
- 2 teaspoons flour
- 1/2 cup freshly squeezed lemon juice
- 2 tablespoons Dijon mustard
- 1 tablespoon prepared yellow mustard
- 2 tablespoons honey (optional)

Heat ham according to package directions.

Meanwhile, melt butter in a small saucepan over medium heat. Whisk in flour until blended. Add lemon juice, Dijon and yellow mustard, and honey; whisk until smooth and slightly thickened.

Remove foil from the ham. Brush half of the glaze over the top of the ham; bake 10 minutes longer.

Serve the ham with the remaining glaze. Makes about 10 servings.

# Croissants Croque Monsieur
## Vie de France

**2 large Vie de France* butter croissants**
**Dijon mustard**
**4 ounces Black Forest ham, sliced**
**4 ounces Gruyère cheese, sliced**
**1 tablespoon butter**
**2 tablespoons grated Gruyère cheese**
**2 tablespoons grated Parmesan cheese**

***BÉCHAMEL SAUCE***
**2 tablespoons butter**
**2 tablespoons flour**
**1 cup milk**
**Pinch of ground nutmeg**
**Kosher salt and freshly ground black pepper**

To prepare the béchamel, melt butter in a saucepan over medium heat. Add flour and cook, stirring, for 1 minute. Slowly add milk, whisking constantly. Add nutmeg. Increase the heat to medium-high and boil until it thickens. Season to taste with salt and pepper. Set aside.

Preheat the broiler.

Slice croissants in half horizontally. Lightly spread mustard on bottom halves. Top with ham and Gruyère slices. Cover with the croissant tops.

Melt butter in a skillet over medium-high heat. Add sandwiches and cook for about 2 minutes on each side, or until lightly browned. Transfer to a baking sheet.

Spoon the béchamel over the sandwiches, then top with grated cheeses. Broil until the cheese begins to brown, about 2 minutes. Makes 2 servings.

** Brands may vary by region; substitute a similar product.*

## Sausage and Chicken Cannelloni

### New York Style Sausage

- 2 teaspoons olive oil
- 1 pound New York Style* Italian sausages, casings removed
- 1 pound boneless, skinless chicken thighs
- Salt and ground black pepper
- 1/2 cup white wine
- 4 pounds ricotta
- 1/2 cup finely chopped fresh parsley
- 1/2 cup finely chopped fresh basil
- 2 medium garlic bulbs, roasted, mashed well (see note)
- 1 tablespoon granulated garlic
- 2/3 cup grated Romano or Parmesan cheese
- 1 egg, beaten
- 1 leek
- 16-20 prepared crepes
- 1 15-ounce jar Alfredo sauce
- 2 cups marinara sauce
- Chopped fresh parsley or basil sprigs, for garnish

Preheat oven to 350°F.

Heat oil in a sauté pan over medium heat. Add sausage and cook until lightly browned, stirring to crumble. Remove from the pan with a slotted spoon and set aside.

Place chicken in the pan with the sausage drippings. Add salt and pepper to taste. Sauté until the chicken is done. Add wine and cook until it has evaporated. Remove the chicken from the pan. When cool, cut into 1/2-inch chunks.

In a large bowl, combine sausage, chicken, ricotta, parsley, basil, roasted garlic, granulated garlic, grated cheese, egg, 1 teaspoon pepper and salt to taste; mix well. Set aside.

Wash and clean leek. Boil in water until tender but firm, 20-30 seconds. From the green part of the leek, cut 16-20 strips 6 inches long by 1/4 inch wide.

Place 1/3 cup of filling in the center of each crepe. Gather the edges together and tie with a leek ribbon into a little sack.

Line the bottom of a 15-by-9-inch casserole dish with half of the Alfredo sauce. Place the crepe sacks in the casserole 3/4 inch apart. Top each with a tablespoon of marinara sauce. Top with the remaining Alfredo sauce. Bake for 30 minutes, or until heated through.

Garnish with parsley or basil sprigs. Serve with the remaining marinara sauce on the side.
Makes 8-10 servings.

**Note:** To roast garlic, cut 1/4 inch off the tops of the garlic bulbs. Coat with olive oil. Wrap in foil and roast in a 350°F oven for 50-60 minutes, or until tender.

** Brands may vary by region; substitute a similar product.*

## Italian Sausage with Corn, Poblano Peppers and Roasted Potatoes

### Premio

- 4 large baking potatoes
- 4 large poblano peppers
- 1 pound frozen corn kernels, thawed, divided
- 2 pounds Premio* mild Italian sausages, sliced into thick rounds
- 2 tablespoons olive oil
- 1 large onion, sliced
- 6 garlic cloves, chopped
- 1 cup chicken broth
- Salt and pepper
- Sour cream, for serving
- 1/2 cup chopped green onions, for serving

Preheat oven to 375°F.

Bake potatoes for 35 minutes. Set aside.

Trim and seed peppers. Arrange on a sheet pan and broil until the skin blisters. Cool, peel, slice into rings and reserve, saving any juices.

Puree half of corn in a food processor, adding a little broth if needed. Set aside.

In a large skillet, brown sausage in oil over high heat; remove when still pink. Reduce heat, add onions and sauté until soft. Add garlic and cook until soft. Add remaining corn kernels and broth. Season to taste with salt and pepper. Bring to a simmer.

Peel potatoes, quarter and add to the pan, along with peppers and any juices. Simmer until potatoes are tender.

Return sausage and juices to the pan, add pureed corn and simmer for 5-10 minutes, or until cooked through. Adjust seasoning.

Top with sour cream and green onions.
Makes 4-6 servings.

** Brands may vary by region; substitute a similar product.*

# Italian Sausage, Wild Mushroom and Spinach Risotto

Premio

1 cup Arborio rice
Butter
1 large onion, diced, divided
1 cup white wine (optional)
3 cups chicken broth, hot
1/4 cup dried porcini mushrooms, soaked in hot water to cover
Olive oil
2 pounds Premio* mild Italian sausages
3 garlic cloves, chopped
8 ounces shiitake mushroom caps, cleaned and quartered
1 cup tomato sauce
8 ounces spinach leaves, picked over and washed
Salt and pepper
Grated Parmesan or Romano cheese

Prepare risotto according to the directions on the rice package, using butter, half the onions, wine, broth and soaked porcini with their liquid. When the risotto is almost cooked, remove from the heat and reserve.

Heat a heavy skillet or casserole over high heat; add oil to coat. Split half of the sausages lengthwise and cut each into 6 pieces. Add to the pan and cook until browned but still pink in the center. Remove from the pan and reserve.

Remove the remaining sausages from their casings and crumble. Add to the hot pan and cook, stirring to break up the meat. Add the remaining onions and garlic; cook for 5 minutes.

Add shiitakes and stir until wilted. Moisten slightly with a small amount of broth if needed.

Add tomato sauce and bring to a simmer. Return sausage pieces to the pan. Add spinach and stir until wilted. Season to taste with salt and pepper.

Meanwhile, reheat the risotto, check the seasoning, and toss with butter and grated cheese to taste. Serve in large bowls and top with the sausage mixture. Makes 4-6 servings.

** Brands may vary by region; substitute a similar product.*

## Sausage, Ricotta and Mozzarella Lasagna

### Classico

- 1 15-ounce container ricotta cheese
- 1 egg, lightly beaten
- Salt and pepper
- Cooking spray
- 1 large red bell pepper, chopped, or about 2 1/2 cups
- 1 medium onion, chopped, or about 2 cups
- 4 garlic cloves, minced
- 1 1/2 pounds mixed sweet and hot Italian-style bulk sausage
- 6 cups Classico* Tomato & Basil Pasta Sauce
- 1/2 cup dry red wine (or water or beef broth)
- 12 no-boil lasagna noodles
- 4 cups shredded mozzarella cheese
- 1/4 cup grated Parmesan cheese

In a medium bowl, mix together ricotta and egg. Season to taste with salt and pepper. Cover and set aside.

Coat a large skillet with cooking spray and heat over medium-high heat. Add peppers, onions and garlic; cook for 2-3 minutes, stirring occasionally. Add sausage and cook for 4-6 minutes, or until cooked through, stirring until small crumbles form. Stir in pasta sauce and wine. Reduce the heat to medium and simmer for 10 minutes, or until heated through, stirring occasionally. Remove from the heat.

Preheat oven to 375°F.

Spread 1 cup of sauce evenly over the bottom of a 13-by-9-inch baking dish. Arrange 3 lasagna noodles on the sauce and spoon about 2 cups of sauce over the top. Layer with 1/3 of the ricotta mixture, 1 cup of mozzarella, 3 lasagna noodles and 1/3 of the remaining sauce. Repeat the layers twice, making sure the pasta is completely coated with sauce on top. Sprinkle with Parmesan and the remaining 1 cup of mozzarella.

Cover tightly with foil and bake for 20 minutes. Remove the foil and bake for an additional 15 minutes, or until hot and bubbly. Let rest for 5-10 minutes before serving. Makes 12 servings.

** Brands may vary by region; substitute a similar product.*

## Potato Lasagna

### Alsum Farms & Produce, Inc./RPE

- 2 tablespoons olive oil
- 2 garlic cloves, minced
- 1/2 teaspoon salt
- 1/2 teaspoon pepper
- 5 large Wisconsin* baking potatoes, sliced 1/4 inch thick
- 1 pound lean ground beef
- 1 large onion, chopped
- Italian seasoning, garlic salt and pepper to taste
- 1 26-ounce jar pasta sauce (any flavor)
- 1 15-ounce container ricotta
- 1 10-ounce package frozen chopped spinach, thawed and drained well
- 2 cups (8 ounces) shredded mozzarella
- 2 tablespoons grated Parmesan

Preheat oven to 425°F.

In a large bowl, combine oil, garlic, salt and pepper. Add potatoes and toss to coat. Spread in an ungreased 15-by-10-inch baking pan. Cover tightly with foil. Bake for 35-40 minutes, or until tender. Let cool for 15 minutes.

Reduce oven temperature to 350°F.

In a large skillet, brown beef with onions and seasonings; drain well. Add pasta sauce and simmer on low for about 10 minutes.

Stir together ricotta and spinach.

Arrange 1/3 of potatoes evenly in a greased 9-by-13-inch baking dish. Layer with 1/2 of spinach mixture, 1/3 of meat sauce and 1/3 of mozzarella. Repeat the next layer with 1/2 of spinach mixture, 1/3 of meat sauce and 1/3 of mozzarella. Top with remaining potatoes, meat sauce and mozzarella. Sprinkle with Parmesan.

Bake, uncovered, for 35-40 minutes, or until bubbly. Let stand for 5 minutes before serving. Makes 8-10 servings.

** Brands may vary by region; substitute a similar product.*

## Brie and Leek Wild Alaskan Salmon Lasagna

Trident Seafoods

- 3 6-ounce cans Kirkland Signature* Wild Alaskan Sockeye Salmon
- 2 tablespoons butter
- 4 leeks, sliced
- 2 garlic cloves, crushed
- Salt and pepper
- 6-8 precooked lasagna sheets

*CHEESE SAUCE*

- 2 tablespoons butter
- 1/2 cup flour
- 3 cups milk
- 5 ounces mature Brie cheese, skin removed, cut in small dice, divided

Preheat oven to 375°F.

Drain salmon and break into large chunks. Set aside.

In a large frying pan, melt butter over low heat. Add leeks and garlic; cook, stirring often, for about 5 minutes, or until the leeks are soft. Season to taste with salt and pepper.

To prepare the cheese sauce, melt butter in a saucepan over medium-high heat. Stir in flour. Add milk, whisking constantly, until the sauce boils and thickens. Reduce the heat to low and cook gently for another minute. Remove from the heat and stir in half the cheese. Season to taste with salt and pepper.

Spoon half the leek mixture into a 13-by-9-inch baking dish and scatter half the salmon chunks over the top. Cover with half the lasagna sheets. Pour half the cheese sauce over the lasagna. Repeat the layers, finishing with the cheese sauce. Sprinkle the remaining diced cheese evenly over the top.

Bake for 40-45 minutes, or until golden brown. Makes 4-6 servings.

** Brands may vary by region; substitute a similar product.*

## Four-Cheese Ravioli Chicken and Mushroom Bake

Kirkland Signature/Seviroli Foods

- 1 10.75-ounce can condensed mushroom soup
- 1 cup water
- 1 12-ounce can evaporated milk
- 2 4-ounce cans sliced mushrooms, drained
- 1/4 teaspoon salt
- 1/8 teaspoon ground pepper
- 1/2 teaspoon porcini powder (optional, see tip)
- 1 bag Kirkland Signature frozen Four-Cheese Ravioli
- 8 ounces shredded provolone cheese
- 12 ounces diced cooked chicken
- 1/4 cup panko bread crumbs (or regular bread crumbs)
- Chopped fresh parsley, for garnish

Preheat oven to 350°F. Grease the bottom of a 12-by-9-inch baking dish.

In a medium bowl, combine soup, water, evaporated milk, mushrooms, salt, pepper and porcini powder. Stir until well blended, about 1 minute.

Place a layer of ravioli in the bottom of the pan (8-12 pieces). Top with 1/3 of the mushroom mixture, 1/3 of the provolone and 1/2 of the chicken. Repeat the layers. Finish with the remaining mushroom mixture and provolone. Sprinkle bread crumbs evenly on top.

Cover with foil and bake for 30 minutes. Remove foil and bake for 10 minutes, or until internal temperature is 165°F.

Remove from the oven and let stand for 5 minutes. Sprinkle with parsley. Makes 6-8 servings.

**Tip:** You can make your own porcini powder by grinding dried porcini mushrooms in a coffee grinder to a fine texture.

# Spinach Ravioli with Sautéed Tomatoes and Basil Pesto
## Monterey Pasta Company/CIBO Naturals

**2 tablespoons extra-virgin olive oil**

**1 pint grape tomatoes or cherry tomatoes, rinsed and dried (very important)**

**1/2 teaspoon salt**

**Half of a 38-ounce package Monterey Pasta Company* Made with Organic Spinach & Cheese Ravioli**

**1/2 cup Kirkland Signature/CIBO Naturals Basil Pesto**

**2 tablespoons shredded or grated Parmesan cheese**

Heat oil in a large skillet over medium heat. Add tomatoes and salt. Cook, stirring, until the tomatoes split open and give off their juice. Continue to cook and stir until the tomato juice becomes syrupy, about 10 minutes.

While the tomatoes are cooking, boil water for the ravioli. Cook ravioli according to package directions (about 4 minutes). Drain and toss gently with pesto.

While the ravioli is cooking, carefully transfer the tomatoes to a blender or food processor and blend until very smooth. Keep warm.

To serve, spread half of the tomato sauce on a large platter. Top with the pesto-coated ravioli and dollop the remaining tomato sauce on top. Sprinkle with Parmesan. Makes 4 servings.

** Brands may vary by region; substitute a similar product.*

# Straw and Hay Fettuccine Alfredo

## Kirkland Signature/Arthur Schuman/Citterio

- 2 tablespoons extra-virgin olive oil
- 3 garlic cloves, minced
- 4 tablespoons butter
- 1 1/2 cups heavy cream
- 1 cup grated Kirkland Signature Parmigiano Reggiano, plus more for shaving
- 1/8 teaspoon grated nutmeg
- 1/8 teaspoon crushed red pepper flakes (optional)
- 1/2 teaspoon salt
- 1/4 teaspoon freshly ground black pepper
- 1/2 pound fettuccine
- 1/2 pound spinach fettuccine
- 6 ounces Citterio Prosciutto di Parma, roughly chopped

Bring 6 quarts of cold salted water to a boil.

In a large skillet, heat oil over medium heat. Add garlic and sauté gently for 3 minutes.

Add butter, heavy cream, grated Parmigiano Reggiano, nutmeg, red pepper, salt and pepper to the pan. Lower the heat to medium-low and stir to incorporate all ingredients. Continue stirring until all the cheese has melted into the sauce.

Cook pasta according to package directions until al dente; drain in a colander.

Add the pasta to the sauce, and stir well to coat evenly. Add prosciutto and gently toss. Transfer to a serving dish.

Using a peeler, shave 5-6 curls of cheese from the wedge of Parmigiano Reggiano directly onto the pasta. Serve immediately. Makes 4-6 servings.

KIRKLAND Signature CITTERIO
arthur schuman inc.

## Traditional Pepperoni Pizza Bagels
Einstein Brothers Bagels/Noah's Bagels

- **3/4-1 1/8 cups your favorite tomato sauce**
- **6 Kirkland Signature plain, onion or honey wheat bagels, cut in half**
- **2-2 1/4 cups shredded mozzarella cheese**
- **60 slices pepperoni**

Preheat oven to 350°F.

Spread 1-1 1/2 tablespoons of sauce on each bagel half.

Top each half with 2 heaping tablespoons mozzarella.

Place 5 slices of pepperoni on each bagel half.

Set bagels on a baking sheet and bake for 7-9 minutes, or until the cheese is bubbly and starting to brown. Makes 6 servings.

Quick & Easy

## Steak Lover's Grilled Pizza
McCormick

- **1 pound boneless beef sirloin steak**
- **4 teaspoons Grill Mates Montreal Steak Seasoning, divided**
- **1 onion, cut into ½-inch-thick slices**
- **1 red *or* yellow bell pepper, seeded and quartered**
- **1 tablespoon plus 1 teaspoon olive oil, divided**
- **2 cups shredded Monterey Jack cheese**
- **1 prepared thin pizza crust (12-inch)**

Preheat the grill.

Sprinkle steak with 3 teaspoons of the steak seasoning. Brush vegetables with 1 teaspoon of the oil.

Grill the steak over medium heat for 7 minutes per side, or until cooked to taste. Grill the vegetables for 8 minutes, or until tender. Cut the steak and vegetables into bite-size pieces.

Mix cheese and remaining 1 teaspoon steak seasoning.

Brush top of pizza crust with remaining 1 tablespoon olive oil. Place oiled-side down on the grill. Close the lid and grill over medium heat for 1 minute, or until grill marks appear on the bottom of the crust. Flip the crust over, using tongs.

Layer the crust with half of the cheese, then the steak and vegetables. Top with the remaining cheese. Close the lid and grill for 4 minutes, or until the cheese is melted. (Check often to avoid burning. Rotate the pizza, if necessary.) Serve immediately. Makes 8 servings.

# British Columbia Sweet Bell Pepper and Roma Tomato Pizza

## BC Hot House/The Oppenheimer Group

- 1 large uncooked pizza crust (12 inches)
- 4-5 BC Hot House* Roma tomatoes, sliced
- Pinch of coarse sea salt
- 1 cup julienned SunSelect* sweet bell peppers
- 1/2 cup crumbled feta cheese
- 1/3 cup black olives, pitted and roughly chopped
- 1/2 cup sun-dried tomatoes, roughly chopped
- 1 cup grated mozzarella cheese
- 1/2 cup fresh basil, torn or julienned

*SAUCE*

- 2 tablespoons extra-virgin olive oil
- 1/3 cup chopped white onion
- 1 garlic clove, crushed
- 4 BC Hot House* Roma tomatoes, roughly chopped
- 1/2 teaspoon dried thyme
- Salt and freshly ground black pepper
- 1 tablespoon roughly torn fresh basil, or 1 teaspoon dried

To prepare the sauce, heat oil in a medium-hot saucepan. Add onions and garlic; cook until the onions are transparent. Add tomatoes, thyme, and salt and pepper to taste; cook over medium heat until the tomatoes start to break down slightly. Lower the heat and let simmer and reduce for 20 minutes. Puree the mixture. Check seasoning and stir in basil. This can be refrigerated for 2-3 days.

Preheat oven to 385°F.

Spread the sauce on the pizza dough. Layer the tomato slices over the dough. Sprinkle with sea salt. Arrange peppers, feta, olives and sun-dried tomatoes on top. Sprinkle with mozzarella.

Place on a pizza pan. Bake for 15-20 minutes, or until the dough has browned on the bottom and the mozzarella is bubbling. Top with fresh basil and serve.
Makes 3-4 servings.

** Brands may vary by region; substitute a similar product.*

*expect the world from us*

## Vegetarian White Pizza Bagels

### Einstein Brothers Bagels/Noah's Bagels

- **1 teaspoon minced garlic**
- **Kosher salt**
- **1/2 teaspoon coarsely ground black pepper, divided**
- **1/2 teaspoon dried basil**
- **1/2 teaspoon dried oregano**
- **2 tablespoons milk**
- **8 ounces cream cheese, softened**
- **2 tablespoons butter**
- **8 ounces sliced mushrooms**
- **1 tablespoon balsamic vinegar**
- **6 Kirkland Signature plain, onion or honey wheat bagels, cut in half**
- **1 1/2 cups shredded mozzarella**
- **3/4 cup artichoke hearts cut in 1/2-inch pieces**
- **3/4 cup roasted red peppers cut in 1/2-inch pieces**

Preheat oven to 350°F.

In a bowl, mix garlic, salt to taste, 1/4 teaspoon pepper, basil, oregano, milk and cream cheese. Set aside.

Melt butter in a sauté pan over medium-high heat. Add 1/4 teaspoon salt and 1/4 teaspoon pepper. After 15-30 seconds, add mushrooms and toss to coat. Sauté for 8-10 minutes, or until substantially reduced in volume and golden brown. Stir in vinegar and heat for another 30 seconds.

Spread cream cheese mixture on bagel halves. Top with mozzarella, artichokes, red peppers and mushrooms.

Place on a baking sheet and bake for 7-9 minutes, or until the cheese is bubbly and starting to brown. Makes 6 servings.

**Tip:** For a vegan version, substitute olive oil, hummus and soy cheese for the butter, cream cheese mixture and mozzarella.

## Cheese Lemon Pizza

### Paramount Citrus

- **4 Paramount Citrus* lemons**
- **Flour**
- **Pizza dough for 1 crust**
- **Olive oil**
- **4 garlic cloves, crushed**
- **2 jalapeños, thinly sliced**
- **1 red bell pepper, thinly sliced**
- **2 cups Italian three-cheese blend**
- **1 cup fresh parsley, chopped**

Preheat oven to 425°F.

Grate the peel from 1 lemon. Peel and thinly slice the remaining 3 lemons and remove the seeds. Set aside.

On a lightly floured surface, pat the dough out, forming a thin 10- to 12-inch-round crust. Brush with oil and sprinkle with the grated lemon peel.

In a large skillet, heat enough oil to coat the pan over medium heat. Add lemon slices, garlic, jalapeños and bell pepper; sauté for 2 minutes. Spread the mixture evenly over the pizza crust.

Spread cheese evenly over the pizza and then sprinkle with parsley.

Bake for about 20 minutes, or until the crust is crisp and the cheese bubbles. Slice and serve.
Makes 4 servings.

** Brands may vary by region; substitute a similar product.*

## Grilled Open-Faced Mediterranean Sandwiches

Chicken of the Sea

- 1/4 cup light mayonnaise
- 1/2 tablespoon prepared pesto
- Dash of crushed red pepper
- 1 7-ounce can Chicken of the Sea* chunk light tuna in water or solid white tuna in water, drained
- 1/4 cup vinaigrette dressing
- 4 slices sourdough bread
- 1 cup jarred roasted bell peppers, drained
- 1 1/3 cups 1/2-inch sliced eggplant, grilled
- 1 1/3 cups 1/2-inch sliced zucchini, grilled
- 1/2 cup sliced pepperoncini, drained
- 1 cup shredded 3-cheese Italian blend
- 4 small sprigs fresh basil, for garnish

Preheat the broiler.

In a resealable container, combine mayonnaise, pesto and red pepper.

In a bowl, gently mix tuna with vinaigrette.

For each sandwich, place a slice of bread on a foil-lined baking sheet. Spread pesto mayonnaise on the bread. Layer each sandwich with 1/4 cup roasted bell peppers, about 5 slices each eggplant and zucchini, about 1/3 cup tuna mixture, pepperoncini (about 4-5 rings) and 1/4 cup shredded cheese.

Broil for 2-3 minutes, or until the cheese has melted. Garnish with basil sprigs and serve immediately. Makes 4 servings.

**Tip:** This can also be served as an appetizer on French bread; just reduce the toppings accordingly.

** Brands may vary by region; substitute a similar product.*

## Oven-Baked Mahi Mahi Sandwiches

Orca Bay

- Nonstick cooking spray
- 4 Orca Bay* frozen mahi mahi portions, thawed
- 1/2 cup all-purpose flour
- 1/2 teaspoon sea salt
- 2 eggs
- 3/4 cup Italian-seasoned dry bread crumbs
- 2 tablespoons butter, melted
- 4 soft hamburger buns or hoagie rolls
- 4 slices American cheese
- 4 tablespoons tartar sauce, or to taste

Preheat oven to 375°F. Coat a baking sheet with cooking spray.

Pat dry the thawed mahi mahi with paper towels.

Combine flour and salt in a shallow bowl. Beat eggs in a second bowl. Place bread crumbs and melted butter in a third bowl and mix until blended.

Dip the fish in the flour, turning to coat evenly; remove excess flour. Dip in the eggs, coating evenly. Dip in the buttered bread crumbs, turning to coat evenly. Press the crumbs into the fish, tapping off excess.

Place the fish on the baking sheet. Spray the fish generously with cooking spray.

Bake for 18-22 minutes (145°F internally). Remove from the oven.

Preheat the broiler on high. Toast insides of hamburger buns until golden brown.

Place a slice of cheese on each fish portion. Broil until the cheese melts. Transfer to the buns, top with tartar sauce, add bun tops and serve. Makes 4 servings.

** Brands may vary by region; substitute a similar product.*

## Southwest Albacore Tuna Burgers

### Kirkland Signature

- **2 7-ounce cans Kirkland Signature solid white albacore tuna, drained and flaked**
- **2 large fresh eggs, lightly beaten**
- **1/2 cup crushed tortilla chips, yellow or white corn**
- **1/4 cup chopped fresh cilantro**
- **1/4 cup diced red bell pepper**
- **1 tablespoon lemon juice**
- **1 tablespoon taco seasoning**
- **1/4 cup vegetable oil for frying, or enough to cover bottom of skillet**
- **4 hamburger buns, toasted**
- **1 cup shredded lettuce**
- **1/4 cup mayonnaise (optional)**
- **1/4 cup salsa (optional)**

In a large bowl, combine tuna, eggs, tortilla chips, cilantro, bell pepper, lemon juice and taco seasoning; stir well. Divide the mixture evenly and shape firmly into 4 patties.

Heat oil in a skillet over medium heat. (If using an electric skillet, set at 375°F.) Add tuna patties and sauté for 2 minutes on each side, or until golden brown.

Serve on toasted hamburger buns with shredded lettuce, mayonnaise and salsa. Makes 4 servings.

**Tip:** Refrigerating the tuna mixture will make shaping the patties easier.

**Nutritional information:** Each plain patty has 270 calories, 32 g protein, 11 g carbohydrates, 11 g fat, 2.5 g saturated fat, 155 mg cholesterol, <1 g fiber, 420 mg sodium. Each serving of patty, bun and condiments has 500 calories, 37 g protein, 34 g carbohydrates, 24 g fat, 4 g saturated fat, 160 mg cholesterol, 2 g fiber, 850 mg sodium.

## Wasabi Cucumber Salmon Burgers

### Trident Seafoods

- **4 Trident Seafoods* frozen 4-ounce salmon burgers**
- **4 sesame seed buns, toasted**
- **4 slices tomato**
- **16 slices peeled cucumber**
- **4 slices red onion**
- **4 romaine lettuce leaves, shredded**
- **Pickled ginger, for serving**

***SAUCE***

- **1 1/2 tablespoons wasabi powder**
- **2 tablespoons mayonnaise**
- **2 tablespoons sour cream**
- **1 tablespoon Dijon mustard**
- **1 tablespoon minced green onion**
- **Salt and pepper**

To prepare the sauce, combine wasabi, mayonnaise, sour cream, mustard, green onion, and salt and pepper to taste in a small bowl. Cover and refrigerate for at least 2 hours before serving.

Preheat the grill to 400°F or an oiled sauté pan over medium-high heat.

Cook frozen salmon burgers for 4-4 1/2 minutes on each side, or until the internal temperature is 145°F.

To serve, place 1 tablespoon of sauce on each toasted bun and add salmon burgers. Garnish with tomato, cucumber, red onion and lettuce. Serve with pickled ginger on the side. Makes 4 servings.

** Brands may vary by region; substitute a similar product.*

## Steelhead Sliders

### AquaGold Seafood/Michael Cutler

- **1 fresh steelhead fillet (1 1/2 pounds)**
- **1 tablespoon *each* finely diced red, green and yellow bell pepper**
- **1 large egg**
- **Salt and pepper**
- **2 cups fresh white bread crumbs, divided**
- **4 tablespoons olive oil, divided**
- **2 large yellow onions, thinly sliced**
- **1 cup light mayonnaise (not salad dressing)**
- **1 medium chipotle pepper in adobo sauce**
- **1 dozen slider buns**

Remove skin and dark meat from steelhead. Mince very fine by hand. Place in a bowl and mix with bell peppers, egg, and salt and pepper to taste.

Add 1 cup bread crumbs and stir just until blended. Form into twelve 3-inch patties.

Heat 2 tablespoons oil in a large skillet over medium-low heat. Add onions and sauté until tender and golden brown, about 20 minutes. Season to taste with salt and pepper.

In a small food processor, puree mayonnaise, chipotle pepper and 1 teaspoon adobo sauce.

When onions are done, remove from the pan and set aside. Add 2 tablespoons oil to the skillet. Dredge the patties in 1 cup bread crumbs, covering each side lightly. Cook over medium heat until done, about 3 minutes per side.

To serve, place a spoonful of adobo mayo on each bun, add a steelhead patty and top with sautéed onions. Serve immediately. Makes 4 servings.

## Greek Turkey Burgers with Spiced Yogurt Sauce
McCormick

- **1 pound ground turkey**
- **1/2 cup reduced-fat feta cheese**
- **2 teaspoons McCormick oregano leaves**
- **1/2 teaspoon McCormick thyme leaves**
- **1/2 teaspoon McCormick ground black pepper, plus more to taste**
- **2 teaspoons olive oil**
- **1/4 cup plain low-fat yogurt**
- **McCormick ground cumin**
- **Sea salt from McCormick Sea Salt Grinder**
- **4 whole-wheat hamburger rolls, toasted**
- **Red leaf lettuce, tomato slices and cucumber slices, for topping (optional)**

In a large bowl, mix ground turkey, feta, oregano, thyme and 1/2 teaspoon pepper. Shape into 4 patties.

Heat oil in a large nonstick skillet on medium heat until hot. Add the patties and cook for 4-5 minutes on each side, or until the burgers are cooked through (internal temperature of 165°F).

To prepare the sauce, season yogurt to taste with cumin, sea salt and pepper.

Serve the burgers on toasted rolls. Top each burger with 1 tablespoon of the yogurt mixture. Garnish with desired toppings. Makes 4 servings.

## Pork Burgers on Focaccia with Cheddar and Arugula
Tillamook

- **4 teaspoons butter, softened**
- **4 3-by-3-inch squares focaccia bread, cut in half horizontally**
- **1 pound ground pork**
- **Salt and pepper**
- **1 teaspoon olive oil**
- **4 slices Tillamook Medium Cheddar Cheese**
- **1/4 cup prepared olive tapenade**
- **1/2 cup roasted red peppers cut in 1/4-inch-wide slices**
- **1 cup baby arugula**

Preheat the broiler.

Butter focaccia halves and toast under the broiler, butter side up, until golden. Set aside.

Gently form meat into four 1/2-inch-thick patties. Season to taste with salt and pepper.

Heat a skillet or grill pan over medium-high heat; add oil and swirl to coat the pan. Cook the patties for 4 minutes on each side, or until a thermometer inserted in the center reads 160°F. Top each patty with a cheese slice. Turn off the heat and cover until the cheese melts.

Spread 1 tablespoon of tapenade on the bottom half of each focaccia. Place a patty on each and top with equal portions of red peppers and arugula. Top with the remaining focaccia halves and serve immediately. Makes 4 burgers.

**Tillamook®**

## Green Chile Cheese Burgers

### Kirkland Signature/Orleans International

**4-5 fresh poblano chiles**
**4-5 serrano chiles**
**Oil (any kind)**
**2 pounds Kirkland Signature ground chuck or 80% lean ground beef**
**Salt and pepper**
**4 hamburger buns**
**8 slices American cheese**
**Sliced red onions, tomatoes, kosher dill pickles and leaf lettuce, for topping (optional)**

Preheat the broiler.

Place chiles on a baking sheet. Coat lightly with oil. Broil the chiles, turning occasionally, until the skin is discolored and blistered all over, about 10 minutes for the serranos and 20 minutes for the poblanos. Transfer to a glass bowl, cover lightly with foil or plastic wrap and let steam for 15-20 minutes. Peel the blistered skin away; don't worry if some of the black remains. Do not wash or rinse the chiles. Discard the stems and seed pods. Slice the chiles into strips about 1/2 inch wide and cut into a small dice.

Preheat a grill or frying pan.

Form ground beef into patties. Season to taste with salt and pepper. Grill or fry over medium to medium-high heat.

In another small skillet, reheat the chiles (this adds flavor and reduces the amount of heat they release). When the burgers are close to being done, lightly toast the buns. Spoon the chiles liberally on top of the burgers. Put 2 slices of cheese on top and let it melt completely so the chiles are held in place.

Add onions, tomatoes, pickles and lettuce. Makes 4 servings.

# Grilled Steakhouse Sliders
## Kirkland Signature

**8 slices Kirkland Signature bacon**
**1/2 cup Italian-seasoned dry bread crumbs**
**1/4 cup Kirkland Signature milk**
**1 1/2 pounds Kirkland Signature ground beef**
**1 teaspoon table salt**
**1/2 teaspoon ground black pepper**
**8 small rolls or buns**

Fry bacon in a large skillet over medium heat until crisp, about 8 minutes. Transfer to a paper-towel-lined plate. Spoon 3 tablespoons of bacon fat from the skillet into a heatproof bowl and place in the refrigerator.

Place bread crumbs in a small bowl, add milk and let the mixture sit until saturated, about 5 minutes. Mash the bread crumbs and milk until a smooth paste forms.

Crumble beef into a medium bowl. Season with salt and pepper, then add bread crumb paste and the reserved bacon fat. Using a fork or your hands, knead the meat so that the ingredients are well mixed. Divide into 8 equal patties.

Preheat the grill to medium.

Grill the patties for 2-4 minutes, then flip and grill the other side for about 3 minutes for medium or 4 minutes for well-done.

Serve with your favorite buns and condiments, topped with bacon if desired.
Makes 4 servings.

**Note:** The bacon grease can cause grill flare-ups. Have a squirt bottle on hand to douse any flames.

## Lime Cilantro Guacamole Cheeseburgers

Market Source

*GUACAMOLE*

**2 ripe avocados, halved and pitted**

**Juice of 1 medium Market Source* lime**

**1 teaspoon chili powder**

**1 jalapeño, minced**

**1/2 cup chopped fresh cilantro**

**1/2 teaspoon minced garlic**

**1/2 teaspoon salt**

**Black pepper to taste**

*BURGERS*

**2 pounds lean ground beef**

**Juice of 1 medium Market Source* lime**

**1 tablespoon minced garlic**

**1/2 cup diced onion**

**1/2 cup diced tomato**

**6 slices Monterey Jack cheese**

**6 hamburger buns**

Preheat the grill to medium.

To prepare the guacamole, scoop the avocado flesh into a bowl and mash. Add all remaining ingredients and mix until well blended.

To prepare the burgers, combine ground beef, lime juice, garlic, onions and tomatoes in a bowl; stir to blend. Shape into 6 patties.

Grill the burgers until cooked to taste. Add a slice of cheese to each burger during the last minute of cooking.

Toast the hamburger buns.

Serve the burgers on the toasted buns with a spoonful of guacamole on top. Makes 6 servings.

** Brands may vary by region; substitute a similar product.*

## Chicken, Apple and Basil Sausage Patties

Pennsylvania Apple/New York Apple

**1 tablespoon olive oil**

**1 1/2 cups finely chopped, unpeeled Eastern* Jonagold apples**

**1/2 cup finely chopped sweet onion**

**2 small garlic cloves, minced (about 3/4 teaspoon)**

**1/3 cup very finely chopped fresh basil**

**1 teaspoon rubbed sage**

**1/2 teaspoon salt**

**1/2 teaspoon ground coriander**

**1/4 teaspoon freshly ground black pepper**

**1 1/2 pounds ground chicken or turkey (white and dark meat)**

Heat oil in a medium skillet over medium-high heat. Add apples and onions. Cook for about 2 minutes, or until nearly tender, stirring occasionally. Add garlic; cook for 30 seconds. Transfer the mixture to a large bowl and let cool to room temperature.

Stir basil, sage, salt, coriander and pepper into the apple mixture. Add ground chicken; mix with hands until just combined (do not overwork). With damp hands, form into sixteen 1/2-inch-thick patties. Transfer to a tray or baking sheet lined with plastic wrap. Cover and refrigerate or freeze until ready to use.

Heat a nonstick skillet over medium heat. Add patties and cook for 6-8 minutes, or until an instant-read thermometer inserted near the center reads 165°F, turning the patties over halfway through cooking. Drain on paper towels. Makes 8 servings.

**Tip:** You can freeze the patties for later use. Thaw them in the refrigerator.

** Brands may vary by region; substitute a similar product.*

# Vegetarian Couscous-Stuffed Ancient Sweets

Mastronardi Produce/SUNSET

Cooking spray

6 SUNSET Ancient Sweets* peppers

Salt

*STUFFING*

1 cup vegetable or low-sodium chicken broth

2 teaspoons kosher salt

1 tablespoon olive oil

2 tablespoons lemon juice

1 tablespoon curry powder

1 tablespoon minced garlic

1/4 teaspoon cayenne pepper

3/4 cup dry couscous

1 cup canned garbanzo beans, drained well

2 large celery ribs, cut in 1/4-inch dice

3 green onions, thinly sliced

1 cup dried cranberries, chopped

1/2 cup dried apricots, chopped

1 cup chopped walnuts, toasted

1 cup crumbled feta cheese

1 egg, lightly beaten

Preheat oven to 375°F. Spray a baking sheet with cooking spray.

Slit peppers vertically down the center, leaving the stem intact. Gently spread peppers open and carefully remove the seeds. Season the insides lightly with salt.

To prepare the stuffing, combine broth, salt, oil, lemon juice, curry powder, garlic and cayenne pepper in a small saucepan. Bring to a quick boil over high heat. Stir in couscous. Immediately remove from the heat and quickly cover with a tight-fitting lid or plastic wrap. Set a timer for 15 minutes.

When the couscous is cooked, remove the lid and fluff with a fork. Transfer the couscous to a large bowl, add the remaining ingredients and toss to combine. Lightly pack the mixture into the peppers.

Place the peppers on the baking sheet and bake for about 15-20 minutes, or until the filling is hot and the peppers are tender. Makes 6 servings.

**Tip:** Add chopped fresh basil or dill to the filling for a delicious twist.

** Brands may vary by region; substitute a similar product.*

# Sicilian Waldorf Chicken Salad Sandwiches

## La Brea Bakery

- 1/2 cup pine nuts
- 1 cup mayonnaise
- 1 1/2 teaspoons Dijon mustard
- 2 tablespoons extra-virgin olive oil
- 3-4 tablespoons fresh lemon juice, divided
- Kosher salt
- 3-4 cups roasted chicken cut in bite-size pieces
- 1 celery stalk, cut into 1/4-inch dice
- 1/2 cup dried currants
- 1/4 cup finely chopped fresh Italian parsley
- Fresh cracked black pepper
- 8 slices La Brea Bakery* Whole Grain Loaf

Adjust the oven rack to the middle position. Preheat oven to 325°F.

Spread pine nuts on a baking sheet and toast in the oven for 8 minutes, or until lightly browned. Let cool.

In a small bowl, stir together mayonnaise, mustard, oil, 1 tablespoon lemon juice and salt to taste. Add more lemon juice, mustard or salt to taste.

In a large bowl, combine chicken and 1/2 to 1 cup of the mayonnaise mixture. Add pine nuts, celery, currants, parsley and 2-3 tablespoons lemon juice; toss to coat, adding more dressing if necessary to coat the chicken thoroughly. Season the salad with salt, pepper and lemon juice to taste.

Spread about 1-2 tablespoons of the mayonnaise mixture over half of the bread slices. Arrange the chicken salad on top and cover with the top slice of bread. Cut each sandwich in half on the diagonal. Makes 4 servings.

** Brands may vary by region; substitute a similar product.*

# Decadent desserts, done right

**Sandra Lee**
Sandra Lee is editor in chief of *Sandra Lee Semi-Homemade* magazine, the host of two TV shows (*Semi-Homemade Cooking* and *Sandra's Money Saving Meals*) and a *New York Times* bestselling author of 20 books. Her latest books are *Semi-Homemade: The Complete Cookbook* and *Semi-Homemade: Comfort Food.*

**By Sandra Lee**

DESSERT IS THE CROWNING achievement of a great meal. In my mind, it's time to be decadent and let the beauty of the presentation, whether it's a cake or a cobbler, take center stage and thrill your guests.

I don't have a long list of hard rules when it comes to dessert, but a few tips can help ensure that your dessert represents the fitting end to the perfect meal. Experiment with different dessert ideas, find creative ways to present them and include fine coffee, and you can't go wrong. Here are some questions I am often asked and suggestions for you to consider.

**How do you decide what to serve?**
Choose what you know everybody in the room loves. The safest bet is a white cake. The number-two safe bet is chocolate.

**What goes best with what foods?**
I don't usually consider pairings when it comes to the main dish and dessert. That said, there are desserts that work best in certain seasons: Carrot and spice cakes are beautiful for October and November. Red velvet and white cakes are lovely for Christmas. White cakes, cupcakes and lemon cakes are perfect for spring. And think of shortcakes, tartlets and fruit desserts for summer.

The beautiful thing about cobblers and trifles is that they are safe bets year-round. They can be served cold in the summer and warm in the winter as a comfort food.

**Is there a proper timing for serving?**
If you're entertaining a big crowd, serve dessert right after dinner with coffee. But sometimes you might want to retire to the living room and have dessert on a sofa. It depends on whether you want a relaxed or more formal setting. The only rule is not before dinner!

**What about presentation?**
I always use a cake as the centerpiece on my table. It can be beautiful, and a cake fills your house with that homey, delicious, wonderful fragrance. We eat first with our eyes and our noses, then with our palates. Desserts are beautiful served on a pedestal or in individual containers.

A cupcake service can be as easy as a coffee cup turned upside down with a saucer on top, for a plate pedestal. Or it can be as elaborate as a big cake pedestal topped with a smaller one. You place cupcakes around the bottom, and your cake presentation on top. It depends on what you want to communicate.

**Any rules never to be broken?**
I always like to double the recipe. There's always going to be some nibbling. Making two desserts gives you one serving for now and one for later, and definitely ensures that you always have enough. Somebody is going to want seconds, and somebody's little fingers are going to get into those cupcakes when you're not looking.

## Apple Crumble Tart
### Domex Superfresh Growers

**2 cups all-purpose flour**
**3/4 cup confectioners' sugar**
**Pinch of salt**
**3/4 cup unsalted butter, at room temperature**
**1 teaspoon pure vanilla extract**
**1/2 cup packed light brown sugar**
**1/2 teaspoon ground cinnamon**
**1/4 teaspoon ground cloves**
**2 pounds Superfresh Growers* Fuji apples**

Preheat oven to 375°F.

Combine flour, confectioners' sugar and salt in a food processor and pulse to blend. Cut butter into pieces and add to the processor with the vanilla. Pulse until the butter is finely blended with the flour and the mixture has the texture of coarse sand with a few small pebbles.

Set aside 1 cup of the mixture and pour the rest into a 10-inch deep-dish pie pan. Press the dough firmly onto the bottom and sides of the pan. If your fingers stick to the dough, lightly dust them with flour.

Add brown sugar, cinnamon and cloves to the remaining dough mixture and stir to evenly blend.

Peel and core apples, then cut into 1/8-inch slices (a mandoline slicer is ideal for quickly making thin, even slices). Arrange the apple slices in the tart shell in even layers. After every 3 layers, sprinkle 2 tablespoons of the brown sugar mixture over the apples. Make the final layer tidy, overlapping the slices in an attractive pattern. Sprinkle the last of the brown sugar mixture on top.

Bake until the apples are very tender and the top is lightly browned, about 50 minutes. Set aside to cool, then cut into wedges to serve. Makes 8-10 servings.

** Brands may vary by region; substitute a similar product.*

## Strawberry Tartlets
### Naturipe Farms

**1/2 cup ricotta cheese**
**2 tablespoons creamy vanilla yogurt**
**1 egg white**
**2 teaspoons lemon extract, divided**
**15 mini filo shells**
**1 1/2 cups chopped fresh Naturipe Farms* strawberries**
**1/4 cup shaved or finely chopped premium bittersweet chocolate**

Preheat oven to 350°F.

In a small bowl, stir together ricotta and yogurt. Blend in egg white and 1 teaspoon lemon extract.

Spoon about 2 teaspoons of filling into each filo tart shell. Place on a cookie sheet and bake for 10 minutes, or until the filling sets. Let cool on a rack.

Meanwhile, gently toss strawberries with 1 teaspoon lemon extract.

Just before serving, spoon 1 tablespoon of the strawberry mixture onto each tart. Top with chocolate. Makes 15 tarts.

**Tip:** Substitute low-fat ricotta and yogurt.

** Brands may vary by region; substitute a similar product.*

# Red Grape Tart

## Kirschenman

1 envelope unflavored gelatin
$1/4$ cup granulated sugar
1 $1/2$ cups ruby Port
1 tablespoon lemon juice
1 3-ounce package cream cheese
$1/2$ cup whipping cream
$1/4$ cup confectioners' sugar
2 $1/4$ pounds Kirschenman red seedless grapes
Whipped cream, for serving (optional)

*ALMOND CRUST*

$1/3$ cup whole almonds
$1/4$ cup granulated sugar
1 cup flour
$1/2$ cup butter, cut in pieces
1 egg yolk

Preheat oven to 325°F.

To prepare the crust, finely grind almonds in a food processor. Add sugar, flour and butter; pulse until combined. Add egg yolk and process until the dough forms a ball. Press over the bottom and sides of a 13-inch tart pan or 1 $1/2$ inches up the sides of a 10-inch cheesecake pan with a removable bottom. Bake until golden, about 25 minutes. Let cool.

In a 2-quart saucepan, combine gelatin and sugar. Stir in Port. Bring to a boil, then remove from the heat and add lemon juice. Chill until the mixture has the consistency of egg whites.

Beat cream cheese to soften. Gradually add cream and confectioners' sugar, beating at high speed until well blended. Spread over the crust. Arrange grapes on top. Spoon thickened gelatin over grapes. Chill until gelatin sets, at least 2 hours or overnight. Serve with whipped cream. Makes 8-10 servings.

# Cranberry Parfait Pie

## Kirkland Signature/Cliffstar

1 cup Kirkland Signature cranberry juice cocktail
1 6-ounce package strawberry-flavored gelatin
1 cup whole-berry cranberry sauce
$1/2$ cup vanilla ice cream
1 9-inch prepared graham cracker crust
$1/2$ cup heavy cream
$1/4$ cup sugar
1 teaspoon vanilla extract

Heat juice in a medium saucepan over low heat.

Stir in gelatin until dissolved. Cook, stirring occasionally, until thickened, 15-20 minutes. Transfer to a medium bowl and beat with an electric mixer until fluffy.

In a blender or food processor, finely chop cranberry sauce. Add the gelatin mixture and ice cream; mix until well blended.

Transfer the blended mixture to the crust. Chill in the refrigerator for 2-3 hours.

In a medium bowl, whip together heavy cream, sugar and vanilla. To serve, top the pie with whipped cream. Makes 8 servings.

# My 4 Boys Blueberry High Pie
## Townsend Farms

**Pastry dough for 1-crust 9-inch pie**
**4 cups Townsend Farms* fresh or frozen blueberries**
**2/3 cup sugar**
**7 tablespoons cornstarch (10 if using frozen berries)**
**1/2 teaspoon ground cinnamon**
**2 tablespoons lemon juice**
**3 tablespoons water**

***TOPPING***
**1/4 cup sugar**
**1/2 cup flour**
**1/4 cup butter**

Preheat oven to 375°F.

Line a 9-inch pie pan with pastry dough.

If you're using frozen berries, sprinkle 3 tablespoons of cornstarch over the bottom of the crust before adding berries. Pour berries into the crust.

In a bowl, combine sugar, 7 tablespoons cornstarch and cinnamon; mix well. Stir in lemon juice and water. Pour over the blueberries.

To prepare the topping, mix together sugar and flour in a bowl. Cut in butter until the mixture is crumbly. Sprinkle over the pie.

Bake for 1 hour, or until the top is golden brown and the filling is bubbly. Let cool on a rack. Refrigerate when cool. Makes 8 servings.

** Brands may vary by region; substitute a similar product.*

# California Apricot Date Pie

SunDate/Blossom Hill

- Pastry dough for single-crust 9-inch pie
- 1 cup sugar
- 3 tablespoons all-purpose flour
- 2 1/2 cups halved fresh Blossom Hill* apricots
- 3/4 cup halved fresh SunDate* Medjool dates
- 1 tablespoon fresh lemon juice
- 2 tablespoons butter, cut in 1/2-inch cubes
- Heavy cream, whipped cream or ice cream, for serving (optional)

Preheat oven to 425°F.

Line a 9-inch pie pan with pastry dough, crimping the edges.

In a small bowl, combine sugar and flour.

Fill the piecrust with apricot halves and mingle date halves in random spaces between the apricots. Sprinkle with the sugar/flour mixture. Dribble lemon juice over all. Dot with butter cubes.

Place the pie on a shallow baking pan or sheet and bake for 25-35 minutes, or until the filling is bubbling and the crust is golden brown.

Serve with fresh heavy cream, whipped cream or ice cream. Makes 6 servings.

** Brands may vary by region; substitute a similar product.*

# Blueberry Cherry Yogurt Pie with Walnut Topping

Grower Direct Marketing/Victoria Island Farms

- Pastry dough for single-crust 9-inch pie
- 1 cup plain Greek yogurt
- 3/4 cup sugar
- 3 1/2 tablespoons all-purpose flour
- 1 egg plus 1 yolk, beaten to blend
- 1 teaspoon vanilla
- 1/4 teaspoon salt
- 1 1/2 cups fresh Victoria Island Farms* blueberries
- 1 cup Grower Direct* fresh sweet cherries, pitted and chopped

*TOPPING*

- 7 tablespoons all-purpose flour
- 5 tablespoons chilled unsalted butter, cut into pieces
- 3 tablespoons sugar
- 3/4 cup chopped walnuts

Preheat oven to 400°F.

Transfer pastry dough to a deep-dish 9-inch glass pie plate. Press to fit and trim as needed. Fold edges under and crimp. Line the crust with foil; fill with beans or pie weights. Bake until the sides are set, about 12 minutes. Remove foil and beans.

In a medium bowl, combine yogurt, sugar, flour, eggs, vanilla and salt; mix until blended. Stir in blueberries and cherries. Spoon into the crust. Bake until the filling is just set, about 25 minutes.

To prepare the topping, mix flour, butter and sugar in a medium bowl with your fingers until small clumps form. Mix in walnuts. Sprinkle over the pie. Bake until the topping is lightly browned, about 12 minutes.

Serve at room temperature or slightly chilled—do not serve hot. Makes 8 servings.

** Brands may vary by region; substitute a similar product.*

## Mini Apple Pies
### Sage Fruit

- **2 refrigerated piecrusts (for 9-inch pie)**
- **4 large tart Sage Fruit* apples, peeled and grated**
- **1/2 cup sugar**
- **1 teaspoon ground cinnamon**
- **1 cup rolled oats**
- **3 ounces toffee bits**

***TOPPING***

- **4 ounces cream cheese**
- **1/2 cup dark brown sugar**
- **1/2 cup granulated sugar**
- **1/2 teaspoon vanilla extract**

Preheat oven to 350°F. Grease a 12-cup muffin pan.

Cut piecrust dough into 12 equal pieces and line each muffin cup.

In a bowl, combine apples, sugar, cinnamon and oats. Fill each crust to the top with the apple mixture.

Bake for 20 minutes.

To prepare the topping, combine cream cheese, sugars and vanilla in a bowl and beat until well blended.

After 20 minutes, remove the pan from the oven and spread the topping on the mini pies. Sprinkle with toffee bits. Bake 5 minutes longer, or until the edges are golden brown. Makes 12 servings.

** Brands may vary by region; substitute a similar product.*

## Fresh Cherry Turnovers
### M&R Company

- **1 17.3-ounce package puff pastry sheets**
- **1/4 cup packed light brown sugar**
- **1/2 cup sour cream**
- **1 tablespoon cherry brandy**
- **1 1/2 pounds fresh M&R* cherries (80-85 cherries)**

Thaw puff pastry according to package directions.

Preheat oven to 400°F.

Lay each pastry sheet out on a clean, smooth surface and cut into quarters.

In a medium bowl, stir together brown sugar, sour cream and cherry brandy.

Stem, pit and cut cherries in half. Gently stir into the sour cream mixture.

Place an equal amount of the cherry mixture in the center of each piece of pastry. Fold in half to form a triangle. Seal by folding the bottom edges of the pastry over the top and pinching together.

Place on a lightly greased baking sheet and bake for 15-18 minutes, or until golden brown. Makes 8 servings.

*Recipe developed by Lindsay Tkacsik.*
** Brands may vary by region; substitute a similar product.*

## Vineyard Cobbler
### Pandol Bros., Inc.

**6 cups Pandol red seedless grapes, stemmed and rinsed**

**1/4 cup red wine**

**1/4 cup sugar**

**1 teaspoon ground cinnamon**

**2 tablespoons tapioca**

**1 teaspoon vanilla extract**

**1 1/2 tablespoons butter, melted**

***CRUST***

**1 1/3 cups flour**

**1/2 cup sugar**

**1/2 cup coarsely chopped pecans**

**1/2 cup butter, melted**

Preheat oven to 375°F.

In a large bowl, combine grapes, wine, sugar, cinnamon, tapioca and vanilla. Pour into a greased 8-by-8-inch glass baking dish. Pour melted butter evenly over the top.

To prepare the crust, combine flour, sugar and pecans in a bowl and mix well. Add melted butter and stir until crumbly and well blended. Sprinkle evenly over the fruit mixture.

Bake until the filling is bubbly and the topping is golden brown, about 30 minutes. Makes 12 servings.

**Nutritional information:** Each serving has 281 calories, 2.5 g protein, 39.7 g carbohydrates, 13.3 g fat.

*Recipe developed by Shani Hibbard, Pandol Bros. employee.*

## Three-Berry Crisp
### Kirkland Signature/Rader Farms

**3 cups Kirkland Signature/Rader Farms Nature's Three Berries (frozen red raspberries, blueberries and Marion blackberries)**

**1 teaspoon flour**

**1 tablespoon tapioca**

***TOPPING***

**3/4 cup rolled oats**

**3/4 cup packed dark brown sugar**

**1/2 cup butter, melted**

**1/2 cup flour**

**1 teaspoon ground cinnamon**

Preheat oven to 350°F. Grease an 8-by-8-inch square pan.

To prepare the topping, combine oats, brown sugar, melted butter, flour and cinnamon in a large bowl. Mix with a spoon until well blended.

In a separate bowl, stir together frozen berries, flour and tapioca. Gently pour the berries into the prepared pan.

Spread the topping evenly over the berries.

Bake on the middle oven rack for 30-35 minutes, or until the top is golden brown. Makes 6-8 servings.

*Recipe courtesy of Debbie Sklar.*

# Banana Nut Pudding Parfait

J&J Snack Foods

1 4.6-ounce package vanilla pudding
6 large bananas, sliced, divided
1/2 pinch ground nutmeg
1/2 pinch ground cinnamon
1 dozen Kirkland Signature Double Nut White Chunk Cookies
Whipped cream, for garnish

Prepare pudding according to package directions. Remove from the heat and stir in 3 sliced bananas, nutmeg and cinnamon. Let cool.

Cut 2 cookies into quarters and reserve for garnish. Coarsely crumble the remaining 10 cookies.

Layer parfait glasses with banana pudding, crushed cookies and the remaining banana slices, ending with a layer of pudding.

Garnish each serving with a dollop of whipped cream and 1/4 of a cookie.

Makes 6-8 servings.

Quick & Easy

# Yogurt Parfait
Kashi

- 1/4 cup (about 5) fresh or frozen strawberries, sliced
- 1/4 cup fresh or frozen blueberries
- 1/4 cup (about 5) fresh or frozen raspberries
- 6 ounces (or 1 small container) plain nonfat yogurt or soy yogurt
- 1 cup Kashi GOLEAN Crunch cereal
- 2 sprigs fresh mint, for garnish

In a 12-ounce parfait or sundae-style glass, alternately layer the fruit, yogurt and cereal. Repeat until you use all the ingredients.

Garnish with mint sprigs. Makes 1 serving.

**Nutritional information:** Each serving has 270 calories, 16 g protein, 53 g carbohydrates, 2.5 g fat, 0 g saturated fat, 0 mg cholesterol, 10 g fiber, 240 mg sodium.

# Chocolate Velvet Mousse
## Splenda

- 3 ounces unsweetened chocolate
- 1 cup low-fat milk
- 1/4 cup egg substitute
- 1/2 cup Splenda No Calorie Sweetener, granulated
- 1 teaspoon cornstarch
- 2 tablespoons orange liqueur (Grand Marnier, Curaçao, Triple Sec or brandy)
- 1/2 cup heavy cream
- 3 cups sliced fresh strawberries

Place chocolate and milk in a medium saucepan. Heat over medium heat until the chocolate melts. Set aside.

In a small mixing bowl, stir together egg substitute, Splenda, cornstarch and liqueur. Add to the chocolate mixture, stirring constantly. Cook over medium heat, stirring constantly, until the mixture begins to thicken (about 3-4 minutes).

Remove from the heat and pour into the bowl of a blender or food processor. Blend or process briefly (10-20 seconds) to make a creamier texture. Pour into a medium bowl and cover. Refrigerate for 2-3 hours, or until cool.

Whip cream until stiff. Fold into the chocolate mixture. Refrigerate overnight to set. This can be refrigerated for 3 days.

To serve, layer strawberries and mousse in 6 stemmed or wine glasses. Makes 6 servings.

# Tiramisu Parfaits
## Folgers

- 3/4 cup semisweet chocolate chips
- 1 14-ounce can Eagle Brand Sweetened Condensed Milk, divided
- 3/4 cup strong brewed Folgers Classic Roast Coffee, divided (see note)
- 1 3-ounce package ladyfingers (24), cut crosswise into quarters
- 1 8-ounce container mascarpone or cream cheese, softened
- 1 1/2 cups heavy cream, divided
- 1/2 teaspoon vanilla extract
- Strawberries, for garnish
- Grated semisweet chocolate, for garnish (optional)

In a microwave-safe bowl, combine chocolate chips, 1/2 cup sweetened condensed milk and 1/4 cup coffee. Microwave on high for 45-60 seconds, or until warm. Stir until smooth. Cool.

Place ladyfinger pieces in a medium bowl. Drizzle evenly with 1/4 cup coffee, 1 tablespoon at a time, tossing with a fork after each addition.

In a large bowl, beat mascarpone, 1/4 cup coffee and remaining sweetened condensed milk with an electric mixer. Add 1 cup cream and vanilla; beat until soft peaks form.

Spoon one-third of mascarpone mixture into 8 parfait glasses. Top with half of chocolate mixture and half of ladyfingers. Repeat the layers. Top with remaining mascarpone mixture.

Chill, covered, for at least 2 hours. Beat 1/2 cup cream until stiff peaks form. Top parfaits with whipped cream and strawberries. For a special touch, garnish with grated chocolate. Makes 8 servings.

**Note:** To make strong brewed coffee, use 1/4 cup ground coffee for each 1 1/2 cups water. To substitute Folgers Instant Coffee Crystals, combine 1 tablespoon coffee crystals and 3/4 cup boiling water.

## A Summer's Dream Kiwi and Grape Trifle

### Trucco/Castle Rock Vineyards

- **2 3.4-ounce packages instant vanilla pudding**
- **8 Trucco* Italian kiwifruit, peeled and sliced**
- **24 ounces pound cake, cut into 1/2-inch cubes**
- **2 pounds Castle Rock Vineyards* red seedless grapes, washed and stemmed**
- **2 8-ounce cans crushed pineapple, well drained**
- **1 ripe banana, sliced**
- **16 ounces frozen whipped topping, thawed**

Prepare the pudding according to package directions and place in the refrigerator.

In a large glass bowl, put a layer of kiwifruit slices along the bottom edge of the bowl.

Place 4 cups pound cake cubes in the center of the bowl.

Place a single row of grapes along the sides of the bowl on top of the kiwifruit.

Fill the center of the bowl with grapes.

Add a layer of pineapple, a layer of vanilla pudding, a layer of sliced bananas and then a layer of whipped topping.

Repeat the layers, beginning with kiwifruit slices placed along the sides of the bowl and ending with whipped topping. Use any remaining kiwifruit and grapes as a garnish.

Refrigerate for 4 hours before serving.

Makes 10-12 servings.

** Brands may vary by region; substitute a similar product.*

## Zabaione with Sugared Cherries

### Morada Produce

- **28 Morada Produce* Bing cherries, divided**
- **4 tablespoons sugar, divided**
- **2 teaspoons water**
- **4 large egg yolks**
- **2 tablespoons cherry brandy**
- **1 teaspoon fresh lemon juice**
- **Pinch of salt**

Rinse 12 cherries with retained stems, do not dry, and coat in 1 tablespoon sugar. Set aside.

Pit and chop the remaining cherries. Place in a small skillet over medium heat and cook for about 5 minutes. Strain the cherries to obtain 1 tablespoon juice.

To make the zabaione—a light Italian custard—combine the cherry juice, remaining 3 tablespoons sugar, water, egg yolks, brandy, lemon juice and salt in a large metal bowl. Beat with a handheld mixer until the mixture has a foamy texture. Then set the bowl over a saucepan of barely simmering water and beat at medium-high speed until the mixture has doubled in volume and forms a thick ribbon when the beaters are lifted, about 12 minutes. Remove from the heat and whisk for a couple of minutes. Let cool for 10 minutes.

Divide the warm chopped cooked cherries among 4 glasses. Spoon the zabaione over the top. Garnish with the sugared cherries and serve warm.

Makes 4 servings.

** Brands may vary by region; substitute a similar product.*

# Sautéed Nectarines and Coconut Panna Cotta

Aconex

6 medium nectarines, halved, pitted, each cut into 6 wedges
2 tablespoons sugar
2 tablespoons orange juice
1/2 teaspoon grated orange peel
Toasted coconut (optional)

*PANNA COTTA*
2 tablespoons cold water
1 envelope unflavored gelatin (about 1 tablespoon)
2 cups heavy cream
1 cup coconut milk
1/3 cup sugar
1 vanilla bean, split lengthwise
1 teaspoon coconut extract

To prepare the panna cotta, place water in a very small saucepan. Sprinkle with gelatin and let stand about 1 minute to soften. Heat over low heat until the gelatin is dissolved, then remove from the heat.

In a large saucepan, combine cream, coconut milk and sugar. Scrape vanilla bean seeds into the pan; add the bean pod. Bring to a boil over medium-high heat, stirring. Remove from the heat and stir in the gelatin mixture and coconut extract. Remove the vanilla bean pod. Spoon into eight 1/2-cup ramekins. Let cool to room temperature. Chill the ramekins, covered, at least 4 hours or overnight.

Place nectarines in a large sauté pan and sprinkle with sugar. Cook, stirring, over medium heat. When the sugar is caramelized, add orange juice and peel, toss well and remove from the heat.

Dip the ramekins, one at a time, into a bowl of hot water for 3 seconds. Run a thin knife around the edge of each ramekin and invert onto the center of a small plate. Serve the panna cotta with sautéed nectarines. Top with toasted coconut, if desired. Makes 8 servings.

## Cuties Ginger Bites

Sun Pacific

**8 ounces spreadable cream cheese**

**1/4 cup sugar**

**1/3 cup minced crystallized ginger**

**4 fresh Cuties* clementines, peeled and separated into segments**

**Thinly sliced fresh Cuties clementine peel, for garnish**

In a small bowl, stir together cream cheese, sugar and ginger.

Spread about 1 1/2 teaspoons of the cream cheese mixture on each Cutie segment.

Arrange on a serving plate. Garnish with peel. Makes about 44 pieces.

** Brands may vary by region; substitute a similar product.*

## Fruit Juice Gelatin Cutouts

Apple & Eve

**1 ounce unflavored gelatin**

**1/4 cup honey**

**6 Apple & Eve* Fruitables Berry Berry juice boxes**

**16 ounces strawberries, sliced**

**6 ounces raspberries**

**6 ounces blackberries**

In a large bowl, mix gelatin and honey with the juice from 2 juice boxes.

Pour the juice from the remaining 4 juice boxes into a saucepan and bring to a boil. Pour into the gelatin mixture and stir until dissolved. Let cool.

Arrange berries on the bottom of a 13-by-9-inch pan. Pour the gelatin mixture over the berries. Chill until firm.

Cut into fun shapes with cookie cutters. Makes 6-8 servings.

**Tip:** Substitute any flavor of Apple & Eve Fruitables juice boxes and their respective fruits, such as mandarin oranges, sliced pineapple or diced apples.

** Brands may vary by region; substitute a similar product.*

# Churro Dessert Kabobs

## J&J Snack Foods

**Toothpicks**

**1 pint large fresh strawberries with leaves**

**8 large marshmallows**

**5 ounces milk chocolate chips**

**2 teaspoons shortening**

**Small block of Styrofoam**

**2 Double Twisted Churros,* cut into 2-inch pieces**

**4 long wooden skewers**

Insert toothpicks into the tops of the strawberries and marshmallows.

In a double boiler, melt chocolate chips and shortening, stirring occasionally, until smooth.

Holding them by the toothpicks, dip the strawberries and marshmallows into the chocolate mixture.

Turn the strawberries and marshmallows upside down and insert the toothpick into the Styrofoam while the chocolate cools and hardens.

To assemble the kabobs, thread churros pieces, strawberries and marshmallows onto the skewers. Makes 4 servings.

** Churros are available at the Food Court or in the freezer case at some Costcos.*

## Baked Apple Dumplings with Maple Caramel Sauce

### Columbia Marketing International

**4 CMI* Granny Smith apples (or other tart baking apple)**
**4 teaspoons unsalted butter**
**1/2 cup pure maple syrup, divided**
**2 tablespoons golden raisins**
**2 tablespoons brown sugar**
**2 tablespoons chopped pecans**
**2 packages refrigerated pie dough (4 crusts)**
**7 whole cloves, divided**
**1 egg white**
**1/2 teaspoon water**
**1/3 cup dry white wine**
**1-inch-thick slice fresh ginger**
**1 cinnamon stick**
**Whipped cream or vanilla ice cream, for serving**

Preheat oven to 375°F.

Peel and core apples from the stem side with a melon baller, leaving about 1/4 inch at the bottom (do not go all the way through). Make a few vertical cuts with a paring knife inside the core area.

Place a teaspoon of butter and a teaspoon of maple syrup inside each apple.

Mix together raisins, brown sugar and pecans; stuff equally into the apples.

Cut each piece of pie dough into a 7-inch square. Place apples on dough and bring the dough up over the top, pressing to shape, crimping and sealing all edges.

Cut out leaf shapes from the remaining dough. Use a paring knife to score the leaves and create veins. Attach leaves to the top of each wrapped apple and place a whole clove on each for a stem.

Place the dumplings in a shallow baking pan. Whisk egg white with water; brush over the dumplings. Place the remaining maple syrup, wine, ginger, 3 cloves and cinnamon stick in the pan. Bake for 30-40 minutes, or until the dumplings' crust is golden brown.

Brush the dumplings with sauce from the pan. Serve with whipped cream or ice cream. Makes 4 servings.

*Recipe courtesy of Chef David Toal of Ravenous Catering, Wenatchee, Washington.*
** Brands may vary by region; substitute a similar product.*

## Medjool Date Triangles

### AMC Direct

**2 cups roughly chopped Fancy Medjool Dates**
**Grated peel and juice of 1 lemon**
**1 heaping tablespoon brown sugar**
**1 8-ounce sheet puff pastry**
**1 egg, beaten**
**Confectioners' sugar**

Preheat oven to 375°F.

In a bowl, combine dates, grated lemon peel, lemon juice and brown sugar; mix to blend.

Cut pastry into 3 strips roughly 4 inches wide and then into 4-inch squares. Place a small amount of the date mixture on each square. Brush the edges with the beaten egg. Fold into triangles and seal the edges, then brush additional egg over the triangles as a glaze.

Place the triangles on a baking sheet. Bake for 15 minutes, or until golden.

Dust with confectioners' sugar. Serve warm. Makes 9 servings.

## Grape Parfait Ring
Four Star Fruit

- **1 pint heavy cream**
- **1 teaspoon lemon extract**
- **1 cup pasteurized egg product**
- **3/4 cup sugar**
- **1/3 cup white grape juice**
- **3 cups Four Star Fruit* green, black or red seedless grapes, rinsed and halved**

In a large bowl, whip cream and lemon extract until fluffy. Set aside.

In a separate bowl, beat pasteurized egg product until medium-soft peaks form.

In a small saucepan, combine sugar and grape juice. Bring to a boil and cook for 2 minutes, stirring constantly. Cool the syrup for 1 minute. With the mixer running, slowly add the syrup to the eggs; beat on high for 1 minute.

Fold the egg mixture into the whipped cream.

Spoon the filling into a 9-inch or larger savarin (ring) mold; smooth the top. Cover with plastic wrap and freeze until solid (about an hour).

Remove from the mold and fill the center with grapes. Serve immediately. Makes 8-10 servings.

*Recipe developed by Kati Neville.*
** Brands may vary by region; substitute a similar product.*

## Grapefruit Alaska
Greene River Marketing/Tropicana

- **4 large Tropicana* red grapefruits**
- **2 teaspoons dark rum**
- **1/2 cup heavy cream, whipped**
- **3 egg whites**
- **1 teaspoon cornstarch**
- **1/4 teaspoon cream of tartar**
- **1/4 cup sugar**
- **8 cherries, for topping**

Preheat oven to 350°F.

Cut grapefruits in half horizontally and remove the sections. Remove the membranes. Return the grapefruit sections to the grapefruit halves. Drizzle with rum. Spread 1 tablespoon of whipped cream over each grapefruit. Place on a foil-lined baking sheet.

In a large mixing bowl, beat egg whites, cornstarch and cream of tartar on medium speed until soft peaks form. Gradually beat in sugar, 1 tablespoon at a time, on high until stiff peaks form and the sugar is dissolved. Mound 1/2 cup on each grapefruit half, spreading to the edges to seal.

Bake for 15 minutes, or until the meringue is golden brown. Top with cherries. Serve immediately. Makes 8 servings.

** Brands may vary by region; substitute a similar product.*

# Bananas Foster Bread Pudding

## Panné Provincio

- 1 Panné Provincio* French baguette, cut into 1-inch pieces
- 1/2 cup golden raisins
- 1/2 cup dark rum
- 4 large eggs
- 1 cup granulated sugar
- 3 cups whole milk
- 1 cup heavy cream
- 1 tablespoon vanilla extract
- 1 teaspoon ground cinnamon
- Nonstick cooking spray

*SAUCE*

- 6 tablespoons butter
- 1/3 cup light brown sugar (not packed)
- 1/2 cup dark rum
- 4 firm bananas, peeled and sliced

Preheat oven to 400°F.

Spread bread pieces in a single layer on a baking sheet. Bake for 14-16 minutes, or until crisp and lightly golden. Remove from the oven and let cool completely. Place bread pieces in an extra-large bowl; set aside.

In a small microwave-safe bowl, combine raisins and rum. Microwave on high for 1-2 minutes, or until bubbly. Let stand for 20 minutes.

In a large bowl, whisk eggs and granulated sugar. Whisk in milk, cream, vanilla and cinnamon.

Add the raisins to the bread pieces. Pour the milk mixture over the top. Gently mix to combine. Cover and refrigerate at least 8 hours or overnight.

Preheat oven to 350°F. Lightly spray a 13-inch oval baker with cooking spray.

Spoon the bread mixture into the baker; pour any remaining liquid over the top. Bake for 45-50 minutes, or until just golden brown. Remove from the oven and set aside.

To prepare the sauce, melt butter in a large skillet over medium heat. Add brown sugar and cook for 2-3 minutes, until the sugar dissolves. Stir in rum, then add bananas. Cook for 2 minutes, stirring occasionally. Gently tip the pan away from you and carefully ignite the rum. Shake the pan gently back and forth until the flame subsides.

Spoon the pudding into dessert bowls. Top with bananas and sauce. Serve warm. Makes 10 servings.

**Tip:** If the pudding begins to brown during baking, place a piece of foil over the top.

** Brands may vary by region; substitute a similar product.*

## Banana Nut Bread Pudding

Dawn Food Products

- 2 Kirkland Signature banana nut muffins
- 1/2 cup sugar
- 1/2 cup whole milk
- 1 cup heavy cream
- 3 large eggs
- 1/2 teaspoon ground cinnamon
- 1/2 teaspoon vanilla extract
- 1 medium banana, mashed

Cut muffins into bite-size pieces; set aside.

In a medium mixing bowl, combine sugar, milk, cream, eggs, cinnamon and vanilla. Add banana and mix until well blended.

Add muffin pieces to the mixture and fold in, making sure everything is evenly moistened.

Cover and let soak for 1 hour in the refrigerator.

Preheat oven to 325°F. Grease six 4-ounce ramekins; place on a baking sheet.

After 1 hour, give the pudding mixture a stir and divide evenly among the ramekins.

Bake until golden brown, 35-40 minutes. Makes 6 servings.

## Fig Napoleons

Stellar Distributing/Earth Source Trading

- Half of a 17.3-ounce package puff pastry sheets (1 sheet)
- 6-8 ounces mascarpone cheese
- 2 tablespoons honey
- 2 cups Stellar Distributing fresh figs (or 6 ounces dried figs), diced into 1/4- to 1/2-inch pieces, plus 2 figs, sliced, for garnish
- 1 cup whipped dessert topping
- 1 tablespoon butter, melted
- Juice and grated peel of 1 Earth Source Trading lime
- 1/2 cup confectioners' sugar

Thaw puff pastry at room temperature for 40 minutes, or until it's easy to handle.

Preheat oven to 400°F.

Unfold pastry on a lightly floured surface. Cut into 3 strips along fold marks. Cut each strip into 2 rectangles and place 2 inches apart on a baking sheet. Bake for 15 minutes, or until golden brown. Remove from the baking sheet and cool on a wire rack.

Beat together mascarpone and honey until fluffy. Gently stir in diced figs and whipped topping.

In a small bowl, mix melted butter, lime juice and confectioners' sugar for the glaze.

Split each pastry into 2 layers. Divide and spread the fig mixture on 6 bottom pastry layers. Add the top layers and a slice of fig. Drizzle the glaze over all and sprinkle with lime zest. Makes 6 servings.

**Tip:** You can substitute 6 ounces of soft cream cheese, mixed with 2 tablespoons milk or cream, for the mascarpone.

*Recipe developed by Christine W. Jackson, food stylist.*

## Blueberry, Blackberry and Mango Dessert with Mascarpone Cream

Alpine Fresh

- **2 cups Alpine Fresh* blueberries**
- **2 cups Alpine Fresh* blackberries**
- **1 pound Alpine Fresh* fresh-cut mango, cut into small cubes (or about 4 Alpine Fresh* mangoes, peeled and cubed)**
- **1/4 cup sugar**
- **Grated peel and juice of 1 large lemon**
- **1/2 cup fresh orange juice**
- **1/2 teaspoon almond extract**
- **8 ounces mascarpone cheese (or whipped cream cheese)**
- **1 tablespoon honey or agave nectar**
- **1/3 cup heavy cream**
- **1 teaspoon vanilla extract**
- **1/2 vanilla bean**

Rinse and drain berries. Combine with mango cubes in a large bowl.

In a small bowl, whisk together sugar, lemon juice, orange juice and almond extract. Pour over the fruit and gently toss.

Beat together mascarpone and honey. Add heavy cream and vanilla. Scrape in seeds from vanilla bean. Blend until smooth.

Serve the fruit mixture in bowls. Place a dollop of the mascarpone cream on each serving and garnish with grated lemon peel. Makes 8 servings.

**Tip:** You can serve the fruit over slices of pound cake for a decadent twist.

*Recipe developed by Christine W. Jackson, food stylist.*
** Brands may vary by region; substitute a similar product.*

## Colleen's Fruit Sauce

Kingsburg Orchards

- **1 1/2 cups sugar**
- **6 tablespoons flour**
- **4 cups apricot nectar (see note)**
- **3 large or extra-large eggs, well beaten**
- **3 tablespoons butter**
- **1-1 1/2 cups whipped cream**
- **Kingsburg Orchards* pluots, yellow peaches and/or white nectarines, pitted and sliced**

In a saucepan, combine sugar, flour, apricot nectar and eggs; whisk to blend well. Cook over medium heat, whisking constantly, until it thickens. Add butter and stir until blended. Let cool.

Fold in whipped cream.

Serve with pluots, peaches and/or nectarines. Makes 6 servings.

**Tip:** For a thicker or thinner sauce, vary the amount of apricot nectar from 3 to 5 cups.

** Brands may vary by region; substitute a similar product.*

# Summer Berry Sundaes

Andrew & Williamson/Curry & Company/ SunnyRidge

**2 cups strawberries, divided**
**3/4 cup raspberries, divided**
**3/4 cup blackberries, divided**
**3/4 cup blueberries, divided**
**3 tablespoons sugar**
**1 teaspoon lemon juice**
**3 cups vanilla ice cream (or nonfat vanilla frozen yogurt)**

Wash and stem berries.

In a blender, puree 1 1/2 cups strawberries, 1/2 cup raspberries, 1/2 cup blackberries and 1/2 cup blueberries with sugar and lemon juice.

To prepare the garnish, slice the remaining strawberries in half and mix with the remaining raspberries, blackberries and blueberries.

Serve the puree over the ice cream and garnish with the fresh berry mix. Makes 4-6 servings.

Quick & Easy

Andrew & Williamson Fresh Produce
SunnyRidge
Curry & Company

# Family-Style Fresh Fruit Sundae

BakeMark USA

- 8 ounces whipping cream, plus more for garnish
- 6 ounces strawberry or blueberry yogurt
- 1 Kirkland Signature Butter Pound Cake
- 8-10 strawberries, plus more for garnish
- 4 ounces blueberries

*GLAZE*

- 1/2 cup sugar
- 1 1/4 cups water, divided
- 2 teaspoons cornstarch
- 2 teaspoons pure vanilla extract

To prepare the glaze, combine sugar and 1 cup water in a saucepan. Bring to a boil, then remove from the heat. Add cornstarch to 1/4 cup water and stir until completely dissolved. Add to the saucepan, return to the heat and bring to a full boil. Remove from the heat and stir in vanilla. Let cool.

Whip cream until stiff peaks form. Add yogurt and stir until well blended.

Slice cake into 8 even slices. Place 4 slices in the bottom of a deep 8-inch glass bowl. Spoon a generous amount of glaze over the slices.

Slice 4-5 strawberries in half, dip in the glaze and place against the sides of the bowl with the cut side showing.

Place half of the yogurt filling over the pound cake slices and sprinkle with blueberries.

Repeat with another layer of pound cake, glaze strawberries, yogurt filling and blueberries.

Decorate with whole strawberries and blueberries dipped in glaze and whipped cream.
Makes 10-12 servings.

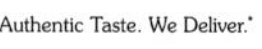


# Milk Chocolate Caramel Macadamia Ice Cream

Kirkland Signature

- 1 64-ounce tub Kirkland Signature premium vanilla ice cream
- 2 cups finely chopped Kirkland Signature Milk Chocolate Salted Caramel Macadamia Clusters

Place a 4-quart bowl in the freezer for 2 hours.

Remove ice cream from the freezer and let soften at room temperature for 15 minutes.

Remove the bowl from the freezer and empty the softened ice cream into it.

Pour chopped macadamia clusters over the ice cream. Using 2 large spoons, quickly blend the ingredients.

Spoon the ice cream mixture back into the original tub, replace the lid and freeze overnight. (Place any extra mixture in another container.) Makes 18 servings.

**Tip:** When softening the ice cream for blending, do not let it melt excessively. It should still be soft-frozen when you are mixing it with the chopped macadamia clusters.

# Peach Ice Cream
## Trinity Fruit

12 fresh Trinity* peaches
2 1/2 cups sugar
1 tablespoon vanilla extract
1 quart half-and-half
1/2 pint whipping cream

*TOPPING*
4 cups peeled, sliced Trinity peaches
1 cup sugar
2 tablespoons peach schnapps

Peel peaches and remove the pits. Mash the fruit thoroughly.

In a bowl, combine mashed peaches, sugar and vanilla; stir to blend. Pour into an ice cream maker. Add half-and-half and whipping cream. Process according to manufacturer's instructions.

To prepare the topping, combine all ingredients in a saucepan. Cook over medium heat until the peaches are soft.

Serve the ice cream with a spoonful of warm peach topping, if desired. Makes 8 servings.

*Ice cream recipe created by Donna Shebelut; topping recipe created by Bobby Minas.*
** Brands may vary by region; substitute a similar product.*

# Spicy Plum Compote and Ice Cream Cake

Aconex

**2 pounds red-skinned plums, halved, pitted, each cut into 6 wedges**
**1 1/2 cups carménère or merlot wine**
**1 1/2 cups water**
**1 1/4 cups sugar**
**1 vanilla bean, split lengthwise**
**1 teaspoon pink peppercorns**
**Grated peel of 1 orange**
**3/4 pound plain sponge cake**
**2 pints vanilla ice cream, softened**
**2 tablespoons confectioners' sugar**

Place plums in a large bowl.

In a large saucepan, combine wine, water and sugar. Scrape in seeds from vanilla bean; add the pod, pink peppercorns and grated orange peel. Stir over medium heat until the sugar dissolves. Increase the heat and boil until reduced to 2 2/3 cups, about 20 minutes. Pour the hot wine mixture over the plums. Let cool. Cover and chill for 2 hours.

Line a 9-inch square cake pan with plastic wrap. Cut sponge cake into thin slices and use half of the slices to line the bottom of the pan. Patch it where you must, but try to keep the slices as large as possible.

Strain the compote through a colander and reserve the juices. Scatter half of the compote over the cake, then spoon the ice cream on top, pushing it to the corners. Smooth the top and then add the remaining compote. Cover with the remaining slices of cake. Press down to compress the fruit and ice cream.

Cover tightly with plastic wrap and freeze for a good hour. Remove the cake from the freezer 30 minutes before serving.

To serve, remove the cake from the pan, dust with confectioners' sugar and slice with a large knife. Serve with the reserved compote juices. Makes 6-8 servings.

**Tip:** The cake will keep in the freezer for up to a week. Once it is frozen, remove it from the pan and wrap in plastic freezer wrap and then foil.

## Raspberry-Infused Tiramisu with Madeleines

Sugar Bowl Bakery

- **6 egg yolks**
- **3/4 -1 cup sugar**
- **3 ounces sweet Marsala or Grand Marnier (optional)**
- **9 1/2 ounces mascarpone cheese, softened**
- **8 ounces cream cheese, softened**
- **3 tablespoons raspberry preserves, preferably seedless**
- **2 1/3 cups heavy whipping cream**
- **1 1/2 teaspoons vanilla extract**
- **1 28-ounce tub Sugar Bowl Bakery* Madeleines (about 32 pieces)**
- **1/4 cup Torani coffee syrup**
- **Cocoa powder and cinnamon, for garnish**

Combine egg yolks, sugar and liqueur in a bowl. Set over a pan of simmering water and whip until thick and light (140°F). Remove from the heat and whip until cool over an ice-water bath.

Fold in mascarpone, cream cheese and raspberry preserves.

Whip cream to soft peaks; add vanilla. Fold into the mascarpone mixture.

To assemble, place 16 Madeleines in the bottom of an 8-by-8-inch pan. Brush with coffee syrup. Top with half of the mascarpone mixture, spreading evenly.

Top with the remaining 16 Madeleines. Brush with coffee syrup. Spread with a layer of the remaining mascarpone mixture.

Refrigerate until set, at least 3-4 hours, preferably overnight. Top with cocoa powder and cinnamon. Makes 15 servings.

** Brands may vary by region; substitute a similar product.*

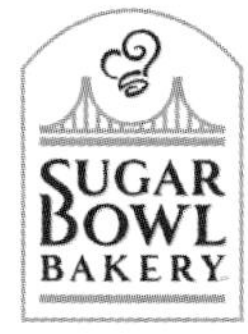


## Croissant Amandine

Vie de France

- **1/4 teaspoon butter, softened**
- **1/2 teaspoon almond paste**
- **1 large Vie de France* butter croissant**
- **1/4 teaspoon granulated sugar**
- **1/2 teaspoon slivered almonds**
- **1/8 teaspoon confectioners' sugar**
- **Vanilla bean ice cream, for serving**

Preheat oven to 350°F.

Blend butter and almond paste until smooth.

Slice croissant in half horizontally and spread the almond paste mixture on both sides.

Sprinkle with granulated sugar and put the croissant halves back together. Place slivered almonds on top.

Heat the croissant in the oven for 2-3 minutes. Sprinkle with confectioners' sugar and serve warm with a scoop of ice cream. Makes 1 serving.

** Brands may vary by region; substitute a similar product.*

# Chocolate Chip Tiramisu

Kirkland Signature

- 6 cups mascarpone cheese
- 1 cup confectioners' sugar, divided
- 2 teaspoons Grand Marnier
- 24 chocolate chip cookies (3-inch diameter)
- 1 cup strong brewed coffee
- 1 quart heavy whipping cream
- 18 ladyfingers, cut in half diagonally
- 3 tablespoons Kirkland Signature Saigon Cinnamon
- Shaved chocolate curls, for garnish

Line a 12-by-10-inch pan with parchment paper.

In a bowl, combine mascarpone, 3/4 cup confectioners' sugar and Grand Marnier. Whisk to blend well. Spread a 1/2-inch layer of mascarpone in the pan.

Dip chocolate chip cookies in coffee for up to 15 seconds. Place a layer of the cookies on the mascarpone. Repeat with 2 more layers of mascarpone and cookies, for a total of 6 layers.

Cover and freeze until stiff.

In a bowl, combine whipping cream and 1/4 cup confectioners' sugar. Whisk until medium peaks form.

Tip the frozen pan onto a flat surface. Spread the whipped cream over the top and sides of the tiramisu.

Evenly place ladyfingers, pointing up, around the perimeter of the tiramisu. Dust the top evenly with cinnamon. Garnish with chocolate curls. Serve chilled. Makes 15 servings.

## Orange Crumb Cake
Tropicana

**1 cup all-purpose flour**
**1/2 cup sugar**
**4 tablespoons butter, at room temperature**
**1 teaspoon ground cinnamon**
**1 teaspoon baking powder**
**Dash of salt**
**1 large egg**
**1/2 cup Tropicana* orange juice**
**1 teaspoon finely grated orange peel**

Preheat oven to 350°F. Grease and flour an 8-inch square baking pan.

In a bowl, combine flour, sugar and butter with a pastry blender or fork until the mixture resembles meal.

Measure 1/2 cup of the crumb mixture and move to a separate cup or bowl. Blend in the cinnamon. Set aside.

To the main crumb mixture add baking powder and salt; blend well.

Beat egg with orange juice until well blended. Stir with grated orange peel into the crumb mixture just until the dry ingredients are moistened.

Pour the batter into the prepared pan. Sprinkle the reserved cinnamon-crumb mixture over the batter. Bake for 20-25 minutes, or until a toothpick or cake tester inserted in the center comes out clean. Makes 8 servings.

** Brands may vary by region; substitute a similar product.*

Tropicana

## Quick Fresh Fruit Upside-Down Cake
Unifrutti of America

**2 tablespoons butter**
**Flour**
**1 9-ounce package single-layer yellow cake mix**
**2 cups mixed Chilean* fresh fruit (such as halved grapes, blueberries, sliced nectarines and peaches)**
**1/4 cup apricot preserves or red currant jelly, melted, divided**
**Whipped cream or ice cream, for serving (optional)**

Preheat oven to 350°F.

Spread butter evenly over the bottom of a round 8-inch cake pan; dust with flour.

Prepare the cake batter according to package directions.

Arrange fruit decoratively in the prepared pan. Drizzle with 2 tablespoons of the melted preserves. Spoon the cake batter evenly over the fruit. Tap the pan on the counter to distribute the batter evenly.

Bake until the center of the cake springs back when gently pressed, about 35 minutes. Cool the cake in the pan on a rack for 10 minutes. Loosen the edges and invert onto a serving plate.

Heat the remaining preserves; drizzle over the cake. Serve with whipped cream or ice cream, if desired. Makes 8 servings.

** Brands may vary by region; substitute a similar product.*

## Amazing Carrot Cake
### Kirkland Signature/Bolthouse Farms

- 4 large eggs
- 1 1/2 cups granulated sugar
- 1/2 cup packed light brown sugar
- 3/4 cup vegetable oil
- 3/4 cup Kirkland Signature* Organic 100% Carrot Juice Organic
- 1 teaspoon vanilla extract
- 2 cups flour
- 1 teaspoon baking powder
- 1 teaspoon baking soda
- 1 tablespoon ground cinnamon
- 1/2 teaspoon ground ginger
- 1/2 teaspoon salt
- 3 cups shredded carrots
- 1 cup walnuts, chopped

*CREAM CHEESE ICING*

- 8 ounces cream cheese, softened
- 1/4 cup butter, softened
- 1 teaspoon vanilla extract
- 1 pound confectioners' sugar

Preheat oven to 350°F. Grease a 13-by-9-inch pan.

In a large mixing bowl, beat eggs until frothy. Add granulated sugar and brown sugar gradually, beating until well blended. Add oil, juice and vanilla; beat until blended.

In another bowl, sift together flour, baking powder, baking soda, cinnamon, ginger and salt; add to the egg mixture and beat just until blended. Stir in carrots and walnuts.

Pour the mixture into the prepared pan. Bake for 50 minutes, or until a toothpick inserted in the center comes out clean. Let cool on a rack.

To prepare the icing, beat cream cheese, butter and vanilla until smooth. Gradually add sugar, beating until smooth. Spread on the cooled cake.

Makes 12-15 servings.

** Brands may vary by region; substitute a similar product.*

## Upside-Down Mango Ginger Cake
### Ready Pac

- 1 32-ounce package Ready Pac* mango
- 2 tablespoons frozen orange juice concentrate, thawed
- 2 teaspoons fresh lime juice
- 3 tablespoons butter
- 1/4 cup packed brown sugar
- 1 14 1/2-ounce package gingerbread mix
- 1 cup water
- 1 egg

Preheat oven to 350°F.

In a large bowl, combine 12-15 mango slices, orange juice concentrate and lime juice. Toss to mix and let stand for 10 minutes.

Place butter in a 9-by-2-inch round cake pan. Set the pan in the oven until the butter has melted. Remove from the oven and sprinkle brown sugar over the butter.

Arrange the mango slices in an attractive pattern over the sugar.

Prepare gingerbread according to package directions, using the water and egg. Pour the batter over the mangoes.

Bake for 35-40 minutes, or until a wooden toothpick inserted in the center comes out clean. Let cool for 5 minutes, then invert on a platter.

To serve, cut the cake in wedges. Serve warm or at room temperature. Makes 8 servings.

** Brands may vary by region; substitute a similar product.*

## Rum Cake with Granola Streusel
CSM Bakery Products

- 1 18 1/2-ounce package yellow cake mix
- 1 3.4-ounce package instant vanilla pudding
- 4 eggs
- 1/2 cup cold water
- 1/2 cup vegetable oil
- 1/2 cup light or dark rum
- 1 cup coarsely chopped Kirkland Signature granola snack mix
- Sweetened whipped cream, for serving

Preheat oven to 325°F. Grease and lightly flour a 10-inch tube or 12-cup springform pan.

In a large bowl, combine cake mix, pudding mix, eggs, water, oil and rum. Beat until well blended.

Pour half of the batter into the prepared pan. Sprinkle with granola. Pour the remaining batter over the granola streusel.

Bake for 1 hour, or until a tester inserted in the center comes out clean. Let cool in the pan on a wire rack.

Serve with a dollop of whipped cream. Makes 12-16 servings.

Bakery Products NA

# Old-Fashioned Coffee Pound Cake

## Starbucks Coffee

**4 cups flour**

**1 1/2 teaspoons Calumet baking powder**

**1 teaspoon salt**

**1 teaspoon ground cinnamon**

**2 cups (4 sticks) butter, softened**

**2 1/2 cups granulated sugar**

**7 large eggs**

**1 cup strong freshly brewed Starbucks coffee, cooled**

**2 tablespoons confectioners' sugar**

Preheat oven to 350°F. Grease a 10-inch tube pan or 12-cup fluted tube pan.

In a bowl, mix flour, baking powder, salt and cinnamon until well blended; set aside.

Beat butter and granulated sugar in a large bowl with an electric mixer on medium speed until light and fluffy. Add eggs one at a time, beating well after each addition. Add the flour mixture alternately with the coffee, beating until well blended after each addition.

Pour into the prepared pan.

Bake for 90 minutes, or until a toothpick inserted near the center comes out clean. Let cool for 10 minutes. Loosen the cake from the sides and gently remove from the pan. Let cool completely on a wire rack.

Sprinkle with confectioners' sugar. Makes 20 servings.

## Fruity Chocolate Shortcake
Dole

- **2 $1/2$ cups biscuit mix**
- **$1/2$ cup granulated sugar**
- **$1/3$ cup cocoa powder**
- **1 cup milk**
- **1 medium Dole* banana, mashed ($1/3$ cup)**
- **3 tablespoons butter or margarine, melted**
- **3 cups Dole* mangoes, bananas or fresh Tropical Gold* pineapple chunks**
- **2 tablespoons packed brown sugar**
- **1 8-ounce tub frozen nondairy whipped topping, thawed**

Preheat oven to 425°F. Grease two 8-inch round cake pans.

In a bowl, stir together biscuit mix, granulated sugar and cocoa powder. Stir in milk, mashed banana and melted butter until the mixture is well combined.

Pour the batter into the prepared pans. Bake for 12-14 minutes, or until a wooden pick inserted in the center comes out clean. Let cool for 5 minutes. Carefully remove the cake from the pans; let cool on racks.

In a bowl, stir together fresh fruit and brown sugar.

Place 1 shortcake layer on a serving plate. Spread half of the whipped topping over the cake layer. Spoon half of the fruit mixture over the topping. Top with the second cake layer. Repeat with the remaining whipped topping and fruit.

Serve immediately, or refrigerate for up to 1 hour. Makes 8 servings.

**Nutritional information:** Each serving has 404 calories, 5 g protein, 59 g carbohydrates, 17 g fat, 10 g saturated fat, 16 mg cholesterol, 552 mg sodium.

** Brands may vary by region; substitute a similar product.*

## Chocolate Syrup Swirl Cake
The Hershey Company

- **1 cup (2 sticks) butter or margarine, softened**
- **2 cups sugar**
- **2 teaspoons vanilla extract**
- **3 large eggs**
- **2 $3/4$ cups all-purpose flour**
- **1 $1/4$ teaspoons baking soda, divided**
- **$1/2$ teaspoon salt**
- **1 cup buttermilk or sour milk (see note)**
- **1 cup Hershey's Syrup**
- **1 cup sweetened coconut flakes (optional)**

Preheat oven to 350°F. Grease and flour a 12-cup fluted tube pan or 10-inch tube pan.

Combine butter, sugar and vanilla in a large bowl; beat until fluffy. Add eggs and beat well.

Stir together flour, 1 teaspoon baking soda and salt. Add alternately with buttermilk to the butter mixture, beating until well blended.

Measure 2 cups batter into a small bowl; stir in syrup and remaining $1/4$ teaspoon baking soda. Add coconut, if desired, to the remaining vanilla batter; pour into the prepared pan. Pour the chocolate batter over the vanilla batter in the pan; do not mix.

Bake for 60-70 minutes, or until a wooden pick inserted in the center comes out clean. Cool for 15 minutes, then remove from the pan to a wire rack. Let cool completely; glaze or frost as desired. Makes 20 servings.

**Note:** To make sour milk, use 1 tablespoon white vinegar plus milk to equal 1 cup.

# Oreo Cake
## Kirkland Signature

**Kirkland Signature filled chocolate cake with buttercream icing**
**2 Oreo cookies**
**1 tablespoon Hershey's chocolate syrup**
**Dollop of whipped cream**
**1 cherry**

Cut a 2-by-6-inch wedge from the cake.

Crush 1 Oreo cookie and sprinkle over the top of the cake.

Garnish with chocolate syrup.

Place a dollop of whipped cream beside the cake, top with the cherry and place the whole cookie on the side. Makes 1 serving.

# Double Chocolate Peanut Butter Supreme Dessert
## Jif

**Crisco Original No-Stick Cooking Spray**
**1 15.9-ounce package Pillsbury Supreme Chocolate Extreme Premium Brownie Mix**
**1/3 cup Crisco Pure Vegetable Oil**
**3 tablespoons water**
**1 large egg**
**1 cup Jif* Creamy Peanut Butter**
**1/2 teaspoon vanilla extract**
**1 cup confectioners' sugar**
**2 tablespoons Smucker's Hot Fudge Topping**

Preheat oven to 350°F. Coat an 8-inch springform pan with no-stick cooking spray.

Prepare brownie mix according to package directions, using the packet of chocolate-flavored syrup, oil, water and egg. Spread into the prepared pan. Bake for 34-37 minutes, or until a toothpick inserted in the center comes out clean. Let cool completely on a wire rack.

In a medium bowl, beat peanut butter and vanilla with an electric mixer until smooth. Gradually add confectioners' sugar; beat for 1 minute.

Remove the outer edge of the springform pan. Spread the peanut butter mixture over the top of the cooled brownie. Chill for about 30 minutes, or until firm.

Place hot fudge topping in a small resealable plastic bag. Knead until smooth. Cut a small corner off the bag. Drizzle over the peanut butter layer.

Cut into wedges. Makes 12-14 servings.

** Brands may vary by region; substitute a similar product.*

# Chocolate Bliss Cheesecake

Kraft

- 18 Oreo Cookies, crushed (about 1 1/2 cups)
- 2 tablespoons butter or margarine, melted
- 3 8-ounce packages Philadelphia Cream Cheese, softened
- 3/4 cup sugar
- 1 teaspoon vanilla extract
- 1 package (8 squares) Baker's Semi-Sweet Chocolate, melted, cooled slightly
- 3 large eggs

Preheat oven to 325°F.

Mix cookie crumbs and butter. Press onto the bottom of a 9-inch springform pan.

Beat cream cheese, sugar and vanilla with a mixer until well blended. Add chocolate and mix well.

Add eggs one at a time, mixing on low speed after each addition just until blended. Pour over the crust.

Bake for 55-60 minutes, or until the center is almost set. Run a knife around the rim of the pan to loosen the cake; let cool before removing the rim. Refrigerate for 4 hours. Makes 12 servings.

## Party-Perfect Cupcakes
### Kirkland Signature/Jelly Belly

- 1 16-ounce container vanilla frosting
- Assorted food colors
- 4 jumbo cupcakes, baked 1 each in blue, red, green and orange paper liners
- 4 standard cupcakes, baked 1 each in blue, red, green and orange paper liners
- 4 mini cupcakes, baked 1 each in blue, red, green and orange paper liners
- Kirkland Signature/ Jelly Belly beans, about 3 ounces (1/3 cup) each, in Berry Blue, Blueberry, Cotton Candy, Very Cherry, Kiwi, Crushed Pineapple and Orange Sherbet
- 4 wavy birthday candles (optional)

Divide frosting into 4 mixing bowls. Tint each bowl a different pastel color (blue, pink, green and orange) with the food color.

Working on one tier at a time, spread the tinted frosting on cupcakes in like-colored paper liners. Using matching colors, arrange alternate-color Jelly Belly beans around the outer edge of each cupcake, one lengthwise and one crosswise.

Stack the cupcakes, pressing the top cupcake into the frosting to secure. Insert a candle in the top cupcake, if desired. Makes 4 servings.

## Mango Cobbler Bars
### Profood

- 1 1/2 cups butter, softened
- 3/4 cup sugar, divided
- 3 cups sifted all-purpose flour
- 4 cups Philippine Brand* dried mangoes (30-ounce bag)
- 1/4 cup all-purpose flour
- 1 1/2 teaspoons ground cinnamon
- Pinch of nutmeg

Preheat oven to 350°F.

In a large bowl, cream together butter and 1/2 cup sugar. Blend in 3 cups flour. Press half of the mixture into the bottom of a 13-by-9-inch baking dish.

Place dried mangoes in a bowl and cover with boiled hot water. Let stand for 10 minutes, or until softened. Drain and cut into bite-size pieces.

In a medium bowl, stir together mangoes, 1/4 cup sugar, 1/4 cup flour, cinnamon and nutmeg until well combined.

Pour the mango mixture over the shortbread in the pan. Sprinkle with the remaining shortbread mixture. Press down lightly.

Bake for 1 hour, or until the topping is golden brown. Let cool for 15 minutes in the pan before cutting into bars. Makes 10-12 servings.

** Brands may vary by region; substitute a similar product.*

## Fruit and Nut Granola Bars
### Kirkland Signature

- **2 cups old-fashioned oatmeal**
- **1/2 cup toasted wheat germ**
- **2 tablespoons unsalted butter**
- **2/3 cup honey**
- **1/4 cup packed light brown sugar**
- **1 1/2 teaspoons pure vanilla extract**
- **1/4 teaspoon kosher salt**
- **1/2 cup peanut butter**
- **3 cups (half of 30-ounce pouch) Kirkland Signature Wholesome Fruit & Nuts**

Preheat oven to 350°F. Butter a 12-by-8-inch baking dish and line with parchment paper.

Spread oatmeal on a sheet pan and bake for 10-15 minutes, stirring every 5 minutes, until lightly browned. Transfer to a large mixing bowl and stir in toasted wheat germ.

Reduce oven temperature to 300°F.

In a small saucepan, combine butter, honey, brown sugar, vanilla and salt; bring to a boil over medium heat. Cook, stirring, for 1 minute. Remove from the heat and stir in peanut butter. Pour over the toasted oatmeal mixture. Add fruit and nut mix and stir until blended.

Pour into the prepared pan, lightly pressing into an even layer. Bake for 25-30 minutes, or until light golden brown.

Let cool completely (about 3 hours). Cut into 2-inch squares. Store in an airtight container for up to a week. Makes 24 servings.

## Honey Raisin Crispies with Soy
### Sun-Maid Growers

- **1/2 cup soy butter**
- **1/2 cup honey**
- **3 tablespoons packed brown sugar**
- **1 teaspoon vanilla extract**
- **2 1/2 cups toasted rice cereal**
- **2 cups old-fashioned oats (uncooked)**
- **3/4 cup Sun-Maid Natural Raisins**

Line an 8-inch square pan with foil, extending the foil over opposite ends of the pan (or lightly coat with cooking spray).

Place soy butter, honey and brown sugar in a large microwave-safe bowl. Microwave on high for 2 minutes, or until bubbly and heated through. Remove from the microwave.

Add vanilla and stir until the mixture is smooth.

Add cereal, oats and raisins. Gently stir, without crushing the cereal, until the mixture is evenly blended.

Press the warm mixture very firmly into the prepared pan. Let cool at room temperature or refrigerate for 30 minutes.

Lift out of the pan and cut into bars. Store the bars in plastic wrap or a tightly covered container at room temperature or in the refrigerator. Makes 16 bars.

**Tip:** This is a healthy snack bar that is gluten free.

# Chocolate Cherry Brownies
## Primavera

- 1 standard-size (18.3-21 ounces) package brownie mix
- 1 cup pitted and diced Prima Frutta* fresh sweet cherries
- 3/4 cup coarsely chopped walnuts, divided
- 1/2 pint heavy whipping cream
- 3 tablespoons confectioners' sugar
- 1 teaspoon vanilla extract

*CHOCOLATE SAUCE*

- 1/2 cup unsweetened cocoa
- 1 1/4 cups granulated sugar
- 1/2 cup milk
- 1 teaspoon vanilla extract

Prepare brownies according to package directions, stirring in cherries and 1/2 cup walnuts. Bake in an 8-by-8-inch baking dish.

To prepare the chocolate sauce, stir together cocoa, sugar and milk in a small saucepan. Bring to a boil over medium heat. Remove from the heat and stir in vanilla. Continue stirring until the sauce thickens and coats the back of the spoon. Let cool.

Whip cream with a beater. When it thickens, add confectioners' sugar and vanilla; continue beating until fluffy.

When the brownies are cool, cut into 9 squares. Drizzle 1 teaspoon chocolate sauce on each brownie. Add 2 tablespoons whipped cream, then drizzle with more chocolate sauce. Sprinkle walnuts on top. Makes 9 servings.

** Brands may vary by region; substitute a similar product.*

## Crunchy Granola Cookies
### Nature's Path Organic Foods

- $1/4$ teaspoon vegetable oil
- $1/2$ cup (1 stick) butter, at room temperature
- $1/2$ cup packed dark brown sugar
- 1 large egg
- 1 teaspoon pure vanilla extract
- 1 cup all-purpose flour
- $1/2$ teaspoon baking soda
- $1/2$ teaspoon ground cinnamon
- 1 $1/3$ cups Nature's Path Organic Pumpkin Flax Plus Granola Organic
- $1/2$ cup raisins

Position rack in the center of the oven. Preheat oven to 350°F. Lightly grease a large cookie sheet with oil.

In a large bowl, combine butter and brown sugar; cream until light and fluffy. Beat in egg and vanilla.

In a separate bowl, combine flour, baking soda and cinnamon. Break up clumps of granola and add to the flour mixture, stirring until evenly distributed.

Add the flour mixture and raisins to the butter mixture. Stir until thoroughly combined.

Drop tablespoonfuls of dough 1 $1/2$ inches apart on the prepared cookie sheet. Bake for 5 minutes. Rotate the pan and continue baking until the top edges and bottoms of cookies are golden brown, 2-4 minutes longer. Transfer cookies to a cooling rack.

Store in a cool place in an airtight container for up to 1 week, or freeze in a tightly sealed plastic bag for up to 3 months. Makes about 30 cookies.

## Oatmeal Walnut Cookies
### Diamond Foods

- 3 cups Kirkland Signature walnuts
- 1 cup (2 sticks) unsalted butter, at room temperature
- 1 cup packed light brown sugar
- $1/3$ cup granulated sugar
- 2 large eggs
- 1 tablespoon vanilla extract
- 1 $1/2$ cups flour
- 1 teaspoon baking soda
- 2 teaspoons ground cinnamon
- $1/4$ teaspoon ground nutmeg
- $1/2$ teaspoon salt
- 3 cups old-fashioned oats
- 1 cup sweetened dried cranberries

Preheat oven to 350°F.

Spread walnuts evenly on a baking sheet or in a shallow pan. Bake, stirring once or twice, until lightly browned and fragrant, 7-10 minutes. Coarsely chop and set aside.

In a large bowl, cream butter and sugars until light and fluffy. Add eggs and vanilla; beat well.

In a separate bowl, combine flour, baking soda, cinnamon, nutmeg, salt and oats. Add to the butter mixture and stir well to combine. Stir in dried cranberries and toasted walnuts.

Drop cookie dough by tablespoonfuls onto a parchment-lined cookie sheet. Bake for 12-15 minutes, or until the edges start to brown. Cool on a wire rack. Makes about 36 cookies.

## Cookie Kisses

Skippy

- 2 1/2 cups quick-cooking oats
- 1 1/4 cups all-purpose flour
- 1 teaspoon baking powder
- 1 teaspoon baking soda
- 1/4 teaspoon salt
- 1 cup Skippy* Creamy or Super Chunk Peanut Butter
- 1 cup Shedd's Spread* Country Crock Spread
- 1 cup granulated sugar
- 1 cup firmly packed light brown sugar
- 2 large eggs
- 2 teaspoons Kirkland Signature vanilla extract
- 72 chocolate candy kisses

Preheat oven to 350°F.

In a small bowl, combine oats, flour, baking powder, baking soda and salt; set aside.

In a large bowl, beat peanut butter and spread with an electric mixer on medium speed until smooth. Beat in sugars, then eggs and vanilla until blended. Beat in the flour mixture just until blended.

Drop the dough by level tablespoonfuls onto ungreased baking sheets, 2 inches apart.

Bake for 13 minutes, or until golden. Immediately press a chocolate kiss firmly into the center of each cookie. Remove the cookies to a wire rack and let cool completely. Makes 6 dozen cookies.

** Brands may vary by region; substitute a similar product.*

## Granola and Apricot Chocolate Clusters

CSM Bakery Products

- 3 cups coarsely chopped Kirkland Signature granola snack mix
- 1 cup chopped dried apricots (each apricot cut into 8 pieces)
- 1 cup Nutella hazelnut spread
- 1 tablespoon butter
- 2/3 cup light corn syrup
- 2/3 cup sugar
- Coconut: 1/2 cup per 12 chocolate balls (optional)
- Finely diced walnuts: 1/3 cup per 12 chocolate balls (optional)

Line a tray or pan with waxed paper.

In a large mixing bowl, combine granola and apricots. Set aside.

In a medium mixing bowl, combine Nutella and butter. Set aside.

In a small saucepan, combine corn syrup and sugar. Bring to a boil over medium heat, stirring to dissolve the sugar. When the mixture is at a full boil—not just on the edges—remove immediately from the heat and pour over the Nutella and butter mixture. Quickly stir until fully blended and the butter has melted.

Pour the hot mixture over the granola and apricots, stirring quickly to fully coat. The mixture will be very sticky.

Using a small scoop or teaspoon, scoop out the mixture and shape into 1 1/2-inch balls. Roll in coconut or finely diced walnuts, if desired. Place on waxed paper and let set at room temperature. Makes about 40 clusters.

**Tip:** These are better made at least one day before serving. They can be stored at room temperature.

csm
Bakery Products NA

# Index

# D



# E



# F

## V



## W



## Z

# Supplier Listing

**_ACH Food Companies_**, 40
www.mazola.com
1-866-4MAZOLA

**_Acme Food Sales_**, 82
www.acmefood.com
206-762-5150

**_Aconex_**, 197, 210
www.aconex.cl
562-941-3300

**_AJ Trucco, Inc._**, 196
www.truccodirect.com
866-AJTRUCC

**_Alaska Glacier Seafoods_**, 127
www.alaskaglacierseafoods.com
907-790-3590

**_Alpine Fresh, Inc._**, 54, 59, 67, 86, 206
www.alpinefresh.com
800-292-8777

**_Alsum Farms & Produce, Inc._**, 165
www.alsum.com
920-348-5127

**_AMC Direct Inc._**, 201
www.amcgrupo.eu

**_American Pride Seafoods_**, 139
www.americanprideseafoods.com
508-997-0031

**_Andrew & Williamson Fresh Produce_**, 207
www.andrew-williamson.com
619-661-6004

**_Ann's House of Nuts_**, 60, 145
www.annshouse.com
410-309-6887

**_Anthony Vineyards, Inc._**, 39
www.anthonyvineyards.com

**_Apio, Inc., Eat Smart_**, 70, 152
www.apioinc.com
800-454-1355

**_Apple & Eve_**, 198
www.appleandeve.com
800-969-8018

**_AquaGold Seafood Company, LLC_**, 175
954-888-9445

**_Arthur Schuman_**, 168
www.arthurschuman.com
973-227-0030

**_Atlantic Capes Fisheries_**, 138, 139
www.atlanticcapes.com
508-990-9040

**_Atlantic Veal & Lamb, Inc._**, 155, 156, 157
www.atlanticveal.com
800-222-8325

**_Babé Farms, Inc._**, 63
www.babefarms.com
800-648-6772

**_Bakemark USA_**, 208
www.yourbakemark.com
562-949-1054

**_Bard Valley Date Growers Association_**, 148
www.bardmedjool.com
800-794-4424

**_Basin Gold Cooperative_**, 83
www.basingold.com
509-545-4161

**_BC Hot House Foods, Inc._**, 170
www.bchothouse.com
604-881-4545

**_Bee Sweet Citrus_**, 51
www.beecitrus.com
559-834-5345

**_Bionova Produce_**, 130
www.masterstouch.com
520-761-1578

**_Blossom Hill - Lucich Santos Farms_**, 188
www.blossomhillapricots.com
209-892-6500

**_Bolthouse Farms_**, 214
www.bolthouse.com
800-467-4683

**_Booth Ranches, LLC_**, 126
www.boothranches.com
559-626-7653

**_Borton & Sons, Inc._**, 17
www.bortonfruit.com
509-966-3905

**_Boskovich Farms, Inc._**, 61
www.boskovichfarms.com
805-487-2299

**_Bravante Produce_**, 64
www.bravanteproduce.com
559-638-5075

**_Cal-Maine Foods_**, 12, 13
www.calmainefoods.com
601-948-6813

**_Calavo Growers_**, 78, 79
www.calavo.com
805-525-1245

**_California Avocado Commission_**, 78, 79
www.californiaavocado.com

**_California Pears_**, 148
www.calpear.com
916-441-0432

**_California Walnuts_**, 125
www.walnuts.org
916-932-7070

**_Cardile Bros. Mushroom Company_**, 147
www.cardilebrothersmushrooms.com
610-268-2470

**_Castle Rock Vineyards_**, 196
www.castlerockvineyards.com
661-721-8717

**_Cecelia Packing Corporation_**, 130
www.ceceliapack.com
559-626-5000

**_Cedar Key Aquaculture Farms, Inc._**, 30
www.cedarkeyclams.com
888-252-6735

**_Chelan Fresh Marketing_**, 144
www.chelanfresh.com
509-682-4252

**_Cherry Central_**, 221
www.cherrycentral.com
231-946-1860

**_Chestnut Hill Farms_**, 145
www.chfusa.com
305-592-6969

**_Chicken of the Sea International_**, 172, 173
www.chickenofthesea.com
858-558-9662

**_Chilean Avocado Importers Assoc. & Comite De Paltas_**, 36
www.chileanavocados.org
831-689-0962

**_Chilean Fresh Fruit Association_**, 55
www.chileanfreshfruit.com
707-938-8400

**_Citterio USA_**, 168
www.citterio.com
800-435-8888

**_CM Holtzinger Fruit Co._**, 81
www.holtzingerfruit.com
509-249-4232

**_Columbia Marketing International_**, 200, 201
www.cmiapples.com
509-663-1955

**_ConAgra Foods_**, 47
www.conagrafoods.com
813-241-1500

**_Consolidated Catfish Producers_**, 129
662-962-3101

**_CSM Bakery Products_**, 215, 224
www.csmglobal.com
800-866-3300

**_Curry & Company, Inc._**, 207
www.curryandco.com
503-393-6033

**_D'Arrigo Bros. Co. of California_**, 60
www.andyboy.com
831-455-4500

***Damascus Bakery, Inc.***, 68
www.damascusbakery.com
718-855-1456

***Dawn Food Products***, 191, 205
www.dawnfoods.com
800-292-1362

***Decas Cranberry Products, Inc.***, 221
www.decascranberry.com
800-950-3683

***Del Monte Foods***, 20
www.delmonte.com
800-543-3090

***Del Monte Fresh Produce***, 65
www.freshdelmonte.com,
www.fruits.com
800-950-3683

***Del Rey Avocado***, 78, 79
760-728-8325

***Delano Farms***, 100, 101, 102
www.delanofarmsco.com
661-721-1485

***Diamond Foods, Inc.***, 223
www.diamondnuts.com
209-467-6000

***Diversified Citrus Marketing***, 159
www.diversifiedcitrus.com
866-801-3863

***Divine Flavor, LLC***, 34
www.divineflavor.com
619-616-7410

***Dole Fresh Fruit, Vegetables***, 71, 159, 217
***Packaged Foods***
www.dole.com
800-232-888

***Domex Superfresh Growers***, 184, 185
www.superfreshgrowers.com
509-966-1814

***Don Miguel Mexican Foods***, 35
www.donmiguel.com
714-634-8441

***Duda Farm Fresh Foods***, 79, 123
www.dudafresh.com
559-627-1337

***Dulcinea Farms***, 32
www.dulcinea.com
800-495-1561

***Earth Source Trading, Inc.***, 205
www.earthsourcetrading.com
877-321-8200

***Earthbound Farm***, 108, 109
www.ebfarm.com
800-690-3200

***Einstein Noah Restaurant Group, Inc.***, 169, 171
www.einsteinnoah.com
1-800-BAGEL-ME

***Eurofresh Farms***, 75, 87
www.eurofresh.com
520-384-4621

***Farm Fresh Direct, LLC***, 71
www.farmfreshdirect.net
719-852-2600

***Ferrero USA, Inc.***, 14
www.ferrerousa.com
732-554-4727

***FirstFruits Marketing of WA, LLC***, 50, 51
www.firstfruits.com
509-853-4723

***Folgers***, 195
www.folgers.com
800-937-9745

***Foster Farms***, 93, 94, 95
www.fosterfarms.com
800-255-7227

***Four Star Sales***, 202, 203
www.fourstarfruit.com
661-725-9621

***Fowler Packing Co.***, 67
www.fowlerpacking.com

***Fresh Innovations of California***, 61
www.fresh-innovations.com
888-755-9015 x202

***Freska Produce International, LLC***, 32
www.freskaproduce.com
805-650-1040

***Garofalo Pasta/P&L Imports***, 110, 111, 112
www.pandlimports.com
866-327-2782

***Giorgio Fresh Company***, 147
www.giorgiofoods.com
610-926-2139

***Giumarra Agricom International***, 78, 79
www.giumarra.com
760-480-8502

***GlaxoSmithKline/Alli***, 136
www.gsk.com
412-200-4000

***Gold Coast Packing, Inc.***, 63
www.goldcoastpack.com
805-928-2593

***GoodHeart Brand Foods***, 68
www.goodheart.com
210-637-1963

***Gourmet Trading Company***, 140
www.gourmettrading.net
310-216-7575

***Grant J. Hunt Company***, 42
www.grantjhunt.com
509-575-8770

***Greene River Marketing***, 203

***Grimmway Farms***, 86
www.grimmway.com
800-301-3101

***Grower Direct Marketing***, 188
www.growerdirect.net
209-931-7900

***H.J. Heinz Company***, 150, 154, 165
www.heinz.com
800-255-5750

***Hain Gourmet, Inc.***, 38, 42
www.sensibleportions.com
800-913-6637

***Harbor Seafood***, 141
www.harborseafood.com

***Harvest Food Products Company, Inc.***, 143
www.harvestfoodproducts.com
510-675-0383

***Harvest Manor Farms***, 60, 145
800-445-8338 x525

***Heartland Catfish***, 129
www.heartlandcatfish.com
334-624-4021

***Hershey Company, The***, 217
www.hersheys.com
800-468-1714

***Hickman's Family Farms***, 12, 13
www.hickmanseggs.com

***Hillandale Farms***, 12, 13
www.hillandalefarms.com
717-229-0601

***Horizon International***, 153
651-209-6770

***Hormel Foods***, 21
www.hormel.com
800-523-4635

***Houweling's Hot House***, 36
www.houwelings.com
805-271-5105

***Icicle Seafoods***, 124
www.icicleseafoods.com
206-282-0988

***Index Fresh***, 78, 79
www.IndexFresh.com
909-877-1577

***J&J Snack Foods***, 193, 199
www.jjsnack.com

***Jacobs, Malcolm & Burtt***, 140
415-285-0400

***Monterey Mushrooms, Inc.***, 147
www.montmush.com
800-333-MUSH

***Morada Produce Company***, 196
www.moradaproduce.com
209-546-1816

***Morey's Seafood International, LLC***, 26
www.moreys.com
800-327-9592

***Morton's of Omaha***, 151, 153, 154
www.cargillmeatsolutions.com

***Mountain King Potatoes***, 73
www.mtnking.com
800-395-2004

***Mountain View Fruit Sales/I.M. Ripe***, 62, 63
www.summeripe.com
559-637-9933

***Mucci International Marketing, Inc.***, 25
www.muccipac.ca
866-236-5558

***Multiexport Foods***, 122
www.multiexportfoods.com
888-624-9773

***National Beef Packers LLC***, 151
www.nationalbeef.com
800-448-2333

***Nature's Partner***, 14
www.naturespartner.com
213-627-2900

***Nature's Path Organic Foods, Inc.***, 223
www.naturespath.com

***Naturipe Farms LLC***, 46, 185
www.naturipefarms.com
239-591-1664

***New York Apple Sales, Inc.***, 179
www.newyorkapplesales.com
518-477-7200

***New York Style Sausage***, 162, 163
www.newyorkstylesausage.com
408-745-7675

***NewStar Fresh Foods***, 140
www.newstarfresh.com
831-758-7800

***Nissin Foods***, 74
www.nissinfoods.com
310-527-5713

***Noble Wordwide Citrus***, 159
www.nobletangerines.com
888-289-6625

***Norpac Fisheries Export***, 59
www.norpacexport.com
877-855-7238

***North Coast Seafoods***, 31, 135
www.northcoastseafoods.com

***NuCal Foods***, 12, 13
www.nucalfoods.com
209-254-2200

***Nunes Company, The***, 70
www.foxy.com
800-695-5012

***Oakdell Egg Farms***, 12, 13
www.oakdell.com
801-298-4556

***Ocean Duke Corporation***, 28
www.oceanduke.com
310-534-8878

***Ocean Spray Cranberries, Inc.***, 221
www.oceansprayitg.com
508-923-3202

***Oneonta Starr Ranch Growers***, 84
www.starranch.com
888-ONE-ONTA

***Oppenheimer Group, The***, 170
www.oppyproduce.com
206-284-1705

***Orca Bay Seafoods, Inc.***, 173
www.orcabayseafoods.com
800-932-ORCA

***Pacific Seafood Group***, 98, 99
www.pacseafood.com
888-742-3474

***Pandol Bros, Inc.***, 192
www.pandol.com
661-725-3755

***Paramount Citrus***, 171
www.paramountcitrus.com
661-720-2500

***Paramount Farms***, 80
www.paramountfarms.com
www.almondaccent.com
800-528-6887

***Pennsylvania Apple Marketing Board***, 179
www.pennsylvaniaapples.org
717-783-5418

***Perdue***, 58
www.perdue.com
410-543-3000

***Peterson Cheese***, 20
www.petersoncheese.com
253-735-0313

***Pilgrim's/Gold Kist Farms***, 113, 114, 115
www.pilgrimspride.com

***Premier Citrus Marketing***, 51
772-794-5388

***Premio Foods, Inc.***, 33, 163, 164
www.premiofoods.com
973-427-1106

***Pride Packing Co.***, 126
www.pridepacking.com
800-828-4106

***Primavera Marketing***, 222
www.primafrutta.com
209-931-9420

***Profood USA***, 220
www.profoodcorp.com

***Quaker***, 16
www.quaker.com
877-858-4237

***Quality Ocean International***, 134, 140

***Rain Forest Aquaculture***, 132
www.tilapia.com
877-522-8420

***Rainier Fruit Company***, 72, 73
www.rainierfruit.com

***Ralcorp Frozen Bakery Products***, 57, 204
www.panneprovincio.com

***Ready Pac Foods, Inc.***, 52, 214
www.readypac.com
800-800-4088

***Regatta Tropicals, Ltd***, 51, 56
805-473-1320

***Reser's Fine Foods, Inc.***, 87
www.resers.com
800-333-6431

***Richard Bagdasarian, Inc.***, 56
www.mrgrape.com
760-396-2167

***Rikki Rikki***, 146
www.rikkirikki.com
866-707-4554

***River Ranch Fresh Foods, LLC***, 85
www.riverranchfreshfoods.com
866-767-3931

***Royal Flavor, LLC***, 28
www.royalflavor.com
619-710-2020

***RPE***, 165
www.rpespud.com
800-678-2789

***Rupari Food Services***, 80
954-480-6320

***Sabra Dipping Company***, 24, 25
www.sabra.com
718-932-9000

***Sage Fruit***, 189
www.sagefruit.com
509-248-5828